OXFORD STUDIES IN LANGUAGE CONTACT

Series Editors: Suzanne Romaine, Merton College, Oxford, and
Peter Mühlhäusler, Linacre College, Oxford

Social Motivations for Codeswitching

D0706278

OXFORD STUDIES IN LANGUAGE CONTACT

MOST of the world's speech communities are multilingual, making contact between languages an important force in the everyday lives of most people. Studies of language contact should therefore form an integral part of work in theoretical, social, and historical linguistics. As yet, however, there are insufficient studies to permit typological generalizations.

Oxford Studies in Language Contact aims to fill this gap by making available a collection of research monographs presenting case studies of language contact around the world. The series addresses language contact and its consequences in a broad interdisciplinary context, which includes not only linguistics, but also social, historical, cultural, and psychological perspectives. Topics falling within the scope of the series include: bilingualism, multilingualism, language mixing, codeswitching, diglossia, pidgins and creoles, problems of cross-cultural communication, and language shift and death.

Social Motivations For Codeswitching

Evidence from Africa

CAROL MYERS-SCOTTON

CLARENDON PRESS · OXFORD

*This book has been printed digitally and produced in a standard specification
in order to ensure its continuing availability*

OXFORD
UNIVERSITY PRESS

Great Clarendon Street, Oxford OX2 6DP

Oxford University Press is a department of the University of Oxford.
It furthers the University's objective of excellence in research, scholarship,
and education by publishing worldwide in

Oxford New York

Auckland Cape Town Dar es Salaam Hong Kong Karachi
Kuala Lumpur Madrid Melbourne Mexico City Nairobi
New Delhi Shanghai Taipei Toronto
With offices in
Argentina Austria Brazil Chile Czech Republic France Greece
Guatemala Hungary Italy Japan South Korea Poland Portugal
Singapore Switzerland Thailand Turkey Ukraine Vietnam

Oxford is a registered trade mark of Oxford University Press
in the UK and in certain other countries

Published in the United States
by Oxford University Press Inc., New York

ISBN 0-19-823923-8

This book is dedicated to my parents,
Pearl Mehlhouse Myers (1908–) and Watt Myers (1905–1992)

Preface

THIS is a study of codeswitching between languages. Such switching involves the use of two or more languages in the same conversation, usually within the same conversational turn, or even within the same sentence of that turn. This book deals with one aspect of codeswitching: the socio-psychological uses of such juxtaposed multiple-language production. This aspect of codeswitching also can be studied between dialects or styles (registers) of the same language; in fact, most of the conclusions reached here would apply to dialect- or style-switching; however, looking at switching involving those linguistic varieties is beyond the scope of this book.

The use of the term 'code' in 'codeswitching' is traditional, and nothing more. That I use it does not mean I endorse the view that the messages humans convey with language are entirely revealed in the deciphering of the elements and configurations of the linguistic code. In fact, the book's major premiss is that codeswitching is used to convey intentional (i.e. non-code-based) meanings of a socio-pragmatic nature.

Structural constraints on codeswitching (i.e. where in a sentence a switch is possible) or psycholinguistic aspects of its production are not considered here. They are the subject of another book (Myers–Scotton, 1993*b*).

Also, this book is definitely non–developmental. That is, the growth of the bilingualism necessary for codeswitching to be possible, whether from a community perspective or from the individual speaker's point of view, is not a topic here. Since much of the data comes from Africa, specifically from Kenya and, to a lesser extent, Zimbabwe, the current sociolinguistic profiles of these areas are detailed. But the history of bilingualism/multilingualism in Africa is not addressed; neither are predictions made regarding future patterns of multilingualism or long-term language policy decisions. These are all worthy topics, but subjects for other studies.

The treatment of codeswitching here is intended to be theoretical. It is aimed at an audience interested in socio-pragmatic theories of the representation of communicative intention related to a speaker's presentation/ negotiation of self in relation to other participants in a conversation. This audience will consist primarily of sociolinguists, social anthropologists, and social psychologists—whatever their areal expertise. However, the book also should be of interest—and accessible—to the general Africanist.

The theoretical arguments are supported with copious examples, mainly from African settings. They come largely from my own field-work but also from the work of others. The urban origin of most of the examples has no special effect on the social motivations which apply; it simply happens that examples of codeswitching are more easily found in urban populations because their multi-group makeup fosters more bilingualism, a prerequisite to codeswitching. However, rural populations also may be multilingual and engage in codeswitching. The implicit claim of the book is that the proposed social motivations for codeswitching apply to all populations, whether urban or rural.

While this is not a study in applied linguistics, the results should be of interest to applied linguists involved in such fields as education and language-planning. This is because the book presents codeswitching as a meaningful enterprise showing skill, not linguistic inadequacies.

I would like to acknowledge the help of several organizations and many persons in my writing of this book. Field-work in Kenya and Zimbabwe was conducted at several different times under a Fulbright Research Grant (1983) as well as Social Science Research Grants (1977; 1988) and a University of South Carolina Research and Productive Scholarship Award (1988). Background work under a grant from the Ford Foundation Survey of Language Use in Eastern Africa (1970), during my appointment as a lecturer at Makerere University, Uganda (1968–70), and at the University of Nairobi (1972–3), was also important.

Field-work would have been impossible to accomplish without the help of many individuals. I am above all grateful to the research assistants in Kenya and Zimbabwe who actually gathered conversations, and in particular to Shem Lusimba Mbira, who worked with me for twenty years in Uganda and Kenya (1968–88). I thank him and his family for their extensive hospitality. I also especially thank Janice Bernsten, my collaborator in collecting data in Zimbabwe, and Nigel Crawhall, who kindly supervised the collecting of naturally occurring codeswitching data for me in Zimbabwe. Discussions with Kumbirai Mkanganwi of the University of Zimbabwe were of great value.

I wish to thank those who commented on parts of earlier drafts, especially Janice Bernsten, Hazel Carter, Carol Eastman, Janice Jake, Georges Lüdi, and Patricia Nichols, as well as the series editors. My thanks also go to the staff at Oxford University Press, especially Frances Morphy and Peter Momtchiloff. My students have always given me useful ideas, and I especially thank Yuriko Kite, Sylvester R. Simango, and Wei Long Xing for their help as research assistants. Finally, I value my son, Kenneth Scotton, for many reasons, but particularly for his psychological support while I was writing this book.

C.M.-S.

Columbia, South Carolina
Summer 1991

Contents

Symbols and Abbreviations

[ ]	indicates phonetic transcription
/ /	indicates phonemic transcription
1, 2, 3	1st, 2nd, 3rd person
CL	Class (1, 2, etc.)
CONDIT	Conditional
CONSEC	Consecutive tense
COP	Copula
INFIN	Infinitive marker
NEG	Negative
OBJ	Object
PAST	Past tense
PERF	Perfect aspect
PL	Plural
PRES	Present tense
S	Singular
VP	Verb phrase

I

Introduction

EVERYDAY conversations in two languages are the subject-matter of this volume. All over the world bilinguals carry on such conversations, from Hispanics in Texas, who may alternate between Spanish and English in informal in-group conversations, to West Africans, who may use both Wolof and French in the same conversation on the streets of Dakar, Senegal, to residents in the Swiss capital of Berne, who may change back and forth between Swiss German and French in a service exchange. Contrary to some popular beliefs, such conversations are not mainly a transitional stage in a language shift from dominance in one language to another. It is true that many immigrants who are in the process of language shift do engage in codeswitching, but this form of conversation is also part of the daily lives of many 'stable' bilingual populations as well. Neither is codeswitching only the vehicle of social groups on the socio-economic 'margins' of society; for example, in every nation, successful business people and professionals who happen to have a different home language from the language dominant in the society where they live frequently engage in codeswitching (between these two languages) with friends and business associates who share their linguistic repertoires. Consider Punjabi-origin physicians in Birmingham, England, Lebanese-origin businessmen in Dearborn, Michigan, or Chinese-origin corporate executives in Singapore.

Codeswitching is the term used to identify alternations of linguistic varieties within the same conversation. While some[1] prefer to discuss such alternation under two terms, employing *code-mixing* as well as *codeswitching*, the single term *codeswitching* is used here.

Utterances containing codeswitching show the same 'discourse unity' as utterances in one linguistic variety alone. For example, if the switching is

---

[1] A number of researchers associated with Braj Kachru (cf. Kachru 1978; 1983), but also some others, prefer to label as 'code-mixing' alternations which are intrasentential, although it is not entirely clear whether this applies to all instrasentential CS. While I grant that intrasentential CS puts different psycholinguistic 'stresses' on the language-production system from intersentential CS (a valid reason to differentiate the two), the two types of CS may have similar socio-psychological motivations. For this reason, I prefer 'CS' as a cover term; the two types can be differentiated by the labels 'intersentential' and 'intrasentential' when structural constraints are considered.

within a single sentence, the elements from the two different languages generally are joined together prosodically.[2]

The linguistic varieties participating in codeswitching may be different languages, or dialects or styles of the same language. However, this volume is concerned only with alternations of languages; thus, when the term 'codeswitching' (hereafter CS) is used here, it refers only to such switching.

Most examples come from urban Africa, where knowing and using every day more than one language is commonplace in all walks of life. Example [1] illustrates the type of data to be considered. Two teenage boys from different ethnic groups (Kalenjin and Kikuyu) are chatting after school in Nairobi, Kenya. English and Swahili are the official languages of multilingual Kenya, an East African nation of more than 30 different ethnic groups, each actively using its own language for many interactions. At home, Nairobi schoolboys largely speak their own ethnic group languages to parents and elder relatives; at school, English is the medium of instruction; but with peers (and probably with siblings as well) their interactions are mainly in Swahili, or the CS combination of Swahili/English illustrated here.

[1] (Swahili/English No. 24)[3]

KALENJIN. Kwetu sisi mtu hawezi kuleta *jokes* kama hizo. *Father* sio mtu wa kuchezea. Kabla ya kw-enda *job*, a- -na- -make sure everybody is out of bed.
                before of INFIN-go   3S-PRES-
'At our home no one can do those kinds of jokes. Father is not a man to play with. Before he goes to work, he makes sure that everybody is out of bed.'
KIKUYU. Mimi siku hizi ni-ko   *used* ku-amka *very early* ili niende shule *in time*.
                        1S-COP used INFIN-wake up
Hata wakati wa *holidays* mimi huamka *just the same time*.
'These days I'm used to waking up very early so that I get to school in time. Even during holiday time I usually get up [at] just the same time.'

---

[2] This is an important aspect of the phenomenon of CS, often not mentioned. However, Romaine (1995: 111) does highlight this characteristic of CS in her definition: 'In code-switched discourse, the items in question form part of the same speech act. They are tied together prosodically as well as by semantic and syntactic relations equivalent to those that join passages in a single speech act.' Of course, when CS represents 'a marked choice' (to be discussed in Ch. 5 below), the switched portion may show marked prosody; and, as I indicate elsewhere (e.g. Myers-Scotton 1991a; 1991b; 1993b), CS sometimes includes 'bare forms' which do not observe co-occurrence requirements of the matrix language of the utterance.

[3] Examples from Swahili/English CS which come from the Nairobi corpus of 40 naturally occurring conversations are numbered 1–40.

KALENJIN. Hebu, twende kuwaona Mark na Fred. Wa-li-sema   tu-ko
3PL–PAST–say IPL–COP

na *programme fit*   sana kwa TV.
with programme fit (= good) very on TV
'Hey, let's go and see Mark and Fred. They said that there is a good programme on TV.'

Goals and topics

The major goal of this volume is to answer this research question: what do bilingual speakers gain by conducting a conversation in two languages (i.e. through codeswitching) rather than simply using one language throughout? A theoretical model is presented to explain the socio-psychological motivations behind CS. This model is supported with primary examples from naturally occurring conversations in Nairobi, Kenya. In addition, some conversations from Harare, Zimbabwe, are included. These data represent my own field work and that of my associates; the interpretations of the data come from over twenty years of research in Africa, mainly in East Africa. Examples from other bilingual or multilingual settings in Africa from data sets of other researchers will provide additional evidence. While the data come from Africa, general applicability is claimed for the model explaining them. That is, an overriding premiss of this volume is that CS serves the same general socio-psychological functions everywhere.

The plan of this study is the following. Chapter 2 presents an overview of African languages and patterns of language use, offering specific detail for the areas which are major data sources. The chapter should be of special interest to Africanists, but it also 'situates' the following discussions for the general linguist or social scientist unfamiliar with Africa's linguistic/socio-linguistic profile. This is deemed necessary since it seems clear that CS exploits the socio-psychological attributes which languages assume in a specific community, based on its patterns of language use. The remainder of the book (Chapters 3–6) deals specifically with the socio-psychological motivations of CS. Chapter 3 discusses the development of this aspect of CS as a research topic. Chapter 4 considers how certain general approaches to the pragmatic force of language use serve as a background for my own model of the social motivations of CS. Chapter 5 presents this model, the Markedness Model. Chapter 6 contains concluding remarks.

What counts as codeswitching?

A slightly more technical, more explicit definition of CS than that offered at the outset is now in order. CS is the selection by bilinguals or multilinguals of forms from an embedded language (or languages) in utterances of a matrix language during the same conversation. The matrix language (ML) is the main language in CS utterances in a number of ways, while the embedded language (EL) has the lesser role.[4] How the ML and EL are identified, and general structural aspects of their participation in CS, are the subject of another study (Myers-Scotton, 1993*a*). The general argument is that CS is not qualitatively different from other naturally occurring language data. It differs only in being subject to the added constraints of the Matrix Language Frame Model developed there, which operate in addition to the well-formedness principles of the languages in the specific CS pair.

Stretches of codeswitched material may be intersentential or intrasentential. Intersentential CS involves switches from one language to the other between sentences. (Note the sentence *We can do nothing* in [2].) Intrasentential switches occur within the same sentence, from single-morpheme to clause level. Note in [3] that the verb phrases *si-ko sure*, *na-suspect*, and *zi-ta-open* all show CS within the same constituent. In [4] there is intrasentential CS of entire constituents, the VP complement *one year* and the prepositional phrase *after one year*. The discussion in this volume applies to both inter- and intrasentential CS.

[2] (Swahili/English No. 31)

(Setting: Outside a grocery store in Nairobi West. Three men from different ethnic groups (Kikuyu, Kalenjin, Luyia) have been talking for several minutes already about the recent rains. The Kalenjin has been going on for some time on this subject. The conversation is mainly in Swahili, with switches to English.)

KALENJIN. . . . Pande yetu ya Ruaraka njia zote zilijaa maji hata mimi ilinibidi kutoa vyatu ili kupita sehemu moja iliyokuwa na maji mengi sana . . .
'On our side of Ruaraka all the streets were so full of water that I had to take off [my] shoes in order to cross one part which had a lot of water . . .'
KIKUYU. Haya mambo ya mvua tuwache tu. Sisi hatuna uwezo. *We can do nothing.*

---

[4] The use of the terms 'matrix language' and 'embedded language' is descriptive, and is not intended to imply any theoretical bias. 'Matrix language' was first applied to CS material by Jacobson (1977) and, in the manner used here, by Joshi (1985).

'Let's just leave these matters of the rain. We don't have any power. We can do nothing.'

[3] (Swahili/English No. 36)

(Setting: A Nairobi office. Three young women from different ethnic groups (Luyia, Luo) are conversing. Again, Swahili is the main medium, with switches to English.)

LUYIA I. *Hello, guys.* Shule zitafunguliwa lini?
'Hello, guys. When will the schools be opened?'
LUYIA II. Na kweli, hata mimi si-ko *sure*   lakini n-a-*suspect*   i-ta-kuwa
                     IS-NEG-be *sure* but   IS-PRES-suspect it will be
week kesho.
week tomorrow
'Well, even I am not sure, but I suspect it will be next week.'
LUO. Shule   zi-   ta-*open*   tarehe tatu mwezi wa tano . . .
       schools CL.10[5]-FUT-open date   three
'Schools will open on the third of the fifth month.'
LUYIA II. Nafikiri shule za *primary* na za *secondary* zitatangulia kufungua lakini *colleges* na *polytechnics* zitakuwa za mwisho kufunguliwa.
'I think primary and secondary schools will be the first to open, but colleges and polytechnics will be the last to be opened.'

[4] (Shona/English; Crawhall 1990)

(A female nurse is talking with a male teacher in Harare, Zimbabwe, about people who buy a car outside the country and then sell it soon afterwards. Both are in their twenties. While English, Shona, and Ndebele are the official languages of Zimbabwe, Shona is the main language heard in Harare, which is located in the Shona-speaking area. However, such educated young people typically do not speak Shona alone among peers, even though it is their first language. Instead, they speak a variety consisting of Shona/English CS as the unmarked choice of their informal conversations.)
TEACHER. Kana kuti vamwe vaibva vasvikotengesa.
'Some will sell them soon after arrival.'
NURSE. Ehe.
'Yes.'
TEACHER. Manje hazvibvumirwe waona. Unofanirwa kupedza *one year* uinwo *motor* yacho. Wozotengesa *after one year.*
'That is not allowed, you see. You should spend one year with that car. Then you can sell it after one year.'

---

[5] References to 'classes' (e.g. CL. 10), when morphemes are identified in examples, refer to noun-class prefixes. Bantuists number noun classes by convention.

Comparing CS and borrowing

Singly occurring CS lexemes and single lexical borrowings resemble each other. Lexical borrowings (B forms) are of two types: Cultural B forms stand for objects or concepts new to the culture (see *primary, secondary, colleges,* and *polytechnics* in [3] and *motor* in [4]). Core B forms are taken into a language even though the language already has lexemes of its own to encode the concepts or objects in question. (See *week* [wik] in [3] as a potential core borrowing.)[6] While what is gained by distinguishing CS and borrowing is an issue in discussions of the structural constraints on CS (cf. Myers-Scotton, 1992*a*; 1993*b*), this subject is not relevant to the argument here.

Descriptive and theoretical themes

Although this book deals largely with CS between Swahili and English in Nairobi, Kenya, it is not intended primarily as a study of that data base alone. Rather, the intention is to give both a descriptive and a theoretical overview of CS in general.

The book's descriptive value has two aspects. First, it offers many examples of parts of conversations containing CS from many different language pairs; it thus provides an extensive and varied corpus for testing various claims about the motivations of CS. Second, it provides descriptive depth in its presentation of the Swahili/English data and other African data, and should therefore make a contribution to African studies.

The theoretical value of this study lies in its attempt to explain a major aspect of CS. The book suggests what bilingual speakers achieve by engaging in CS, rather than staying with only one language for a conversation. These proposals are contained in a socio-psychologically based model of code selection, the Markedness Model. The model is intended as relevant beyond CS for all linguistic-code choices; however, this study is focused only on the model's relation to CS.

A major theme will be that CS in general is a type of skilled performance with communicative intent. From the socio-psychological point of view, CS can be characterized as symptomatic either (*a*) of an unwillingness or an

---

[6] Earlier, of course, Swahili borrowed the lexeme *week* from English, but integrated it into Swahili phonotactics as [wiki]; it coexists with *juma* [juma] 'week', an even earlier borrowing from Arabic. The form used here however, is [wik], which may be a 'new' borrowing. In this case, it would be an alternative to both [wiki] and [juma], at least for some social groups.

uncertainty on the speaker's part regarding the commitment to indexing any *single* rights-and-obligations set between participants in a conversation, or (*b*) of a negotiation to change the rights-and-obligations set. This is so because each linguistic variety used in CS has socio-psychological associations, making it indexical of a rights-and-obligations set. For each interaction type in a specific community, this set is derived from salient situational features (e.g. statuses of the participants, topic, setting) and relevant cultural values. Code choices become associated as the unmarked indices of specific rights-and-obligations sets in specific interaction types.

A second theme will be the explanation of why not all speakers in the same community engage in exactly the same CS practices. True, speakers share the same general norms regarding the socio-psychological significance of switching linguistic varieties; this is necessary if they are to interpret with some confidence the communicative intention of CS choices which others make. However, speakers do not make identical choices in their own CS practices because they have differing views regarding the relative costs and rewards of one choice over another.

A final theme is that CS also is always a reminder to the addressee that the speaker has the multiple identities associated with each of the linguistic varieties involved.

Summary

The purpose of this chapter, in addition to providing an overview of the organization and argument of the book, has been to introduce the reader to the material which will count as CS constituents, while also conveying the flavour of the everyday conversations containing them.

2

The African Setting

THE main data sources of this volume are two African nations where English is the main official language, with one or more indigenous languages also sharing official status. In Kenya, Swahili is a co-ordinate official language, and in Zimbabwe, Shona and Ndebele also have official status. In both cases, English has more of the roles in domains of socio-economic conse-quence. For example, English is the medium of instruction of education at all levels, or at least beyond the first few years of primary school. It is also the language of written work, whether in government or business. The CS to be studied largely involves English; however, two examples come from francophone Africa (Wolof/French and Lingala/French).

Two of the reasons English retains prominence in Africa are its inter-national status and an anglophone colonial heritage. Kenya became inde-pendent in 1963, Zimbabwe in 1980. But a more important reason for the position of English and other former colonial languages (French, Portu-guese) in Africa is the indigenous language picture: in such a multilingual area, where no single group of speakers has sufficient dominance, nations find it difficult to agree on an indigenous language as the official language. The former colonial language, therefore, becomes a neutral solution in some respects. Yet it embodies colonialism for some; and for others, especially liberal intellectuals, it is also a negative resolution of the problem: since it is near-impossible to make the alien tongue accessible to everyone, the choice is an élitist solution.

Its large number of languages is one of the most distinctive features of sub-Saharan Africa. Their precise number cannot be stated, for two reasons: there is no generally accepted method for distinguishing between dialect and language; and even if there were, a practice often followed across the world is to use socio-historical criteria, not linguistic ones, in drawing language boundaries. For example, within East Africa, both extremes to the solution of segmenting a linguistic continuum are amply illustrated. In Uganda, although they are mutually intelligible, Acholi and Lango are called separ-ate languages, probably because the peoples see themselves as having differ-ent histories. And in Tanzania, although some of them are *not* mutually

intelligible, the Chaga dialects are called one language, presumably to promote a sense of unity.

Even by a conservative estimate, however, the number of distinct languages
in Africa is well over 800 (Greenberg 1971a: 126). These languages group
into four language families, in terms of their genetic affiliations (see Map 1).

The largest, most far-flung family is Niger–Kordofanian. The bifurca-
tion in this family is very uneven: Kordofanian includes only a pocket of
little-studied languages in Sudan while the other branch, Niger–Congo,
includes all the West African coastal languages as well as the Bantu subgroup.

There are at least 300 Bantu languages, covering much of the continent
from Cameroon in the West to the tip of South Africa. Kenya falls at the
northern boundary of the Bantu group in East and Southern Africa. South
of Kenya, the majority of the population are Bantu speakers; Zimbabwe is
entirely Bantu-speaking. The Bantu languages present many typological differences from their distant relatives on the West African coast. For example,
Bantu languages are inflectional-agglutinating while most West African coastal
languages are highly analytic, showing many single-morpheme words.

A prominent feature of Bantu languages is their noun class system. Today most Bantu languages have about 18 noun classes; but up to 22 classes
are posited for proto-Bantu (Doke 1943; Guthrie 1967–71). Nouns are
marked according to class membership by the prefixes they receive, as well
as by the agreements they govern on their modifiers, and by their pro-forms
occurring as obligatory subject prefixes in verbal assemblies and also as
object prefixes in these assemblies. For example, in the following Swahili
sentence, note the same *m-* prefix (for class 1) on the noun and its modifiers;
the pro-form of the class which appears as a verbal subject prefix is *a-*:

[1] M-toto m-moja m-dogo a-me-anguka
child   one   small   he/she-PERF-fall down
'One small child has fallen down'

Noun classes pair up as singular and plural forms (e.g. Swahili classes 7 and
8: *ki-kombe* 'cup', *vi-kombe* 'cups'). Bantuists have numbered the classes for
easy reference across languages, and these numbers will be used if reference
is made to class prefixes in examples cited in later chapters (e.g. class 6 takes
the *ma-* prefix; this is a plural class which is paired up with class 5, which
takes one of several or more allomorphs (often *ji-/li-/ø-*) as its prefix). The
class 6 prefix *ma-* often is found on collective nouns in Southern Africa; thus,
the Shona may be referred to as the *ma-shona*. In East Africa, the class 2
prefix *wa-* is used more often with peoples (e.g. the *wa-swahili*). Languages
are in class 7 in most Bantu languages, and take a prefix often realized as *ki*

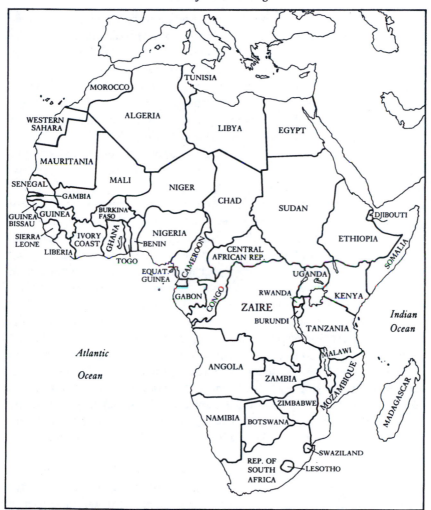

MAP 1. *Africa.*

or *si*. Thus, in the Swahili language itself, the lexeme for the language is *ki-swahili*; and in Zulu the lexeme for the language is *i-si-zulu*. Lexemes for some Bantu languages are in class 11 (e.g. the Luyia cluster in Kenya), showing *lu-* as the characteristic prefix, thus *lw-idakho* or *lu-luyia*.

Bantu languages show many structural and lexical similarities, indicating that the period of their differentiation is relatively short; yet, with some exceptions, varieties denoted as separate languages are not mutually intelligible. Bantuists generally agree on an East–West division within the Bantu group, judging that the eastward Bantu migration (from the Bantu home-land in the area of the Nigeria–Cameroon border) took place during the second millennium BC (Nurse and Spear 1985: 37). Within any single geographical area, of course, there may have been further in- and out-migrations of individual Bantu groups, resulting in a less than homogeneous picture in some places. From the linguistic point of view, this means there may well be several fairly different subgroups of Bantu languages, based on structural differentiations, even within a single nation.

In Kenya, for example, there are three Bantu subgroups, according to Nurse and Phillipson (1980: 41–52). These are (1) Lacustrine, the largest, with at least 16 million speakers, taking in the Luyia group in Kenya as well as Gusii, but also western Tanzanian languages and extending westward to Rundi and Nyarwanda and north-westward to include all the Ugandan Bantu languages; (2) North-east, with 6 million speakers, extending along the Kenyan and much of the Tanzanian coast and including Swahili, going westward to include Sukuma/Nyamwezi and implying historical population movements north and north-east from the west or south-west; and (3) Thagicu, with 5 million speakers in central Kenya, including Kikuyu.[1]

A second major language family in Africa is Afro-Asiatic. This family is as widely dispersed as Niger–Kordofanian, extending from the Middle East to Northern Africa, where it dips down in the West to western Cameroon and Nigeria and again in the East to Sudan, Ethiopia, Somali, Kenya, and even into Tanzania. It has five branches: Semitic (including Arabic and Hebrew in the Middle East, as well as Amharic in Ethiopia), Chad (including Hausa in West Africa), Cushitic (including Somali), Berber (including North African languages as well as Tuareg in Nigeria), and Ancient Egyptian (now extinct).

Central Africa is the centre of a third family, Nilo-Saharan. There are important languages from this family from the West (e.g. Kanuri in north-eastern Nigeria) to the East (e.g. the Nilotic languages in Uganda, Kenya, and Tanzania).

Finally, the fourth indigenous language family in Africa is Khoisan. Its speakers may once have roamed all of eastern and southern Africa as hunters and gatherers. They were pushed into agriculturally marginal areas by the expansion of the Bantu peoples, who are agriculturalists (as well as by the

---

[1] Nurse and Spear (1985: 40) offer a slightly different picture when writing more exclusively about the coastal areas, apparently seeing closer relationships among 3 E. African groups than any has with the Lacustrine group. They refer to an Eastern Bantu group composed of the Rufiji–Ruvuma subgroup (spoken in southern Tanzania), Chaga–Taita (spoken around Mt. Kilimanjaro and to the east), Thagicu (spoken around Mt. Kenya) and North-east coast (including 4 branches).

Afrikaans-speaking farmers in Southern Africa). Today, there are two pockets of Khoisan speakers in Tanzania (Sandawe and Hadza) and the remainder are largely in Southern Africa.

In comparison with areas of West Africa, the nations under study here may appear relatively homogeneous in linguistic terms. West Africa is the most populous area and it also has the most languages; for example, by conservative educated estimates, Nigeria alone has 300 languages. But lack of differentiation in East and Southern Africa may only exist on the surface. Zimbabwe, for example, appears to have only two main indigenous languages, both Bantu languages. Shona mother-tongue speakers account for about 80 per cent of the population, and Ndebele speakers for about 15 per cent. Further, Ndebele speakers are concentrated in the south-western areas around the city of Bulawayo, making most of Zimbabwe Shona-speaking. For administrative purposes, when Zimbabwe was still a colony, it was divided into two main divisions along linguistic lines: Matabeleland and Mashonaland.

Language in Zimbabwe

The apparent linguistic homogeneity in Zimbabwe is, however, deceptive. Shona itself is a 'constructed language'. Shona arose when a standard version was produced in the 1930s, for use by missionaries and government administrators among peoples speaking six relatively closely related linguistic varieties in Zimbabwe (then Southern Rhodesia), as well as in contiguous areas of Mozambique (then Portuguese East Africa) in the east, Zambia in the west, and Botswana in the south-west. Missionary societies working independently of each other in different areas prior to 1930 pushed four distinct dialect clusters into prominence (Karanga, Zezuru, Manyika, and Ndau). Because the General Missionary Conference of Southern Rhodesia could not agree on adopting a single dialect cluster as standard at their meeting in 1928, they asked the government for expert advice. Clement Doke, a well-known Bantuist (and senior lecturer in Bantu philology at the University of the Witwatersrand in Johannesburg, South Africa) was appointed to study the matter. Based on his year's research, Doke produced the first scholarly description of the dialects, and recommended in 1931 that a single unified literary variety be devised to serve the main Shona area, covering the dialects of Zezuru, Karanga, Korekore, Manyika, and Ndau. Doke (1931: 77) excluded Kalanga in the West because of 'long separation from the main section and strong outside influences', citing mutual intelligibility as a problem. Spoken in Matabeleland, Kalanga has been heavily

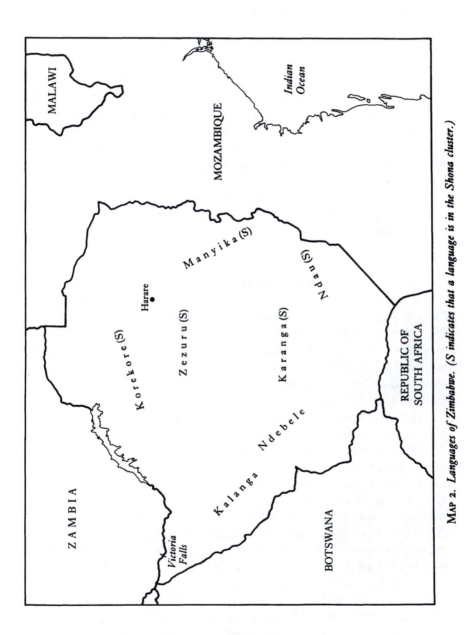

MAP 2. *Languages of Zimbabwe.* *(S indicates that a language is in the Shona cluster.)*

influenced by Ndebele. Today, Shona and Kalanga speakers regard Kalanga as separate from Shona (Ngara 1982: 17).

Doke (1931: 80) recommended that 'the unified grammar be standardized on the basis of Karanga and Zezeru', probably because (as he noted, p. 4) Zezuru had already received more recognition than other varieties, since it was spoken indigenously around the administrative headquarters of Harare (then Salisbury), and because Karanga had a greater population than any other variety.

To name this unified variety, Doke suggested Shona, a name with an uncertain etymology. In doing so, he recognized (p. 78) that 'it [Shona] is not the true name of any of the peoples whom we proposed to group under the term "Shona-speaking peoples"'; he also recognized that 'the name Mashona is not pleasing to the natives'.

Doke (1931: 4) suggested that the inherent unity of the dialects was camouflaged by the different orthographies and word divisions in use by different missionary societies or writers. He stated that there were four distinct translations of the New Testament in use at that time. He estimated that the central dialects shared from 80 to 90 per cent of their vocabulary; even Kalanga shared just under 80 per cent.

Since Doke's recommendations, standardized Shona has been in official use as the appropriate variety to use in any written materials. Intended to represent standard Shona spelling, Hannan's *Standard Shona Dictionary* (1959) included entries from four dialects (Karanga, Korekore, Manyika, and Zezuru). In the introduction to a Shona reader (Carter and Kahari 1972), Carter refers to the variety used in the texts as 'Union Shona', stating it is based on features from the three main dialects (Manyika, Karanga, and Zezuru). She also (p. iv) refers to Union Shona as 'the language everyone writes and nobody speaks'. Interestingly enough, though, the texts are tone-marked.[2] Novels, plays, and poems have been written in the standard dialect, although English is largely the written language of educated Zimbabweans.

Although no spoken standard for Shona ever has been declared, it has long been the case that when the term 'ChiShona' is used, listeners typically understand that 'Zezuru' is intended. Early important grammars of Shona by Fortune were probably influential in crystallizing the association of Zezuru with spoken Shona. Fortune's *An Analytic Grammar of Shona* appeared in 1955 and *Elements of Shona* came out in 1957, both based on the Zezuru dialect. In the grammar appearing alongside their reader, Kahari and Carter (1972) state that the description is based on the Zezuru dialect. And Ngara

---

[2] The texts are tone-marked with Kahari's patterns, which are largely Zezuru (Carter, pers. comm.).

(1982: 17), after the disclaimer that 'It is not the intention of the present writer to give preference to any of the six dialects', goes on to say he will use the Zezuru dialect as a model for a number of reasons (e.g. its geographical centrality), including the fact it is his own dialect.

Speakers still use their various home dialects, and see their linguistic varieties primarily as part of their own ethnic group and only secondarily as part of what is now recognized as the greater Shona community, although more of a sense of community has arisen since independence. But writing in 1973 Gelfand (p. 8) could still state, 'The Shona do not call themselves Shona. They are called the Shona because they speak one or other of the dialects of what the linguists call the Shona cluster of Bantu languages.' However, Ngara (1982: 16) states, 'Educated Shona speakers tend to call themselves by this name.'

Although it is located in Zezuru-speaking territory, Zimbabwe's capital, Harare, is a multilingual urban centre. The city has attracted in-migrants as job-seekers from other dialect areas and the Ndebele-speaking areas, as well as from other nations. For example, for some years Malawians have gone to Harare to look for salaried positions—so much so that (in Chewa) looking for work used to be referred to as 'going *ku-Halale*'. There are also, of course, a number of residents of European origin.

Traditionally, the European farms of what was then Southern Rhodesia and the gold-mines of South Africa have drawn male Bantu-speaking workers from East African nations as far north as Tanzania. The multilingualism of the work forces is one reason for the development of the pidgins used in the mines and on the farms. In Zimbabwe, a pidgin called Chilapalapa is still in some use and is very similar to, if not identical with, Fanagalo spoken in South Africa.

The concentration of Shona mother-tongue speakers in Harare varies a good deal from area to area, according to a survey conducted in 1975–6 by Mkanganwi. In the Highfield and Glen Norah townships, 87 per cent of the residents are first-language speakers of Shona; but some African neighbourhoods include 30 per cent non-Shonas. Today Mkanganwi (1990) estimates for Harare as a whole that the figure for mother-tongue Shona speakers may be as low as 80 per cent. His survey also showed that the Chewa/Nyanja group (from Malawi and eastern Zambia) was the largest other African group, followed by the Ndebele group.

Another source of division beneath the homogeneous surface in Zimbabwe is the relationship between Shona and Ndebele. True, they are both Bantu languages and both within the general grouping of Southern Bantu languages. But Ndebele shows more affiliations with the Bantu languages spoken in South Africa than it does with Shona. Tradition has it that the Ndebele, following their leader Mzilikazi, left Zululand, fleeing from the famous Zulu chief, Chaka, and finally settled in Zimbabwe in about 1837. The Ndebele have made the Bulawayo area their own, to the extent that a number of the people of Shona origin in the Bulawayo area now speak Ndebele as a first language. From Doke (1931: 3) onwards, it has been recognized that Ndebele is a dialect of Zulu from a linguistic point of view. There is a good deal of mutual intelligibility between speakers of Zulu and of Ndebele (Ngara 1982: 19). But the Ndebele feel very strongly that they are a separate nation from the Zulu, and recognize their language as a separate entity. (Interestingly, Zulu was the indigenous language taught in the schools up to 1967 in the Bulawayo area (Ngara 1982: 19).) In Harare the appellation *Ndebele* means 'from Matabeleland' and/or 'fluent in Ndebele and not necessarily a mother-tongue speaker of Ndebele' (Mkanganwi 1990).

Divisions between the Shona and the Ndebele continue to be recognized. A prominent phonological difference between their languages is that Ndebele has a number of the click consonants which also occur in South African Bantu languages. (These were borrowed from the neighbouring Khoisan languages.) Modern political divisions are also along linguistic lines between the Shona and the Ndebele. Thus, for reasons somewhat linguistic, but more psychological, it is not unusual to hear a Shona speaker say, 'Ndebele is very different from Shona! Why, it's easier to learn English.'

Language in Kenya

While Kenya cannot rival the diversification found in West Africa, it has many more languages than Zimbabwe and much deeper linguistically based divisions. Kenya has approximately 34 indigenous languages (Whiteley 1974*b*: 27). More importantly, it shows three different language families.

While Bantu languages are prominent (about 15 out of the 34), more actual physical territory in Kenya is covered by representatives of the Afro-Asiatic and Nilo-Saharan families. These non-Bantu groups are largely speakers of Nilotic languages, classified into three distantly related groups in the Nilo-Saharan family (Greenberg 1963). Western Nilotic languages stretch in a corridor from Sudan to the north-western corner of Tanzania, including Luo in Kenya. One of the four major ethnic groups in Kenya, the Luo are the only non-Bantu one.

While their home area is around the city of Kisumu on the shores of Lake

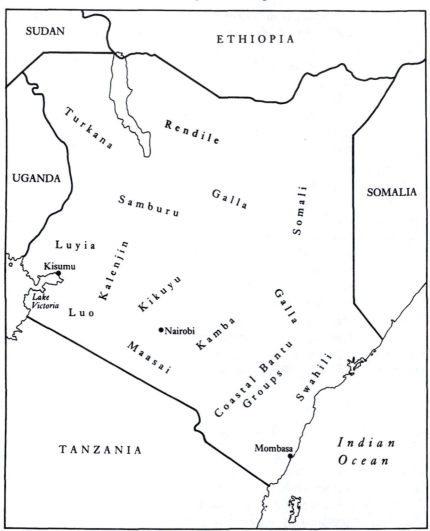

MAP 3. *Major languages of Kenya.*

Victoria in the far west, the Luo form a prominent in-migrant group in other Kenyan cities, especially Mombasa (on the coast of the Indian Ocean) and Nairobi. Perhaps because they have a tradition of good schooling (thanks to early and important missionary presence in their home areas), the Luo have been prominent at the national level in politics and as civil servants. Perhaps because they are non-Bantus, they traditionally have spoken less

Swahili for inter-ethnic purposes than Kenyan Bantu groups; also, their education has equipped them to use English as a lingua franca.

The genetic relations of the other Nilotic languages in Kenya used to be in dispute (note that Whiteley (1974*b*: 23) still persists in calling them 'Para-Nilotic'), but almost all scholars today agree with Greenberg's placement of them within the Nilotic subgroup. The Eastern Nilotic group includes Teso in Kenya and Maasai, as well as several other groups closely related to Maasai, such as Samburu. The Teso are a relatively numerous group in neighboring Uganda, but are only found in Kenya along the Kenya–Uganda border; the smaller Turkana group is in a similar position. The Maasai are a nomadic, cattle-owning group in the central areas of Kenya and Tanzania. Groups related to the Maasai are in north-central Kenya, including the Samburu. While they have received a good deal of attention from Westerners as picturesque nomads, the Maasai and their relatives are not, for Kenyans, a strong presence outside their own traditional areas, and certainly not in urban contexts.

Southern Nilotic languages are found only in Kenya, and include the Kalenjin group. Their home areas are on the western fringe of the Rift Valley, extending the length of Kenya. The Kalenjin group includes most prominently Nandi and Kipsigis. In the past, many Kalenjin varieties wanted to retain their separate identities. But today, especially given the fact that the current president of Kenya, Daniel Arap Moi, is a Kalenjin, most speakers in this group are happy to be called Kalenjin. While the Kalenjin had not previously been prominent in Nairobi affairs, under President Moi, more members of this group hold important positions in the central government in Nairobi. Like their Eastern Nilotic brethren, Kalenjins did not have access to much education in the past and therefore are not numerous in white-collar jobs in Nairobi. But the first Kenyan university outside the Nairobi area, Moi University, was opened in Kalenjin territory, near the city of Eldoret in western Kenya.

Kenya's north-eastern areas are largely Eastern Cushitic-speaking. The varieties spoken can be grouped into either the 'Somali group' or the 'Galla group' (Whiteley 1974*b*: 24). Somali is the main language of the large North-eastern Province, which borders on Somalia. Oromo, a major language in Ethiopia, is in the 'Galla group', and is spoken in Eastern Province, along with related languages. One Southern Cushitic language, Dahalo, is spoken by a very small group near the coast.

Even with the non-Bantu presence, Bantu groups clearly dominate in Kenya and, indeed, in all of East Africa. They represent about 66 per cent of the population in both Kenya and Uganda and over 95 per cent in

Tanzania. Three of the four major ethnic groups in Kenya are Bantu-speaking: Kikuyu, Kamba, and Luyia.

The Kikuyu, with a home area stretching northwards from Nairobi, have been an important force in Kenyan politics and in urban centres since before independence (in 1963). The well-known Mao Mao rebellion of the 1950s was theirs. When independence came, it seemed inevitable that the first president would be the famous Kikuyu statesman, Jomo Kenyatta, who was imprisoned during the Mao Mao rebellion by the British. Like the Luo, but perhaps even more so, since their homelands are in the temperate, well-watered areas favoured by Europeans, the Kikuyu benefited early on from a good, missionary-sponsored educational system. Even today, a disproportionate number of secondary schools and other institutions of higher learning are in the Central Province, traditionally Kikuyu territory. Thanks to their superior education and Kikuyu prominence in the national government, many Kikuyu hold civil-service jobs in Nairobi, as well as in other urban centres. They also became major players in the Nairobi business community. Further, more than any other ethnic group in the whole of East Africa, the Kikuyu have become well known as successful entrepreneurs. In almost any hamlet in Kenya, if there are provisions shops at all, there is at least one Kikuyu-owned shop. Nakuru, the fourth largest city in Kenya (after Nairobi, Mombasa, and Kisumu) is dominated by the Kikuyu today, although it is located in traditional Kalenjin/Maasai territory. This is a post-independence phenomenon.

The Kamba, who come from the area of Eastern Province just to the east of Nairobi, speak a language very closely related to Kikuyu; Parkin (1974a: 185) refers to Kikuyu and Kamba as 'each standing on the "threshold" of learning each other's language'. These two languages are the major members of the Thagicu, (Nurse and Phillipson 1980), a Bantu grouping centred in the Mount Kenya area of central Kenya. It also includes Embu, Meru, and Tharaka. In his study of language-use patterns in Nairobi in the 1970s, Parkin (1974a: 177) found more combined mutual vernacular knowledge between the Kamba and the Kikuyu than for any other ethnic group pair, with 36.5 per cent of all Kamba and Kikuyu in his sample claiming to be able to switch to the other language. But Parkin also notes that the Kikuyu do not learn other groups' vernaculars as much as other groups learn theirs, suggesting that this is a direct result of the Kikuyu national dominance and numerical superiority in Nairobi at the time. Regarding the Kikuyu–Kamba relationship, Parkin (p. 185) writes: 'because Kikuyu are so predominant in Nairobi, they provide the most obvious, numerous and culturally and linguistically convenient source of "patronage" for the Kamba, whose generally low socio-economic status tends to foster their dependence.' There is little reason to think this picture has changed appreciably in the interim.

The other major Bantu group in Kenya is the Luyia, who come from Western Province and spill over the border into Uganda. Their home area borders the Luo to the south, the Kalenjin to the north and east, and largely the Teso in the west. But, while they are separated geographically from other Kenyan Bantu groups, they are part of a large Lacustrine Bantu group extending westward to include all the Ugandan Bantu languages (Luganda, Lunyoro, etc.) and also Gusii in the south-western corner of Kenya. Because I have done field work among the Luyia in their home area, as well as in Nairobi, many of my examples come from Luyia speakers, most especially of the Lwidakho dialect.

Like Shona in Zimbabwe, a standardized variety of Luyia is a creation of the missionaries; in the Luyia case, however, the outcome was not totally successful. There are about 16 or 17 Luyia dialects, depending on how they are counted (Itebete 1974: 89; Angogo 1980: 4), showing differing degrees of mutual intelligibility. For example, Itebete (1974: 89) notes, 'Linguistically it would be difficult to prove that Lwisukha and Lwidakho are separate dialects, unless one took as criteria small differences in vowel quality and quantity and some tonal variations.' And indeed, the central dialects which were chosen to form the basis of the standardized orthography show few differences. But there are sharp transitions at the edges of the Luyia cluster, especially concerning Lubukusu and Luragoli. The name, *Luyia*, is of uncertain origin (Angogo 1980: 2); people today called [βaluyia/waluyia] were earlier called [wakavirondo].

Missionaries began work in the Luyia area in the first decade of the twentieth century, with the Friends arriving first in 1902 and settling at Kaimosi (in Maragoli territory), but followed closely by many other groups. Prior to 1942, four separate orthographies had been devised for four dialect areas, each representing a sphere of missionary influence: (Lu)Hanga, used by the Christian Missionary Society (CMS); (Lu)Nyore, used by the Church of God; (Lu)Ragoli, used by the Friends African Mission (FAM); and (Lu)Wanga, used by the Catholics, who also used other dialects. The first meeting of an Orthography Committee aiming for unification took place in 1941. Eventually, plans called for a 'Luluhya' grammar based on that of the central dialects ((Lu)Marama, (Lu)Shisa, (Lu)Wanga, and (Lu)Tsotso). Archdeaconess L. L. Appleby (of the CMS), a trained linguist, produced a stencilled Luluhya–English vocabulary in 1943. The FAM had been hostile to the project from the beginning, and did not eventually support the standardized version. Later, the Bukusu speakers, among the most populous groups, also pulled out of the standardization exercise, as did other small groups. But as Itebete (1974: 109) points out, the two dialects which broke away, (Lu)Bukusu and (Lu)Ragoli, had from the earliest times been recognized as the two most divergent from the rest of the cluster. Before 1957, a number of primary books were published in the union dialect (now usually written 'Luyia'), but the Ragoli and the Bukusu peoples also produced some of their own reading materials. There still are three orthographies in use, but publications in any of them are very limited.

As matters stand today, the standardization exercise was only a success in so far as it gave peoples from the dialect clusters a common name, the Luyia, and something of a common ethnic identity. But whether people refer to themselves as Luyia, speaking the Luyia language, depends on where they are. In fact, they always speak only their own dialects (unless they know another dialect and choose to speak it with a native speaker of that dialect). In their home areas of western Kenya, people refer to themselves and their speech by their dialectal/ethnic group names. For example, a person may be a Mudakho [mu-daxo] speaking Lwidakho [lw-idaxo]. If they are far from home—living in Nairobi, for example—they refer to themselves and their speech as Luyia. That is, a person who is a Mudakho in his western Kenya homeland becomes a Muluyia in Nairobi, speaking Lu-luyia (or Ki-luyia, if the Swahili name is used).

While these three large Bantu groups (Kikuyu, Kamba, and Luyia) occupy up-country areas in Kenya, the coastal strip along the Indian Ocean is inhabited by a number of smaller Bantu groups, all within the subgroup called Sabaki within the North-Eastern Coastal Bantu group (NECB). The most prominent of these languages is Swahili, of course.

Many non-Bantuists, including some linguists, still erroneously list Swahili as a pidgin/creole which had no existence before there were contacts along the East Africa coast between Bantu-speaking peoples and Arab traders.[3] As Greenberg (1963) has pointed out, in the history of language classification in Africa, it has often been the most widely spoken or most well-known languages which have been erroneously classified. Greenberg was referring particularly to Fulani and also to Hausa. Early students from the time of F. Mueller in the nineteenth century have given Fulani a special status. Greenberg (1963: 24) comments, 'The reasons are not far to seek. The Fulani

---

[3] That the 'creole' hypothesis for Swahili is not dead is exemplified by references to Swahili in Holm (1989), a recent survey of the world's pidgins and creoles. While Holm never states that Swahili developed from a pidgin, he does assert (p. 564): 'The language arose on the coast of East Africa during the eighth century AD out of contact between Arabic-speaking traders and the native Bantu-speaking peoples.' On the same page he states that the hypothesis that Swahili 'originated as a pidgin of the Arabs' slaves and half-caste families has by no means been proven'.

are a conspicuous people, one of the largest tribal groups in Africa, spread in isolated though substantial islands over well-nigh half the breadth of the African continent from Senegal to Wadai, east of Lake Chad.' When the European colonials arrived, the Fulani appeared 'different' to them because they were in political control of large parts of West Africa and they seemed to form a special racial subtype. A Caucasoid origin was posited and Africanist linguists of the early twentieth century, such as Meinhof, attempted to show that the Fulani language was Hamitic, a mixed group. But one of Greenberg's major accomplishments in his classification of African languages was to demonstrate that, linguistically, Fulani fits clearly into the West Atlantic subgroup of the Niger–Congo branch of the Niger–Kordofanian family. Hausa, perhaps an even more conspicuous language than Fulani, was also similarly 'lifted out of context' and considered 'unusual' among African languages. Before Greenberg's work, Hausa was classified only in reference to resemblances to Semitic or Berber languages. While it does have affinities with these languages (they are all in the Afro-Asiatic family Greenberg defined), Greenberg shows that Hausa's closest linguistic relatives are other languages of the Lake Chad area. Hausa and these languages are in the Chad group within what is now called the Afro-Asiatic family.

It is the prominent inclusion of cultural words from Arabic which has tempted lay people and historians alike to classify Swahili as a mixed language. But, as Nurse and Spear (1985: 6) point out, it is a fallacy to think the most important feature of Swahili is its Arabic component. When the basic structures of Swahili are examined (sound system and morphosyntax), it becomes clear that Swahili is genetically related to Bantu languages, not Arabic. Its closest relatives are those languages in the NECB subgroup in coastal Kenya, north-east Tanzania, and the Comoros Islands.

Nurse and Spear (1985: 43) posit a homeland of NECB between Mombasa and mountainous areas slightly inland to the south-west (the Usambara, Taita, and Pare mountains), based on linguistic and archaeological reasoning, including a second-century pottery site. Two of the four branches of NECB are still in this area (Seuta and Pare), while the third (Ruvu) moved south and the fourth (Sabaki) moved north of the Tana River along the northern Kenyan coast (i.e. near the island of Lamu). Gradually, various Sabaki communities moved south. Of the five Sabaki languages, three are confined to the Kenya coast (Elwana, Pokomo, Mijikenda). A fourth, Comorian, is spoken on the Comoros Islands. Swahili is the fifth and obviously most prominent Sabaki language.

As a first language, Swahili is spoken today in a discontinuous pattern along the East African coast; it is spoken all along the Kenyan coast, but then it skips to the southern Tanzanian coast. It is also the mother tongue of various offshore islands, most prominently Lamu in the far north and Mafia (Kilwa) in the far south, with Zanzibar and Pemba in between.

Living on the coast, the Swahili came in contact with Arab sailors and traders. From them, they borrowed some cultural features as well as vocabulary. The result is that Swahili's native speakers, like those of Fulani in West Africa, have a way of life and, thanks to intermarriage, a physical appearance different from inland East African groups.[4] Many have used the Swahili people's culture as another reason for viewing the Swahili language as having a different origin from neighbouring African languages. Most of the Swahili are followers of Islam, and many have Arabic names and facial features.

But it is a mistake to assume that linguistic affinities always follow cultural ones. True, it is undeniable that the Swahili borrowed from the Arabs a number of cultural lexemes, especially relating to jurisprudence, trade, religion, non-indigenous flora, and maritime affairs (Nurse and Spear 1985: 15). Still, following a detailed analysis, Nurse and Hinnebusch (1993) estimate the total proportion for loan-words, both local and foreign, to range from 6 to 23 per cent, the average being 15 per cent. They compare this to 12 per cent as an accepted figure for English and about 13 per cent which they have found for the other Sabaki languages.

In its core vocabulary, and also in its structure, Swahili fits entirely within the Bantu pattern (Whiteley 1969; Nurse and Spear 1985; Nurse and Hinnebusch, 1993). There is no basis at all for arguing that Swahili was ever a creole, with the polygenetic origin that designation applies. True, Swahili appears to have lost some structural features retained by nearby Bantu languages, such as tone as a distinctive feature. But it retains fifteen of the posited twenty-two proto-Bantu noun classes and the concordial system which goes with it, as well as the distinctive Bantu verbal assembly.[5] Also,

---

[4] Nurse and Hinnebusch (1993: 309) point out differences in exposure to other cultures between the Swahili and other E. Africans: 'The background of Swahili is thus different from that of other members of Sabaki, indeed, of most other language communities in East Africa. Most other East African linguistic communities are landlocked and restricted to well delimited and relatively small geographical domains. By contrast, for 1500 years since their diaspora, the littoral communities speaking Swahili have been strung out in a thin and often discontinuous line along a thousand miles of coast. Frequently they do not identify themselves as subsets of Swahili, but rather in local terms. Their linguistic and social interaction with various neighboring peoples or with peoples across the Indian Ocean have been just as significant as their earlier descent from a proto-community.'

[5] Nurse and Hinnebusch (1993: 331) conclude a lengthy discussion by stating that the structural changes that have affected Swahili are not extraordinary, and that evidence suggests 'they have taken place at different times, and are not the result of a single set of circumstances at a single time, such as creolisation would require'. They point out that the Swahili phonemic inventory has been enlarged by 4 fricatives /θ, δ, χ, γ/ borrowed from Arabic, but they see no sign of the borrowing of phonological processes. Also, they see no evidence that Swahili nominal or verbal morphology has directly borrowed anything from Arabic or Persian.

it shows the usual type of systematic correspondences in its structure with its relatives in NECB, which comparative linguists would expect to find in the natural development of any language. Of course, there are varieties of Swahili spoken in up–country areas, especially in Zaïre, which might qualify as pidgins/creoles; but even here this designation is in dispute (e.g. Kapanga 1989).

Nurse and Spear (1985: 49) estimate that an early form of Swahili was probably spoken by the ninth century all the way from northern Kenyan coastal settlements to southern Tanzania. Given the sound changes which have affected Swahili and the sound patterns found in Arabic loans, Nurse and Spear also suggest that Arabic influence was not very intense before the eighteenth century, stating (p. 6): 'The Arabic material is a recent graft onto an old Bantu tree.'

A final reason for assuming Swahili does not fit into the ordinary Bantu mould is its success as a lingua franca. Today, Swahili is probably the most widely spoken African language because of its currency as an inter-ethnic language throughout East Africa (Tanzania, Kenya, and Uganda) and into neighbouring nations (Mozambique, Zambia, Burundi, Rwanda, Zaïre, Somalia, and Southern Sudan). That is, while its native speakers are relatively few, 20 million or more persons speak it as a second language. No doubt because of this position, it is the African language with the most official recognition. It is the national and official language of Tanzania, the national and co-official language in Kenya (sharing official status with English), and the national language in Uganda. In addition, it is one of the four languages in Zaïre with regional official status. As far south as Zambia, and even in West Africa, if a lingua franca is needed, someone will know enough Swahili to cope. Tanzania and Kenya are the Swahili strongholds, of course; but in cities all over eastern Africa, Swahili is over-whelmingly the major indigenous lingua franca. For example, Scotton (1972) found that 97 per cent of workers in a sample studied in the capital of Uganda, Kampala, claimed to speak at least some Swahili. And today, in Bukavu in eastern Zaïre, where almost everyone knows and uses a version of Swahili every day, a language shift to the Bukavu version of Swahili as a mother tongue is under way (Wilt 1989).

The rise of Swahili

Diverse historical circumstances created successive needs for a lingua franca in the East African interior, and Swahili, fortuitously, was on hand to meet these needs.

First, the Arab traders who organized trading caravans to the interior from Zanzibar and nearby points on the Tanzanian coast needed a means of communicating with the indigenous peoples they met along the way. There is no direct evidence regarding language use before the 1840s, but presumably these traders spoke Swahili as their own first language, or at least knew it, and it became the medium of trade (Whiteley 1969). In this way, Swahili was spread across Tanzania, north-west to Uganda, and as far west as Zaïre, although when it reached as far as Shaba Province, where it became a lingua franca in the copper-mines, is in some dispute (Fabian 1986). Note that caravans went west mainly from the Tanzanian coast, not from Kenya, where there were also Swahili speakers in Mombasa and other ports. The reason for this seems to have been that the Kenyan interior was inhabited by unfriendly ethnic groups, prominently the Maasai. But even today in Tanzania, there are still some pockets along the trading route (e.g. in Tabora in the Tanzanian interior) where descendants of caravan members speak Swahili as their mother tongue.

Second, the missionaries who arrived on the coastal scene in the mid- and late nineteenth century also needed a lingua franca. Since they set up initial operations where Swahili was a first language (e.g. Zanzibar and Mombasa), since Swahili was already in place as a lingua franca, and since it had a written literature (in Arabic script, with existing manuscripts dating possibly as far back as the seventeenth century), it is not surprising that the missionaries considered Swahili worthy of their linguistic energies. Several grammars of Swahili were soon produced, the first in 1850 by the CMS missionary, J. L. Krapf, in Mombasa (Krapf 1850). This further enhanced Swahili as a lingua franca.

Third, the colonials also needed a lingua franca to govern. When the Germans arrived to colonize Tanganyika (now Tanzania, including Zanzibar as well as the mainland territory), they envisioned the area as a profitable colony and therefore wanted literate Africans, not expensive expatriates, filling at least the minor civil-service positions. They started with Swahili-speaking personnel from Zanzibar, founded schools that taught Swahili, and required the missionaries to produce Swahili-speaking school graduates. In their administration of East Africa, the British (first in Uganda and Kenya, and then also in Tanganyika when this area became a British protectorate after the First World War) also wanted to use local resources in the civil service; they welcomed the idea of a lower-level, Swahili-speaking cadre.

Many European civil servants and settlers, as well as in-migrants from India, who became shopkeepers and businessmen, learned Swahili, although sometimes a simplified version. Derisive names for such versions were *ki-settla* and *ki-hindi*. Finally, especially in Tanganyika and to an extent in Kenya, Swahili was the natural choice as the vehicle of nationalist mobilization in the push for independence after the Second World War.

A standardized version of Swahili was produced by an inter-territorial conference in 1928. Standard Swahili was based on the Zanzibar dialect. This was partly a political decision; among other things, it meant supporting groups favouring the grammar of the Zanzibar dialect produced by Bishop Edward Steere (1870) at the Universities Mission Centre in Zanzibar. Under the British, English did become the language of post-primary education and of higher administration in East Africa, but the British embraced Swahili as a lingua franca between themselves and the Africans, as well as for the Africans themselves.

Official policy toward the teaching of Swahili in the schools waxed and waned, but in general Swahili was the medium of primary education for Africans; this policy was especially consistent in Tanganyika.[6]

Choosing an official language in Africa

In many ways, both Kenya and Zimbabwe represent the typical African nation in the dilemma with which they are faced in choosing an official language and the inevitably uneasy solution to the problem.

First, there is no single group with both enough numerical and enough political dominance to make its language the natural choice as official. With a very few exceptions (e.g. Somalia, Botswana, Lesotho, Burundi, Rwanda), this is the pattern across Africa; and not even all the exceptions have given primary official status to the dominant indigenous language.

Second, in both Kenya and Zimbabwe there are several groups of enough size and power to dispute the awarding of official status to any other indigenous language. A similar situation prevails in Nigeria, for example; there, the Yoruba, Ibo, and Hausa are major groups, each unwilling to see another group's language prevail. As noted above, Tanzania's demographic makeup was a crucial factor in making Swahili an acceptable choice there.

Third, if there is an indigenous lingua franca which is widely known, it

[6] See Whiteley (1969) for a sketch of the rise of Swahili as a lingua franca; Scotton (1978) discusses Swahili's position in E. Africa in relation to political ideologies. During the late 1960s and early 1970s, Ford Foundation-sponsored language surveys were conducted in 5 African nations. The surveys resulted in 5 volumes: Ladefoged, Glick, and Criper (1971) on Uganda was followed by 4 edited volumes: Whiteley (1974a) on Kenya, Bender *et al.* (1976) on Ethiopia, Ohannessian and Kashoki (1978) on Zambia, and Polome and Hill (1980) on Tanzania. For a recent statement on bilingualism and language policy in Tanzania, Kenya, and Uganda, see Scotton (1988c).

is unacceptable to many as the main official language, either because of its associations with situations in which socio-economic status is not salient or because of its ties to a single ethnic group. In Zaïre, for example, there are four indigenous languages, each with official recognition in a specific region (Lingala, Swahili, Luba, Kongo), but French remains the sole national official language and is the sole medium of higher education and governmental business. And although Nigerian pidgin English is widely known in Nigeria, it has no official role because of its lowly associations as a market language, even though such highly placed persons as university professors report using it for their informal interactions. Also, although Wolof is widely spoken in Senegal, especially in the capital of Dakar, its ties to the Wolof ethnic group militate against its being granted official status.

Fourth, given such conditions, a nation often opts for its former colonial language as its main official language, making English, French, and Portuguese still official languages in most of Africa. The main virtue of the alien official language is its relative ethnic neutrality.

It is important to understand that language choice (including language shift) is predominantly based on political and economic considerations, not emotional ones.[7] That is, people recognize that the official language becomes the vehicle of political participation and socio-economic mobility. The competition among groups for primacy of one language over others, or at least parity with the others, is based on this, not on 'primordial loyalties'. If one ethnic group's language becomes official, its members have a head start. What makes an alien official language attractive is the reasoning that all groups (in theory) start at zero in acquiring it. Still, because of its colonial and élitist associations (more than twenty years after independence, under half the population know the official language across Africa), the alien official language is definitely a negative choice. Real access to this language comes through extended formal education, and such education is tied to privilege.[8]

Given the linguistic diversity outlined above, especially for Kenya, it is clear that selecting an indigenous language as the nation's main official language would be difficult. In Kenya, no language is numerically dominant. The fact that Swahili is the sole official language in Tanzania today, but not in Kenya or Uganda, can be attributed to different linguistic proportions,

[7] In a general discussion of instances of language shift around the world, Edwards (1985) concludes that people typically shift when socio-economic advancement lies with the replacement language.

[8] Scotton (1982c) advances an argument as to why more Africans do not acquire the alien official language informally. Myers-Scotton (1990b) discusses the role of such languages in maintaining 'élite closure', i.e. official and unofficial practices which promote preferential access to socio-economic mobility.

but also to different political goals, at least in the first years after independence.[9] With a largely Bantu population comprising many small groups (Polome and Hill (1980) list 102 Bantu languages as composing 94 per cent of the population), Tanzania found it easy to choose Swahili as its official language. There were no ethnic groups with both enough size and enough political dominance to offer competition, and, as a Bantu language itself, Swahili was not difficult for the many Bantu-speaking peoples to learn. Further, since Swahili was not the mother tongue of any sizeable group (it was the mother tongue of Zanzibar and other offshore islands, but it was not the language of the entire Tanzanian coast, in contrast to its position on the Kenyan coast), choosing Swahili as the official language did not give preferential treatment to many.

In Kenya, however, there were four up-country groups with enough size and political power to resist giving official status to Swahili, the language of coastal peoples of fewer numbers and less power. Also, even though Swahili is the first language of Kenya's coast, the area which produced the greatest traditional Swahili literature, Swahili has often been viewed as alien by up-country Kenyans.

First there is the question of dialect. Of interest for this study is the fact that the Zanzibar-based Standard Swahili is what most up-country Kenyan Africans learned, not a variant of Kenyan coastal Swahili. Recall that it was this variety which was spread up-country by trading caravans and which, in addition, was taught in the schools and used in any government communications. Whiteley (1969: 81) notes that the decision to make the Zanzibar dialect the basis of Standard Swahili engendered a good deal of bitterness: 'during the thirties and forties the Mombasa dialect was associated with separatism and conservatism.' Today, up-country Kenyans still view coastal Swahili in this light. And the Kenyans who argue most loudly for making Swahili Kenya's sole official language are often coastal residents who also advocate their own dialect (not Standard Swahili) as the basis for this variety.

Second, there is the matter of culture. The Moslem culture of the Swahili coast remains alien to most up-country Kenyans, who spurn its relative lack of emphasis on Western education and socio-economic aspirations. It is largely up-country Kenyans with Western-style credentials and values who have captured most positions of power in both government and the business sector.

Finally, up-country Kenyans have always been reluctant to embrace movements in favour of Swahili. First, under colonial rule they could see that

---

[9] See Scotton (1978).

the benefits of learning Swahili consisted only of becoming more useful to
the Europeans as servants, labourers, and clerks. Swahili's image as a language
for master–servant relationships has not entirely faded. It remains the norm
to address in Swahili persons of obviously lower socio-economic status, such
as watchmen, porters, and market sellers. Therefore, while on the one hand
feeling some pride in Swahili as a symbol of their African heritage, educated
Kenyans see English, not Swahili, as a symbol of the aspects of their lives
involving socio-economic mobility.[10] Thus, for example, although Swahili
was made an official language of parliament, alongside English, in 1974, even
today few members of parliament give their speeches in Swahili.

Yet today the picture in Kenya is one in which Swahili is gaining more and
more official recognition. Swahili's status was recently enhanced when in 1988
it was made a compulsory school subject and included among those subjects
examined on the primary school-leaving examination. But whether Swahili's
gain is English's loss is not yet clear. For example, it is possible that any
ground Swahili gains may be at the expense of ethnic-group languages.

There has always been a good deal of rhetoric in Kenya about the official-
language issue, part of the love/hate attitude Kenyans have toward their
colonial heritage and their relations with the Western world. Few weeks
pass without at least one letter to the editor of a newspaper, condemning
continuation of English as the official language. For example, two incidents
related by a University of Nairobi student as taking place in his home area
show the extent of psychological conflict involved in the competition between English and local languages (Scotton 1982*c*: 79):

[2]

My brother was arrested by the police and sent to the chief for making beer without a license. He asked to be forgiven (in the local language) by the chief, who
rejected the plea. I went to the chief's center where I found some policemen at
the door. Nobody was allowed to enter. I spoke English to one of the policemen
and said I wanted to see the chief. The police allowed me in. It was, I strongly
believe, my English that gave me the honor to be allowed in. And it was my
English, during my talk with the chief, that secured the release of my brother.

---

[10] Scotton (1977) reports on an experimental study conducted in Kampala, Uganda, which
showed that, while subjects used a speaker's performance in English to judge his possible occupation, they did not do this with his Swahili performance. Twenty years ago, similar attitudes pre-
vailed in Nairobi; however, today's attitudes need study. But the ramifications of not using Swahili
as a socio-economic marker are clear: people feel freer to express themselves in Swahili than
English, since their linguistic performance is not being judged in a socio-economic sense; but at the
same time Swahili's value is seen as diminished relative to English (i.e. it does not give much of a
'return').

[3]

At a beer party near my home, two boys broke into talk in English. The reaction of the old men was bitter and they said, 'Who are those speaking English? Are they back-biting us? They are proud! Push them out.' Although the boys were not addressing the beer party as such, this was regarded as an insult.

Still, even while Swahili makes headway in the schools, English remains the medium of all examinations and of all higher education (except for some university-level lectures in Swahili classes). Also, while English and Swahili are co-ordinate official languages, and while Swahili, never English, is the language of political speeches to the masses, written government business is in English. There are a few publications in Swahili, including a newspaper, but these are largely read only by coastal residents or 'traditionally minded' persons. The message is clear: to date, education and other forms of modernity are being expressed in English.

For example, a University of Nairobi student doing a research project on patterns of language use reported the following exchange with a a Nairobi bus conductor:

[4] (Myers-Scotton, unpublished data)

(Trying to establish the conductor's reasons for using one language rather than another, she identifies herself as a university student and asks him in Swahili why he had just spoken English, knowing Swahili is the language most used in such service encounters in Nairobi. He responds in English.)

STUDENT (Swahili). Kwa nini unasema Kizungu na yeye?

'Why do you speak English with him?'

(Note: *Ki-zungu* = class 7 prefix + 'European')

CONDUCTOR (English) (said with a laugh). Do you think we don't speak any English? We went to school and we can speak very good English—better than you!

In another conversation on a bus, a passenger gets himself into trouble by trying to speak English, apparently trying to impress his fellow ethnic-group member. When he asks a question in English and gets an answer in English, he does not seem to understand the English word *debts*; at least he remained silent for the rest of the journey:

[5] (Scotton 1979: 74)

SPEAKER I (Kikuyu). Niatia, Mwangi?

'How are you, Mwangi?'

SPEAKER II (Kikuyu). Nikwega.

'Fine.'

SPEAKER I (English). Are you still working in the same place?

SPEAKER II (English). Yes.

SPEAKER I (English). By the way, what sort of work do you do there?
SPEAKER II (English). Dealing with debits.
SPEAKER I (English). What?
SPEAKER II (English). I usually deal with credits and debits of the company.
SPEAKER I (Kikuyu). Ati?
'What?'
SPEAKER II (English). Debts.
SPEAKER I. (Silence.)

Other Kenyan indigenous languages have very little official recognition. About eighteen have been designated official school vernaculars. But the policy to use these as media in the early years of schooling is highly flexible. If the population is mixed, Swahili may be the medium. And in Nairobi schools high up the socio-economic ladder, the sole medium will be English. This is even the policy in some rural schools, the vernacular being used only for certain explanations. The reason is that educators feel the more English the students are exposed to, the better, since the primary school-leaving examination is in English (Scotton 1988*b*: 211). Also, in Africa, as a whole, even rural areas are frequently multilingual to the extent that choosing a single indigenous language as the medium rarely serves the needs of most students. Ohannessian (1978: 300) reports a primary school in the Kabwe rural area of Zambia in which eight different mother tongues are represented among the students.

Compared with Kenya, language policy in Zimbabwe has little volatility. English, Shona, and Ndebele are all official languages; but English seems firmly established in all the major roles in the government, mass communications, and business sectors. In fact, in writing about Zimbabwean language policy McGinley (1987: 160) remarks, 'One of the most telling points that describe the role of English in Zimbabwe is the absence of comment in the media about it. It is not an issue.'

Still, while language policy is not a subject of overt debate, opinions differ. For example, Ngara (1982: 25) asked 60 university students their opinion about language policy; 55 per cent thought Shona should be the (sole) official language, while 43 per cent disagreed. And Mkanganwi (1989: 1) refers to the position of English in Zimbabwe as 'both confused and confusing'. He sees the sentiment for English as élitist because he does not consider it possible to offer all Zimbabweans the same level of instruction in English. He goes on to comment (p. 2):

English is widely used by . . . people of all socio-economic classes, in all domains, not as a communication medium used proficiently with precision, but rather as an 'impressive' medium. Speaking English in Zimbabwe often has little to do with the propositional content of words, phrases or sentences or their denotative meaning, or with the referring property of utterances, but more to do with the mere fact that it is *English* being spoken by the individual. It's English for 'impression' rather than for 'expression'.

Zimbabwe, of course, is only recently independent (1980), and after a bloody war. But, in contrast with Kenya, there is little overt animosity against the former colonial whites who remain. This attitude may be more politic than magnanimous, since the whites continue to control the economy. No doubt this attitude spills over to the language issue. There is also another matter, though: English is really the only choice in Zimbabwe because granting a primary role to Shona, the language of the numerically dominant, would be unacceptable to the Ndebele, who are already politically alienated in the new nation.

In education, English is the medium of instruction in most primary schools from the earliest years. Both Shona and Ndebele are taught as school subjects.

Patterns of bilingualism

Who becomes bilingual in Africa? The simple answer is, almost everyone who is mobile, either in a socio-economic or a geographic sense. While there are monolinguals in Africa, the typical person speaks at least one language in addition to his/her first language, and persons living in urban areas often speak two or three additional languages.[11] Specifics in the following discussion come mainly from Kenya and Zimbabwe and neighbouring areas, but the generalizations apply across the continent. In writing about the sources of bilingualism, Parkin (1974*b*: 163–4) speaks of an 'age syndrome' in reference to Nairobi; and Kashoki (1978: 404) writes about a 'travel syndrome' operating in Zambia. I would include the same factors, but prefer the term 'urban syndrome', since this highlights the effects of salaried work experience and the multi-ethnic nature of everyday interactions.

[11] A survey I conducted in Lagos in the early 1970s not only showed that respondents were often tri- or quadrilingual, but also that they made frequent use of the second languages they knew. That is, people mainly learn languages they see as an *occasion to use*. For example, in the sample studied (N = 187), 77% claimed some ability in English. Of these, 91.5% reported using some English in the previous 2–3 days. For those claiming ability in Pidgin English (74%), 76% reported using it in the previous 2–3 days. While a much smaller percentage claimed to speak Hausa as a second language (29%), what is interesting is that as many as 75% of these persons claimed to have used it in the last 2–3 days (i.e. generally with first-language speakers of Hausa), even though the Hausa area of Nigeria is far to the north of Lagos, a Yoruba-speaking city.

Also, while bilingualism is so widespread in Africa that it inevitably cuts across socio-economic and ethnic groups, one can make certain generalizations using these factors. As a rule, the more education, the more bilingualism. Extended education means learning the official language, since it is the medium of education at least after the first few years of primary school. Also, while those at the top of the educational scale may know fewer languages, since the circles they move in make it possible to rely on the official language for their intergroup communication needs, many educated persons learn the languages of other ethnic groups. Access to these languages is a by-product of education. For some, education involves travel, since many secondary schools are boarding schools. Also, those who have more access to education often live in urban areas, a setting in which their classmates are typically drawn from several ethnic groups. Finally, well-educated persons will probably be employed by the nation's major employer, the government, who may well send them to posts outside their home areas.

Certain attributes of a person's group affect degrees of bilingualism. Africa as a whole is bilingual because it is a continent of many relatively small ethnic groups, each with its own mother tongue—and with socio-economic motivations for maintaining its own language as a means of group identification. Small linguistic groupings the world over produce good second-language learners: witness the Berbers in North Africa and the Danes or Flemish-speaking Belgians in Europe. The reasons are obvious: when the numbers sharing one's first language are small, odds are good that speakers will have to deal with others on a daily basis not sharing that language.

When communication requires bilingualism on someone's part, the accommodation typically falls to the small-group member. Thus, reporting results from a nationwide survey, Heine (1980: 64) notes, 'The highest numbers of Swahili speakers are found in Kenya's linguistic minorities.' And Scotton (1972: 151–2) found that some minority groups in Uganda's capital, Kampala, such as speakers of Teso (an Eastern Nilotic language) know more Ganda and Swahili (Bantu languages which are lingua francas there) than speakers of some Ugandan Bantu languages (for whom these languages should be easier to learn).

It is no surprise that the reverse relationship holds: speakers from large groups are less bilingual. When a group is large, it can expect that most of its interactions are likely to be with ethnic brethren. Therefore, its members learn few other ethnic group languages, and also learn lingua francas in fewer numbers than other groups. For example, a nationwide survey conducted by Heine (1980) showed about 80 per cent of most ethnic groups reporting knowing some Swahili, while only 49 per cent of the Kikuyu so reported. Also, in describing Kenyan rural language-use patterns, Abdulaziz (1982: 105) notes that, in a Kikuyu village only seven miles from multi-ethnic Nairobi and on the main road, 'At home, in spite of the proximity to Nairobi, the children know no other language before school [except Kikuyu] . . . And at the market place, since the buyers and sellers are almost wholly Kikuyu, the language used is Kikuyu.' He notes that, in other rural sites not in Kikuyuland, more than one language often will be heard at markets.

The 'size' of a group's political or socio-economic status is also a factor. For example, Parkin (1974*b*) found that in cross-group communication between Kikuyu and Kamba living in Nairobi, the lower-status group (Kamba) reported more knowledge of Kikuyu than vice versa. The same relationship held between Luo and Luyia group members in Nairobi, with the Luo holding the high statuses and the Luyia learning more Luo.

Further, the 'large-group syndrome' is just as often psychologically based. Thus, in Zimbabwe, even though they are small in comparison with the Shona group (15 per cent as against 80 per cent in the nation as a whole), Ndebele have a sense of self rivalling that of the Shona, supposedly based on their 'warrior tradition'. In Matabeleland, Shona speakers find contacts with locals more possible if they speak Ndebele.

Whatever its basis, the 'large-group syndrome' often leads to inter-ethnic bad feeling, if not overt hostilities, when it is manifested as using one's own language in an inter-ethnic interaction. For example, in Nairobi, members of two large and powerful ethnic groups, the Kikuyu and the Luo, often create animosity by doing this. In the following example, this happens between speakers of these two groups:

[6] (Scotton 1976*a*: 217)

(Three women (two Luos and one Kikuyu) working in close proximity in a government office have been talking. All have from form 4 to form 6 education ('O' level or higher). The Luos have been chatting together in Luo about the illness of the mother of one of them. That reminds her to ask her Kikuyu co-worker something, so she turns to her, now speaking in Swahili. The conversation is in Swahili, except for switches to English.)
LUO I (to the Kikuyu). Inanikumbusha, Jane—kama watu fulani ni kimya! Unakumbuka uliniambia habari ya *chemist* moja ambapo twaweza kupata dawa kwa ajili ya ugonjwa wa mgongo wa mama yangu.
'That reminds me, Jane—the way some people are quiet! You remember you told me about a certain chemist's shop where we could get medicine for my mother's backache.'

KIKUYU. Nyinyi wajaluo—sijui nyinyi mko namna gani. Saa ingine mnazungumza vizuri kama mnataka msaidiwe. Na saa ingine mko *isolated* sana.

'You Luos—I don't know what's with you. Sometimes you converse very nicely if you want to be helped. And other times you are very isolated.'

LUO II. Lakini wewe, Jane—*Sometimes I wonder, the way you envy us. It won't be a wonder if you end up in a Luo man's kitchen.*

'But you, Jane— . . .'

Other major factors in bilingualism which are interrelated with education are sex (males are typically more bilingual than females and typically receive higher education); and age (the under-35s are more likely to have had extended education and more likely to be bilingual).

Finally, travel tends to promote bilingualism (the more travel, the more intergroup contacts). It has already been noted how travel is interrelated with education. It is also related to ethnic-group size and the group's socio-economic position (the smaller the group, the more likely it is that searches for salaried work will involve out-group travel; also, the less powerful the group, the more likely it is that desired employment or patronage will involve travel to an out-group's sphere of influence). For example, many of the night-watchmen in Nairobi are not Kikuyu, the dominant indigenous group, but come from various Nilotic groups of less power, some of them from home areas distant from Nairobi, such as the Samburu. In Mombasa, many of the dock-workers are Luo or Luyia from the other side of Kenya. And in Harare, many of the domestic workers are not first-language speakers of Shona from neighbouring areas, but come from distant ethnic groups, such as the Chewa in Malawi.

The use of lingua francas

The most prevalent pattern of bilingualism in Africa is speaking one's own mother tongue as well as an indigenous lingua franca; a second, but less likely, pattern is combining the alien official language with one's mother tongue. Note that, in either case, speakers have added a lingua franca, not simply the language of a neighbouring ethnic group. One of the most interesting findings in a survey (N = 187) conducted in Lagos, Nigeria, was that, while most people speak more than one language (only 5 per cent spoke no second language), the vast majority spoke the same second languages (Scotton 1975). Since Lagos is largely a Yoruba-based city, it is no surprise that 85 per cent of the non-Yoruba spoke Yoruba. For the sample as a whole, English (77 per cent) and pidgin English (74 per cent) were the main second languages (Scotton 1975). And Whiteley (1974*b*: 51) found that the most common trilingual pattern in a Kenyan study was mother tongue, Swahili, and English; over 50 per cent of persons in 11 out of 20 samples report this pattern. Conversely, persons trilingual in mother tongue and two other ethnic-group languages were very rare.

Few areas of Africa are so isolated that there is not some need to communicate with persons outside one's own ethnic group at some point in one's week, if not day. For example, Whiteley (1974b: 20) points out, 'Even in a completely homogeneous group like the Turkana [*in northern Kenya*], the few stores in Lodwar [*the main shopping centre*] are owned by Meru, Kikuyu, and Luyia, and a similar diversity characterizes the civil servants stationed there.'

As Greenberg (1971b: 201) observes, once a language is established as a lingua franca, it rapidly acquires a momentum which puts other languages out of business:

The single lingua franca tends to become the dominant solution not because anyone plans it that way, but . . . Once it becomes at all widespread, it has the advantage over other lingua francas so that its expansion continues. Thus is there a dynamic quality to the spread of a lingua franca.

This phenomenon points up the fact that people largely add languages with a measure of shrewdness rather than by chance. If a single language is known to be useful for communicating with persons from several different ethnic groups, learning that language is more utilitarian than trying to learn smatterings of the individual ethnic-group languages. That this strategy is employed in Africa is obvious; on a continent of hundreds of languages, it is difficult to find any large areas where in inter-ethnic communication all languages compete in a free-for-all; rather, regional lingua francas arise.

Of course, Swahili and English are the main lingua francas of Kenya, especially in urban areas. In Parkin's (1974a: 148) study of a Nairobi housing estate (N = 349), only one person claimed to know neither Swahili nor English; all the heads of household claimed to know Swahili and 42 per cent also claimed to know English.

Possibly three-quarters or more of all Kenyans have at least a working competence in Swahili, and all urban dwellers know the language well. In a 1968–70 nationwide study, 65 per cent claimed to speak Swahili (Heine 1980: 61). In a report on multilingualism in twenty rural samples, Whiteley (1974b: 59) found well over 80 per cent of half the groups claimed competence in Swahili. Urban studies (Parkin 1974b; Scotton 1982b) report knowledge of Swahili by virtually every respondent.

Smaller numbers know English, with no statistics on speakers available.

Based on various earlier studies, however, (Whiteley 1974*b*; Parkin 1974*a*; Scotton 1982*b*), one can estimate that in Nairobi well over half of the population know English. However, the percentages are much lower in rural areas.

In Zimbabwe, with such a high percentage speaking a Shona dialect as the mother tongue, Shona emerges as the major indigenous lingua franca. Mkanganwi (1990) estimates that about 95 per cent of Harare residents can speak Shona well enough to carry on a conversation; in the immediately surrounding area, the figure is almost 100 per cent. As noted above, people speak their own dialects, although Mkanganwi (1990) comments that the Harare Zezuru dialect 'draws least attention to itself'. The differences among dialects at all levels are sufficient to make certain speakers claim a lack of mutual intelligibility between geographically distant dialects.

Because education has been relatively available in Zimbabwe, however, English is also widely used. For example, Mkanganwi (1990) suggests that no foreigner *needs* to use Shona in order to survive in Harare. In Mkwanganwi (1989) he points out that many second-language speakers use English as their primary language. No studies are available on relative percentages of users, however.

Patterns of bilingualism in other languages

While Africans generally are most fluent in the major lingua francas as their second languages, many of them know other languages as well. For example, even in a relatively remote rural area in western Kenya, where almost everyone is a first-language speaker of a Luyia dialect, 31 per cent (11 out of 36) of persons surveyed reported knowing another Kenyan language in addition to Swahili. And among Luyia living in Nairobi, 46 per cent of those surveyed (18 out of 39) reported knowing a third second language in addition to Swahili and English (Scotton 1982*b*: 128).

As noted above, learning another ethnic group's language is often the result of living in a border area (statistics in Whiteley 1974*b* bear this out); or it depends on a patron–client relationship with members of a more dominant ethnic group (Parkin 1974*b*). Other major sources of this type of bilingualism are holding a salaried position in another group's home area, or intermarriage.

Patterns of language use

There are three different spheres of language use in much of urban Africa: home, neighbourhood, and work. They are still relatively compartmentalized, for bilingualism itself is a sign of social compartmentalization. That is, the executive secretary with her sophisticated hair-style, with her own bailiwick, becomes quite a different person when she goes home to become a mother and wife, tending children and cooking the evening meal. Not only does she exchange her Western dress for the indigenous kanga, a length of brightly patterned cloth, but she also puts aside her fluent English and speaks her mother tongue with her family.

With family members, most urban Africans still speak their mother tongues almost exclusively unless their marriage is inter-ethnic or they are highly educated. However, those at the top of the socio-economic scale know well how to travel the road to success, and speak English (in anglophone Africa) part of the time with their children to improve their chances in school exams.

When neighbours and leisure-time associates are from one's own ethnic group, then the mother tongue is also used in interactions with such persons. Now, however, there is also some codeswitching to Swahili and English in Nairobi and to English in Harare (or to Shona for non-mother tongue speakers). How much switching occurs seems to be a function of the speaker's educational level and occupation, but also of age. For example, schoolchildren are perhaps the speakers who do the most codeswitching, no matter what their socio-economic level. My field-work showed much codeswitching among children. In Nairobi it is especially common in the Eastleigh area, a working-class estate. A slang variety called 'Sheng' also exists in such areas; it is an innovative *mélange* of Swahili as a matrix language with English embeddings (Scotton 1988*a*; Mazrui and Mphande 1990). Mkanganwi (1990) points out it is children in the middle- and upper-class areas in Harare who are prominent users of codeswitching.

The reason for maintaining the mother tongue in the multi-ethnic city is that open networks do not yet characterize most African cities. Instead, people tend to look toward members of their own ethnic groups; they live in the same housing estates and drink in the same bars as persons of shared ethnicity. For example, while there is a national myth of egalitarianism, the fact of life in Nairobi is that those whom residents help to get jobs at their place of work or advance through the ranks are 'people from home'.

With neighbours from other ethnic groups, the situation is quite different. Now, neutral lingua francas are the order of the day: Swahili and English in Nairobi and Shona and English in Harare. English is decidedly a language associated with formal public interactions, so it is not much used for informal situations. Still, Mkanganwi (1989) states: 'Nearly all Zimbabweans use English in one form or another, for one reason or another, in their daily lives.' And, as Scotton (1982*b*: 131) notes about Luyia men working in Nairobi in regard to their inter-ethnic conversations outside of work, 'As one goes up the educational scale, there is a discernible change from reporting Swahili alone to reporting the combination Swahili/English.' In the group having primary education only, the respondents divide equally, with half using only Swahili and half reporting Swahili/English. But within the group with any secondary schooling, those who report Swahili alone account for only 2 out of 47 respondents. It must be remembered, though, that within the combination Swahili/English, more Swahili is generally used; and no matter what the educational level, English is almost never a preferred choice over Swahili for these informal interactions.

In service encounters, the indigenous lingua franca is the order of the day unless both participants share ethnicity. Even then, the norm is decidedly to express ethnic neutrality unless the encounter is very private or special conditions prevail. For example, in the following interaction at the post office, the customer switches to Luo because he has recognized that the clerk is also Luo and the customer needs help. He needs money out of his postal savings account and the regulations allow for only one withdrawal a week.

[7] (Myers-Scotton, unpublished data)

(Setting: the main Nairobi post office. Swahili is used except for switches to Luo, which are italicized.)

CLERK. Ee . . . sema.

'OK . . . what do you want? (literally: 'speak')

CUSTOMER. Nipe fomu ya kuchukua pesa.

'Give me the form for withdrawing money.'

CLERK. Nipe kitabu kwanza.

'Give me [your] passbook first.'

(Customer gives him the passbook.)

CUSTOMER. Hebu, chukua fomu yangu.

'Say, how about taking my form.'

CLERK. Bwana, huwezi kutoa pesa leo kwa sababu hujamaliza siku saba.

'Mister, you can't take out money today because you haven't yet finished seven days [since the last withdrawal].'

CUSTOMER (switching to Luo). *Konya an marach.*

'Help, I'm in trouble.'

CLERK (also speaking Luo now). *Anyalo kony, kik inuo kendo.*

'I can help you, but don't repeat it.'

Quite often some relatively set expressions from English are used in service encounters so that codeswitching prevails. The motivations behind such switching will be discussed in the following chapters.

[8] (Myers-Scotton, unpublished data)

(At the market in Nairobi. A Kikuyu stallholder is speaking to a well-dressed Luo customer. Swahili is the main language, with switches to English.)

STALLHOLDER. Habari, mheshimwa. *Have some vegetables.*

'Hello, respected sir. Have some vegetables.'

CUSTOMER. Mboga gani? Nipe kabeji hizi. *How much is that?*
'Which vegetables? Give me these cabbages. How much is that?'
STALLHOLDER. *Five shillings only.*
CUSTOMER. *That's too much.* Sina pesa.
'That's too much. I don't have [much] money.'
STALLHOLDER. Una pesa ngapi?
'How much money do you have?'
CUSTOMER. *Three shillings only.*
STALLHOLDER. Ongeza shilling moja. *You are my customer.*
'Increase it a shilling. You are my customer.'
CUSTOMER. *I'll give you three fifty.*
STALLHOLDER. Sasa nyinyi mkililia pesa na nyinyi ndio wakubwa wetu. Sasa, nani atatupa pesa? Nyinyi ndio wenye madaraka 'omera'.
'Now if you cry about money and you are our superiors. Now who will give us money? You are indeed the ones having the high ranks of "omera".' (*Omera* is a Luo word of greeting.)

At work, again the ethnically neutral lingua francas prevail. In Nairobi, Swahili is used more than English except in white-collar jobs. For example, Parkin (1974a: 151) reports that less than 4 per cent of his working-class sample (N = 378) claimed never to use Swahili at work, while 76 per cent said it was their main language with fellow workers. Reporting on Luyia men only (N = 39) Scotton (1982b: 132) found that 93 per cent reported using some Swahili, with only 78 per cent reporting some English. The difference in response according to education is significant in both the Nairobi sample and another studied in a provincial capital (Kakamega), with the more educated using more English. One interesting finding is that Swahili and English combined was the single choice most mentioned; this corroborates a hypothesis proposed in Scotton (1976b) to be discussed further in Chapter 5. The hypothesis is that using two linguistic varieties in the same conversation as a 'strategy of neutrality' prevails in uncertain situations.

When speaking with superiors, most strive to use the language most associated with education and authority; this is English for many jobs, but could be Swahili in lower-status jobs. Kariuki (1986) surveyed middle-level government administrators and found they claimed to use much Swahili only with persons of lower status. They were extremely positive about Swahili's usefulness, but gave an equally clear signal that they see it as the language for communicating with the masses.[12] Scotton (1982b: 133) found

[12] Kariuki (1986: 52) found that neither the language used by governmental managers when interacting with their superiors nor the language they used with subordinates showed a significant relationship with their own educational level; there was such a relationship between their educational level and the language used with peers, however. When speaking to superiors, respondents at all educational levels reported either English alone or a combination of English and Swahili. With

that when Luyia respondents had Luyia bosses, English alone was preferred. Additional interviews indicate that bosses prefer to use a neutral
language to mark the relationship as one of the workplace.

Nairobi residents will use their own first language at work when conversing only with ethnic brethren, but it is not used exclusively. At least among
Luyia men surveyed, the choice mentioned most frequently was a combination of English, Swahili, and Luyia (Scotton 1982*b*: 131).

Anecdotal evidence indicates that long-term Nairobi residents grow
accustomed to using Swahili and English so extensively that their use
becomes unconscious. For example, Luyia-speaking residents interviewed
in Luyia (by a first-language speaker of a Luyia variety) did not sustain Luyia
for their responses, but instead switched frequently to Swahili and English.
Ironically, one man, even when asked what language he spoke with his family,
responded with codeswitching to English, very much at variance with the
content of his message. The Lwidakho dialect of Luyia is his matrix language; English (small capitals) and Swahili (italics) are embedded languages.[13]

[9] (Myers-Scotton, unpublished data)

Inzi nomoloma kiluhya khu-FAMILY yanje *na kiswahili kwa majirani*. Nenyanga
vana vanje vosi valome lome lumoloma hsa mama. BECAUSE IT WOULD BE VERY BAD
FOR MY MOTHER TO TALK LULUHYA na vana vijibi mu-kiswahili OR ANY OTHER
LANGUAGE.

'I talk Kiluhya to my family and Kiswahili to the neighbours. I want all my
children to talk my mother tongue because it would be very bad for my mother
to talk Kiluhya and children to respond in Kiswahili or any other language.'

Little evidence is available on language use patterns in Harare. Personal observation indicates that English is very widespread in at least the whitecollar

---

subordinates, respondents with only a primary-school education tended to use Swahili alone, while
those with more education tended to use a combination of English and Swahili and, to a lesser extent,
Swahili alone. About language use with peers, Kariuki found, 'Although English alone or in
combination with Kiswahili is mostly used with the peers, it however seems that the higher
the educational level of the manager, the more the manager interacts with the peers in English alone
than a combination of English and Kiswahili. However, Kiswahili alone and first languages are
rarely used with the peers by respondents at all educational levels.' While these governmental
managers see the need to speak Swahili, they see it as a vehicle of downward accommodation.
Witness the words of a senior government officer reported in Kariuki (1986: 74). Speaking on
behalf of a group of officers who had completed a Swahili writing and presentations course at the
Kenya Institute of Administration, the officer says: 'We as government administrators realize that
if we are not fully competent in the language that those we administer and serve speak, serious
communication problems may arise, and consequently, the goals and objectives of our government
in national development may be adversely affected.'

[13] As indicated in this chapter, the Luyia do not agree on one variety as a standard for the Luyia
cluster, much less on what its orthography would be. Further, orthographies used for any individual Luyia variety are not necessarily consistent. Transcripts in this volume of Luyia material are
in the orthography provided by Shem Lusimba Mbira, my main Kenyan research assistant. Lwidakho,
a Luyia variety, is his first language.

workplace, where its use may be greater in Harare than in Nairobi. One major factor, of course, is the sensitivity of the ethnic issue between the Shona and the Ndebele, and the lack of a relatively ethnically neutral indigenous language to serve the same role as that of Swahili in Kenya. And Ngara (1982: 25) states that, even if the speakers are all Shona-speaking, 'English seems to continue as the language associated with official communication, education and formal situations such as letter writing, speeches and conferences. Educated Africans tend to prefer English to Shona, even for purposes where Shona can function perfectly.'

Mkanganwi (1990) argues that the major code of supposed first-language speakers of Shona who live in Harare is a continuum, including elements of both Shona and English, rather than simply either Shona or English. Certainly, it is true there are a large number of English loan-words in Shona as a whole today, including such core lexemes as numbers. And much of the codeswitching which occurs seems to be of the type characterized in Chapter 5 as 'codeswitching as the unmarked choice', meaning that there is a good deal of switching back and forth. Mkanganwi states (1990): 'All "bilinguals" in Harare codeswitch regularly.'

Overall, this linguistic portrait of urban African workers emerges: they may well speak a second language more than their first language, even if they live with their families. This is because the multi-ethnic nature of African cities and an accompanying sensitivity to ethnic rivalries only find resolution in neutral linguistic choices. Certainly, in Nairobi most people speak Swahili in more situations, and probably more often, than any other language. For white-collar workers, English may be more of a main language for the hours a person spends at work. And in Harare, an educated person may speak English much of the time, while non-Shona first-language speakers must certainly use either Shona or English more than their own languages.

Summary

This chapter has offered a sketch of Africa as a linguistic area, paying special attention to Kenya and Zimbabwe. Genetically related linguistic groupings and their geographical spread have been described. Factors promoting bilingualism have been discussed, along with the types of patterns characterizing bilingualism in Africa. Finally, a survey of where speakers use one language rather than another in the multi-ethnic urban centres of Nairobi and Harare has been included. Against this backdrop, discussion of the social motivations for codeswitching becomes more comprehensible, and the claim that CS is an everyday phenomenon in African communities becomes more justified.

3

The Rise of Codeswitching as
a Research Topic

THIS chapter provides an overview of how study of the socio–psychological motivations for CS evolved to become a major research topic. This development can be attributed to a number of factors, but the stimulation offered by the work of John Gumperz on CS was crucial. Gumperz's own work is discussed in some detail and that of others who have followed him in the attempt to interpret or explain CS is surveyed.

Current interest in CS

Today CS is clearly established as a subject of study from a number of different points of view. In the last ten years, almost all major conferences within linguistics have included at least one paper on CS, and articles on CS appear regularly in many journals within the field. Two collections of articles on CS in book-form recently appeared (Heller 1988a; Jacobson 1990). Two journals have recognized the importance of CS by devoting entire numbers to CS: A recent number of *World Englishes* (1989) is exclusively concerned with articles on CS involving English; *The Journal of Multilingual and Multicultural Development* (1992) has a special number on CS. The European Science Foundation (ESF) has recognized interest in CS by sponsoring a series of three workshops and a symposium on CS (in 1990–1); the papers from each have been published (ESF 1990; 1991a; 1991b; 1991c). The ESF is also sponsoring a volume of 'state of the art' papers on CS (Milroy and Muysken, forthcoming 1995).

The subject of this chapter, the communicative intention of CS, has attracted sociolinguists, social psychologists, and anthropological linguists. Work by Penelope Gardner-Chloros (1985; 1991) represents the sociolinguistic approach. She discusses the bilingual community of Strasbourg, France (Alsatian/French). What makes her approach largely sociolinguistic is that she considers CS as one of the pieces within a larger discussion of patterns of language use and their social correlates. Jane and Kenneth Hill's

(1986) study of the use of Mexicano (Nahuatl) and Spanish in the Malinche Volcano region of Mexico typifies the anthropological approach: they examine CS as one of the ways in which language use reflects social change and cultural values. The recent volume edited by Monica Heller (1988*a*) samples approaches to CS by both sociolinguists and anthropological linguists. Within social psychology few researchers have dealt with CS, with the major exception of those working within speech accommodation theory (SAT), developed by Howard Giles and his associates (e.g. Thakerar, Giles, and Cheshire 1982). The emphasis in most SAT work is on *shifts*, not *switching*, to another style within the same language; that is, the speaker does not alternate varieties, but moves from one to another and then stays with the second. Still, operating within this theoretical framework, Richard Bourhis and his associates have made CS their explicit object of study in a series of studies (e.g. Bourhis *et al.* 1979; Genesee and Bourhis 1982; 1988). Further, Sachdev and Bourhis (1990) devote much attention to studies on CS in their survey of the interest social psychologists have shown in bilingualism.

CS becomes a respectable research topic

One can date current interest in CS from the 1972 publication of a study by Jan Blom and John Gumperz in a collection of readings on sociolinguistics edited by Gumperz and Dell Hymes (1972). Blom and Gumperz (hereafter B & G) deal, not with CS between languages, but with CS between dialects of Norwegian in Hemnesberget, a Norwegian fishing village. The article, however, stimulated a flood of investigation of CS between languages. Preference for studying switching between languages rather than between dialects is not really surprising, since the utterances contributed by each member are generally easily distinguished in CS between languages, therefore making the data more accessible. Of course, it is still the case that, in a bi/multilingual community, different languages are rarely totally discrete; some convergence at some structural level is almost always present.

In many ways, the 1972 B & G article, augmented by a study of CS among Hispanic Americans in California (Gumperz and Hernandez-Chavez 1970; 1978), established Gumperz as the most influential figure in discussions of the social motivations for CS in the 1970s and 1980s. It was not that others had never discussed CS, although treatments were admittedly few and did not always appear in very accessible places (e.g. Clyne 1969; 1972; Hasselmo 1970; 1972); and, in fact, Gumperz himself had previously written on the Norwegian data in 1967 and 1970 publications. But often, if instances of CS were discussed, it was as part of a larger discussion; therefore, they often went relatively unnoticed. For example, Stewart (1968) gives an excellent example of CS between Haitian Creole and French and an interpretation which still stands up today; but the major subject of his article was diglossia in Haiti, not CS.

Rather, the influence of B & G resulted from three factors. The first is somewhat fortuitous, but still crucial: the Gumperz and Hymes reader (1972), in which B & G appeared, became a standard textbook in the new courses in sociolinguistics which were being added to linguistics departments and programmes in the 1970s. (Sociolinguistics had just been established as a subject of study, thanks to Hymes's earlier work in the 'ethnography of speaking' (1962) and William Labov's introduction of the correlation of dialectal variation in a speech community with sociological variables (1966) as a new means of studying language change. Also crucial in raising interest in sociolinguistic topics was the publication of Joshua Fishman's reader (1968), which included influential articles by Hymes, Labov, and Fishman.)

Second, B & G discuss CS neither as aberrant performance nor as unique to exotic cultures. Their research site is a Western society (Norway), and they treat CS not only as a legitimate subject of study but as a phenomenon amenable to analysis. More important, they present CS as a type of *skilled performance*.

Third, and related to the second point, B & G introduced the heuristic constructs of *situational* and *metaphorical* switching to describe types of CS. Whatever the ambiguities or inconsistencies in their use of these terms, they struck other researchers at the time as useful.

What especially seemed to impress other writers on bilingual phenomena as 'right' and fed their imaginations was the idea that a change in linguistic code could serve the same purposes as the use of a metaphorical expression within a monolingual utterance. B & G's characterizations will be discussed more fully shortly.

The prevailing views of CS

The dominant view of CS was simply that it did not exist, least of all as a research topic. If they treated CS at all, earlier studies of language in contact largely considered CS as an interference phenomenon, with 'interference' interpreted in its most literal sense. That is, CS was considered part of the performance of the imperfect bilingual, motivated by inability to carry on a conversation in the language on the floor at the moment. The way in which Uriel Weinreich dismisses CS in his classic work on language contact phenomena (1953) no doubt solidified such views. Now that CS is so widely studied, many recent articles on CS quote Weinreich's brief comment about CS more for its ironic impact today than anything else. Yet Weinreich was only reflecting the attitudes of his time when he dismissed (intrasentential) CS in this way (p. 73):

The ideal bilingual switches from one language to the other according to appropriate changes in the speech situation (interlocutors, topics, etc.), but not in an unchanged speech situation, and certainly not within a single sentence.

Labov, moreover, while he did not disparage CS itself, spoke of CS (1972: 189) as one of the 'puzzling problems' in trying to study linguistic variation within a community; he labels as 'an unconvincing effort' the only type of analysis which he saw as available to the researcher attempting to explain motivations for dialect-switching in the example he cites.

Thanks to such attitudes (and non-attitudes) toward CS before B & G, few linguists may have even *noticed* CS. To take a personal example, even though I was doing field work intermittently from 1964 to 1973 on language use in African multilingual communities, I never recognized CS as a special phenomenon until 1972. Previously, I had obtained interview data on language use among urban workers in Kampala, Uganda, and Lagos, Nigeria, and made extensive observations in multilingual communities. Workers had made statements such as, 'We sometimes mix languages when speaking with fellow workers'. But, operating within what I will call the prevailing 'allocation paradigm' in sociolinguistics for dealing with multilingual situations, I interpreted 'we sometimes mix languages' to mean 'we use language X with such and such persons and language Y with other persons'. Even when I myself observed language in use, as I often did, I managed to 'ignore' CS. Why? I suggest two reasons. First, the current literature on bi/multilingual communities led me to expect a simple allocation within any community of generally one language per speech-event type. Second, my familiarity (through the literature) with language contact phenomena was with borrowing as a 'respectable' phenomenon worthy of study, but not with CS.

What raised my awareness of CS was the field-work of my students at the University of Nairobi in 1972–3. I had sent them out to collect examples of language in use in Nairobi, to answer Fishman's question (1968) of 'who speaks what, where, and when, and to whom'. As were other workers in multilingual settings, I was following the two prevailing models. One was the 'domain model' of Fishman (1968; 1972) which views linguistic choices as predictable on the basis of the domain in which they occur. Fishman

(1972: 441) defines domain in terms of 'institutional contexts and their congruent behavioral co-occurrences'. Examples of domain are family and employment.

A related model was the 'binary-choice' model, exemplified by the tree diagrams with binary branching at the nodes, in such works as Rubin (1968: 526) on choices between Spanish and Guarani in Paraguay, G. Sankoff (1971: 39) on choices among New Guinea languages, and Ervin-Tripp (1972: 219) on choices among American forms of address.

And, while the domain model does not require that only one code be associated with one domain, such is clearly the unmarked choice in that model. In writing about language choice in multilingual societies, Fishman (1972: 437) states:

'Proper' usage dictates that only *one* of the theoretically coavailable languages or varieties *will* be chosen by particular classes of *interlocutors* on particular kinds of *occasion* to discuss particular kinds of *topics*.

And, clearly, the binary-choice model explicitly points to a single language as the outcome for a specified interaction.

Notions about domain and the binary nature of linguistic-code choices (together making up an 'allocation paradigm') were partly due to the influence of two classics on language choice, Ferguson (1959) and R. Brown and Gilman (1960). In Ferguson's widely read paper on diglossia, he stresses the strict allocation of the two varieties to distinctly different functions for a limited set of communities. Rightly or wrongly, many sociolinguists took Ferguson's description of specifically designated communities as a model for bilingual communities elsewhere; the problem was that these researchers assumed that allocation of available varieties in *any* community was strict and usually binary. Also, Brown and Gilman's often-cited discussion of socially conditioned choices between second-person pronouns in European languages as largely binary at any point in time may also have been over-generalized.

My problem was that I was viewing the Nairobi community as at least reminiscent of diglossic communities, and certainly within a cognitive framework based on a combination of the domain and binary-choice models in the 'allocation paradigm'. But my students' field notes included more than just conversations to which one linguistic variety was allocated, the prediction of the domain and binary-choice models. They also reported interactions conducted in two languages without a change in participants, locale, or even topic.[1]

[1] Some of my 'best' examples of CS (the 'bus' e.g. first appearing in Scotton and Ury (1977) and repeated in Ch. 5, below), as well as [4], [5], and [6] in Ch. 2, come from this field-work by my students.

These Nairobi data opened my eyes to CS in a number of ways. First, CS was not just a 'performance error' caused by a lack of ability in the ongoing language; speakers were obviously fluent in both codes they used. Also, CS did not seem to be unprincipled alternation, based on either the speaker's capriciousness or his/her searching for *le mot juste*. As I have indicated above, in the pre-B & G days, these were the only motivations for CS which were discussed—if CS was discussed at all. But also, while CS did not necessarily negate the principles behind both the domain and the binary-choice models (i.e. that language choice does function from a probabilistic point of view on a society-wide basis), its occurrence clearly indicated that associating only one code with one interaction type was too restrictive.

An interest in CS takes hold

Following B & G, a number of studies on the social functions of CS between Spanish and English in the American south-west appeared in the 1970s. Rodolfo Jacobson (1978*a*; 1978*b*), Donald Lance (1970; 1975), and Guadalupe Valdes-Fallis (1976) were among those first publishing on this subject. A number of such articles, including several on Spanish/English among Puerto Ricans in the New York City environs, were collected in Duran (1981).

In the meantime, linguists studying other languages discovered CS. Multilingual Africa seemed a rich source. In their study of Swahili/English bilinguals in the USA, Beardsley and Eastman (1971) found that CS correlated with topic and was set off by markers and pauses. Abdulaziz Mkilifi (1972) published an article ostensibly on a form of diglossia which he calls triglossia; but it is often cited for its examples of Swahili/English CS from Tanzania. Parkin (1974*c*) deals with CS in Nairobi, with examples mainly showing Swahili/English/Luo. And my own first work on CS appeared (Scotton and Ury 1977; Scotton 1979). Agheyisi (1977) considers what she called 'interlarding' of English with Nigerian languages.

The late 1970s and 1980s saw continued interest in the social motivations of CS, but with little change away from the B & G orientation of most studies. Representative of the range of concerns are Calsamiglia and Tuson (1984) on Catalan/Castilian CS in Barcelona; W. Edwards (1983) on dialectal CS in Guyana along a creole continuum; Platt (1977) on contact in Singapore and Malaysia between Chinese dialects, English and Malay; Gibbons (1983; 1987) on Cantonese/English CS in Hong Kong; Kachru (1978; 1983) on contact phenomena between Indian languages and English; Auer (e.g. 1984; 1988) on CS among the children of Italian guest workers in Germany; Clyne on European immigrant languages in contact with English in Australia in a series of publications (e.g. Clyne 1982); and Lüdi (e.g. 1987; 1990) on Turkish and North African migrant workers in Europe. I have already mentioned above the volume edited by Heller (1988*a*) devoted entirely to CS in various communities. Also in a textbook on bilingual phenomena Grosjean (1982) deals extensively with CS, as do Appel and Muysken (1987) in a textbook on language contact. Further, the centrepiece chapter of Romaine's textbook on bilingualism (1995) is on CS.

In addition, starting in the mid-1970s, some of these practitioners as well as other scholars became increasingly interested in constraints on where in a sentence a switch could occur; but the intellectual history of this side of CS research is a subject for Myers-Scotton (1993*b*).

Almost every scholar writing about social motivations of CS in the fifteen years following B & G (and still today) refers to their article. More important, most endorse the divisions within CS proposed therein, situational and metaphorical switching, as the best way to view CS. The publication of a number of the *International Journal of the Sociology of Language* (1983, No. 39) devoted to a discussion/critique of the 1972 article attests to its importance. Writing the focus article, Lawrence Breitborde provides a critique of B & G, and a number of other researchers comment on either B & G or Breitborde, or both.

In an updated statement of his view of CS, Gumperz himself (first in 1976 and then in a later version in 1982) somewhat moves away from discussing CS in terms of the situational and metaphorical divisions. (This is also more the theme of Gumperz and Hernandez-Chavez 1970; 1978.) Gumperz now focuses more on metaphorical CS and its 'contextualization'. He also refers to the two varieties involved in CS as the 'we' and the 'they' codes. Finally, he expands his coverage of CS in this paper to deal with structural constraints on CS. The 1982 chapter on 'Conversational Code-Switching' in his book *Discourse Strategies* (Gumperz 1982) also has been referred to more widely than the work of any other practitioner writing in the 1980s.

The Gumperz interpretation of CS

As I have stated above, B & G gave a psychological boost to the possibility of making sense out of CS. At this time, other sociolinguists (e.g. Fishman and Labov) were studying order in language use only at the macro-level of societies. While their interests were different from those of Gumperz (Fishman, for example, was concerned about language policy and language shift and maintenance, while Labov was interested in language change), the implicit statement in this concentration at the macro-level was that, while linguistic choices do appear to be idiosyncratic if one looks only at individuals, it is only when individual choices are quantified across groups that patterns emerge. B & G were able to convince their audience that even the variation found in individual conversations was in no sense haphazard.

Situational versus metaphorical switching

While the success of B & G is witness that the analysis clearly makes sense to other researchers, it is, in fact, difficult to pin down exactly what is intended by the two most prominent terms figuring in their analysis, 'situational' and 'metaphorical' CS. Especially unclear was how many and diverse might be the motivations included under metaphorical CS. The most explicit statement differentiating the two types is found in the introduction to Gumperz and Hymes (1972: 409): 'In Hemnes [the research site] situational switching involves change in participants and/or strategies, metaphorical switching involves only a change in topical emphasis.' But how does a change 'in strategies' differ from a change in 'topical emphasis'? Situational CS is never really very well defined, but it seems clear that B & G are referring to CS motivated by changes in factors external to the participant's own motivations (e.g. makeup of participants, setting, topic) when situational CS is meant.

And while they continue to talk about 'topic' when mentioning metaphorical CS, it is not really topic which B & G wish to relate to metaphorical CS so much as a 'presentation of self' *in relation to* the topic, or changes in relationship to other participants, I suspect. In the article itself, B & G (1972: 425) say this about metaphorical CS:

The language switch here relates to particular kinds of topics or subject matters rather than to change in social situation. *Characteristically, the situations in question allow for the enactment of two or more different relationships among the same sets of individuals.* [My emphasis.]

And later, in the discussion of the findings of experiments in which they recorded conversations between two groups of local adults and one group of university students (also locals), the motivation for metaphorical switching is no longer topic alone. The point B & G (p. 434) emphasize in their conclusion is that, when the students switch to the standard dialect, they do so because of a topic change, but *also* because use of the standard dialect evokes participants' shared experiences as intellectuals.

Gumperz's ideas extended

The chapter on CS in Gumperz's 1982 collection of essays largely extends or amplifies previously articulated ideas. Here (p. 59), the term 'conversational CS' is introduced. This essay does two things: (1) extending Gumperz's earlier ideas, it emphasizes the creative use of CS; (2) joining in discussion of the latest topic in CS circles, it offers some tentative structural constraints on CS.

Although Gumperz never says so explicitly, considering 'conversational CS' as a creative performance seems to mean that the term is another name for metaphorical switching. At least, this is how others seem to use the term. And Gumperz separates this type of switching from what would count as situational switching, 'a shift in topic and in other extralinguistic context markers that characterize the situation' (p. 98). CS without changes in these markers results in 'partial violation of co-occurrence expectations', and this state of affairs gives rise to inferences' (p. 98). But what the nature of these inferences are and where they come from is not clear.

At other points Gumperz is extremely clear, such as in speaking out against a strictly deterministic view of language choice (p. 61): '[Speakers'] main concern is with the communicative effect of what they are saying.' Speakers somehow 'produce' their own intentional meanings; he writes (p. 61):

Rather than claiming that speakers use language in response to a fixed, predetermined set of prescriptions, it seems more reasonable to assume that they build their own and their audience's abstract understanding of situational norms, to communicate metaphoric information about how they intend their words to be understood.

But at times, he almost gives the impression that 'anything goes', writing (p. 66) that 'only in a relatively few interaction situations . . . is only one code appropriate. Elsewhere, a variety of options occur . . .' But while choices may not be limited, at times he does limit interpretations (p. 70):

if members can agree on interpretations of switching in context and on categorizing others on the basis of their switching, there must be some regularities and shared perceptions on which these judgements can be based.

In concluding the essay, Gumperz makes explicit the important link between CS and monolingual stylistic choices, a theme subsequently highlighted by many other researchers. He also gives an idea of what he means when he says CS is a 'contextualization cue' (p. 98):

Code switching signals contextual information equivalent to what in monolingual settings is conveyed through prosody or other syntactic or lexical processes. It generates the presuppositions in terms of which the content of what is said is decoded.

In summary, this essay contains more a collection of ideas and observations than a single argument. His approach is to offer descriptive examples of CS's creative purposes. He introduces the idea that CS is one of a number of 'contextualization cues' which addressees use to interpret a conversation; but a moment's reflection indicates that, while 'contextualization cue' is a useful label for CS, it is not an explanation.

Gumperz makes something of a virtue out of the need to interpret each example in terms of its own context. One of the few generalizations he provides is to introduce the terms 'we' and 'they' codes (1982: 95). 'They' codes are associated with public interactions, 'we' codes with home and family bonds.

Gumperz does offer a catalogue of the functions of CS, but says it is not exhaustive. It is a disparate catalogue: some headings are structurally based, others refer to motivations. They are: quotations, addressee specification, interjections, reiteration, message qualification, and personalization versus objectivization.

Critiques of Gumperz's views

One has to search far and wide to find any negative reactions to Gumperz's approach to CS. For example, even though it would seem that Gumperz's use of 'we codes' versus 'they codes' creates the obvious problem of implying a stable interpretation for codes in *all* interactions, his followers ignore the problem and go on using the 'we'/'they' distinction (e.g. McClure and McClure 1988: 45). Singh (1983) does raise the static nature of the 'we' and 'they' constructs as an issue.

The few criticisms there are of Gumperz generally take issue with the division between situational and metaphorical switching, and with inconsistencies in their definitions in Blom and Gumperz (1972). Pride (1979: 39–40) states there is lack of clarity in the definitions of the two switching types and also argues that they are not so separate as B & G seem to assume. He writes (p. 40):

The contrast 'situational redefinition' : 'metaphorical enrichment' is perhaps as fundamentally mistaken (at any rate as incomplete) as would be the view that social situations in general cannot CHANGE quite radically upon being given some added —even fleeting—element of 'enrichment'.

I also find problems with situational versus metaphorical switching in Scotton (1983*a*; 1983*b*). In Scotton (1983*a*: 119), I argue, 'If two types of switching are presented as differentially motivated, they imply a model which is bipartite in some sense.' And in Scotton (1983*b*: 121), I state that important *similarities* between situational and metaphorical switching are not explored. Specifically, one would want to argue that codes, in metaphorical switches, receive their social meaning from whatever that meaning is *when they occur in a situational switch*. That is, their metaphorical meaning is *derived from* their unmarked (i.e. situationally based) meaning. Another problem is that I see metaphorical switching as subsuming two quite different motivations for switching which will be explicated in Chapter 5: CS itself as an unmarked choice and CS as a marked choice.

Auer (1984) also offers a critique of the situational/metaphorical distinction, partially along similar lines. He concludes (p. 91):

the distinction between situational and metaphorical code-switching must be criticized from both ends; at the 'situational code-switching' end, the relationship between language choice and situational features is less rigid, more open to re-negotiation, than a one-to-one relationship, at the 'metaphorical code-switching' end, things are less individualistic, less independent of the situation. The distinction collapses and should be replaced by a continuum.

Gumperz's theoretical contribution

There is no question of Gumperz's extremely positive influence on CS research for two major reasons. First, it is perhaps no exaggeration to say that much of the work on CS would not have been done at all without the stimulation of B & G. Second, the B & G approach gave would-be researchers a new model for studying and interpreting data as an alternative to the 'allocation paradigm'. This might be called the 'interactional/interpretative' model, a term derived from Gumperz's own writing. (Note, for example, that the preface to Gumperz (1982: vii) opens with this sentence: 'This book seeks to develop interpretative sociolinguistic approaches to the analysis of real time processes in face to face encounters.')

This model, however, is never really explicated. Rather, it exists in a number of crucial premisses: (1) small-group interactions are the proper research site and naturally occurring data are the object of study; (2) the social meanings of language use are a function of situated contexts; and (3) the use of linguistic choices as a strategy adds intentional meaning to an utterance.

Small-group interactions and natural data

The model champions micro-analysis, emerging at a time in the intellectual history of sociolinguistics and the sociology of language when most analyses were at the macro-level. This model took shape when Labov and his disciples were doing large-scale, interview-based studies at the community level, and Fishman and his followers were also doing similarly large-scale studies in bi/multilingual communities. The objects of macro-research for these two groups were quite different (generally, phonological variables in the case of Labov's group and language use patterns as a whole in the case of Fishman's associates). But their methodologies and theoretical orientations were very similar. They both used survey interviews (crucially involving audio-recordings of the subject's speech in Labov's case); they both tested hypotheses claiming a relation between linguistic variation and the social identities of the subject pool and other situational factors.[2] In contrast, Gumperz preferred to study naturally occurring data in small-group inter-actions, with little attention to the salience of sociological variables.

Social meanings of language use derived from contexts

The Gumperz model considers language use as a function of the dynamics of interactions. This view contrasts with the macro-approaches, which see linguistic variation as derived (exclusively?) from the sociological attributes

---

[2] That is, their premiss is that linguistic variation (i.e. individual choices) are derived from sociological attributes. Early studies using the Labovian approach include Labov's own study of phonological variables in New York City (1966), with social class as the main independent variable; a similar study by Trudgill (1974) in Norwich, England; and Wolfram (1974), who studied phonological and morphological variation in Detroit, with social class and racial group as main independent variables. Earlier examples within the Fishman framework were Fishman, Cooper, and Ma (1971), a study of patterns of language use in a New Jersey Puerto Rican community; and my own study (Scotton 1972) of language-use patterns in the multilingual community of Kampala, Uganda.

of the speaker and the situation. Under the Gumperz model, the speaker is important not so much as an identity-bearing individual but rather as a *participant* in an ongoing interaction.

Linguistic choices as a social strategy

Gumperz's final premiss, one especially important in relation to the Markedness Model I develop in Chapter 5, is that speakers do not use language in the way they do simply because of their social identities or because of other situational factors. Rather, they exploit the possibility of linguistic choices in order to convey intentional meaning of a socio-pragmatic nature. While Gumperz does not refer specifically to intentional meaning, his interpretations of code choices indicate that choosing one variety rather than another has relevance to the message of an intentional nature. To use a term which Gumperz does use himself, code choices are not just choices of content, but are *discourse strategies*.

In this sense, Gumperz was one of the first of a now-growing group of sociolinguists who view linguistic choices as dynamic events. That is, speakers are no longer seen as influenced only by situational factors in making their speech choices (what I call the more or less 'stable' factors, which include the social–identity attributes of the speaker such as age, education, sex, and also factors outside the speaker such as topic and setting). Rather, they also make the choices they do because of what I call the 'dynamic' factors (e.g. whether a long-term or short-term relationship is involved, or whether power or solidarity is salient). This idea will be developed further in Chapter 4.

Major influences in interactional sociolinguistics

Gumperz was no doubt influenced by Dell Hymes in formulating his premiss that to explain linguistic choices means to describe them in their sociocultural contexts. In addition, his methodology is related to that of the ethnomethodologists within sociology and anthropology (e.g. Sacks 1967; Schegloff 1972).

At the same time that Labov and Fishman were becoming well-known for correlating linguistic choices and sociological variables, Hymes was being recognized for his call for studies within what he called 'the ethnography of speaking' (e.g. 1962; 1967). Although Gumperz is cited in reference to CS more than any other researcher, Hymes was the *ultimate* influence (I would argue) on the development of all small-group sociolinguistic studies (and these of course included CS studies). Like Labov and Fishman, Hymes was emphasizing the need to look at language choice as a social phenomenon, but from a very different perspective.

Hymes makes three main points. First, he argues that choices are properly described within a taxonomy providing 'rules of speaking': 'Rules of speaking are the ways in which speakers associate particular modes of speaking, topics or message forms, with particular settings and activities' (1972a: 36). Second, he emphasizes that ways of speaking are a function of the socio-cultural values and patterns of behaviour of the group. It is in this primary emphasis on group values that he differs from Labov and Fishman. That is, Hymes stresses linguistic choices as *situated meaning*, in the sense that they are somehow more a part of the socio-cultural fabric of the group than merely derivable from correlations with a small set of acquired values, such as socio-economic status. Hymes, for example (1972a: 39), refers to 'the community's own theory of linguistic repertoire and speech' as a necessary consideration. Third, Hymes sees the proper method for arriving at 'rules of speaking' as on-the-ground, open-ended description rather than as a testing of specific hypotheses. Favouring an inductive method of research, he writes (1972a: 41), 'A satisfactory understanding of the nature and unity of men must encompass and organize, not abstract from, the diversity.'

Gumperz (1982: vii) clearly endorses this view:

Detailed observation of verbal strategies revealed that an individual's choice of speech style has symbolic value and interpretive consequences that cannot be explained simply by correlating the incidence of linguistic variants with independently determined social and contextual categories.

As something of an extension of his idea that speakers have a sense of 'rules of speaking', Hymes develops another notion which Gumperz employs, especially in his 1982 article. This is Hymes's conceptualization of communicative competence (1972b). There is a general discussion of communicative competence in Chapter 4.

Ethnomethodology also seems an important strand in Gumperz's work. Those ethnomethodologists who are interested in communication now are called 'conversation analysts', and include scholars from several disciplines (e.g. the collection of papers in Atkinson and Heritage 1984).

Ethnomethodology arose as a reaction against large-scale sociological surveys. Methodologically, this school opposed relying on self-reports; theoretically, it claimed that social meanings were constituted 'locally' rather than at the societal level, and that therefore studies should be conducted in small-group interactions. For the conversation analysts (and Gumperz), if social meanings arose in the interaction, then obviously a speaker's linguistic choices would only make sense as part of an ongoing interaction.

In sum, with its emphasis on interactions and their intentional meanings, Gumperz's premisses gave practitioners a framework better suited for studying CS than other current sociolinguistic models. After all, other available models were designed for a macro-approach.[3] Further, since they implied that linguistic choices on any one occasion were binary matters, such models could hardly be suitable for CS data. That most practitioners have followed an approach very similar to that of Gumperz attests to the acceptance of his model as the most appropriate approach to CS so far.

Limitations of the 'interactional model'

Still, the emphasis within Gumperz's writings is primarily descriptive. Further, like Hymes, Gumperz champions the development of open-ended taxonomies as against building models which might provide predictive power to an analysis. Most other CS practitioners have followed Gumperz's lead, providing an unordered list of the stylistic functions of CS (for example, although their overall analysis includes many original and valuable insights, Hill and Hill (1986: 356–87) even follow the exact categories listed in Gumperz 1982 when they discuss motivations for CS). And, as in Gumperz's own writings, in the work of some of his followers it is often not very clear what they intend by the functions listed for CS, or how those functions are interrelated. For example, in Gumperz (1982: 78–81) there is no consideration how such functions as 'objectivization' might overlap with other functions such as 'reiteration'.

Related to this is a second point. Those who favour descriptions and taxonomies often also insist on the value of viewing each datum or interaction 'on its own terms'. One must believe in the possibility of generalizing *across interactions* in order to build explanatory theories, I argue. It is not at all clear that Gumperz has this belief. A theme in Gumperz's 1982 chapter is that CS is a creative strategy. So far so good. But at issue is whether there are patterns in the way that individual actions are socially constrained. It is Gumperz's position on this point which is not clear. For example, in reference

---

[3] I thank Carol Eastman for the observation that the major reason the available approaches were operating on a macro-level was that this level was appropriate to their research goals.

to a specific example, he states (1982: 83): 'Whatever patterning there is in this type of code switching cannot be explained by generalized rules relating conversational functions to instances of code use.' Yet Gumperz also makes statements indicating he does see patterns in the data. For example, he writes (1982: 82): 'What is conveyed varies greatly with context and discourse content. Yet the same kinds of uses or functions tend to recur in what on both linguistic and social grounds are quite distinct situations.'

In concluding this section, let me suggest that the difference between one interpretative approach and another is often only a matter of emphasis. Here in question is the emphasis on creativity and where in the interaction creativity comes into play. The issue, which has relevance far beyond the work of Gumperz, is this: are social meanings so much a product of individual interactions that they are largely locally negotiated? I would claim that answering this question with a 'yes' results from undue emphasis on the surface diversities existing among interactions everywhere. As will become clear in Chapter 5, I also use 'individual negotiation' as a major construct in my model; the difference is that what is open to negotiation are *positions in rights-and-obligations balances* through code choices, not the *communicative intention* of one code choice over another.

No one questions that a thorough description of data is certainly a necessary step in any analysis. But the ultimate goal, surely, must be to attempt to explain data in terms of relations with other data sets. This means operating with the premiss that relations exist among interactions, and that predictions can be made about yet-to-be-examined data. On the level of the individual interaction, it means that speakers can make predictions about the effects of their code choices. If this is the case, then the assumption that data are primarily individualized, and that interactions operate largely 'on their own terms', is questioned.

Conversation analysts, who also stress 'accurate' description over theory, typically analyse interactions as individual units (although they also sometimes arrive at generalizations across interactions such as 'preference organization', as surveyed in Levinson 1983). Conversation analysts use the term 'local management' to reflect their premiss that the interpretation of an interaction is built up in the interaction itself. Gumperz's use of the term 'contextualization' also reflects a similar emphasis on the individuality of the interaction. For example, he writes (1982: 96):

What is signalled are guidelines to suggest lines of reasoning for retrieving other knowledge. The actual judgements of intent are situated, i.e. negotiated, as part of the interactive process and subject to change as more information is brought in.

Peter Auer (1984; 1990), who looks at CS within a conversation analysis framework and makes use of some of Gumperz's ideas, also seems to see individual interactions generating the social meaning of code choices. He writes (1990: 78):

To give an example: if German is habitually used by Italian children in Germany for conversational activities such as joking, innuendo, side remarks, evaluations and assessments, whereas Italian is not, then this conversational usage will both construe and display the values associated with German (e.g. 'peer language'). The interpretation of such code alternation is not imported from outside, it is built up in the conversation itself, and on the basis of similar cases in the coparticipants' experience.

And, certainly, other well-respected sociolinguists also espouse or inspire similar views (for example, Dell Hymes and, most recently, Robert LePage). LePage stresses a focus on individuals making choices, not on overall patterns, in characterizing the sociolinguistic profile of a Caribbean creole community. A main hypothesis of the volume LePage produced with Andrée Tabouret-Keller (1985: 181) is this:

The individual creates for himself the patterns of his linguistic behaviour so as to resemble those of the group or groups with which from time to time he wishes to be identified, or so as to be unlike those from who he wishes to be distinguished.

The problem I see with these views is that it is difficult to reconcile all of this individuality, and the accompanying view that social meaning is locally created, with the empirical fact that, in general, members of the same speech community interpret the same interaction as communicating more or less the same social intention. (Admittedly, however, the thorny issue of defining a speech community is beyond the scope of this book.)

At issue are the mechanisms (both cognitive and social) by which a local negotiation of the social significance of linguistic choices might be accomplished. How are speakers able to do this unless their interactions are conducted against a common social backdrop of shared views of salient situational factors? More to the point, if participants do arrive at similar views regarding interpretations, then this is either very fortuitous *or* it seems likely to be the result of (*a*) participants' having identical cognitive faculties which abstract socio-psychological intent from interactions and (*b*) their having common experiences against which to test and on which to base the abstracting. That is, 'inductees into the community' must have the same cognitive faculties which, when exposed to a set of choices and reactions (by other speakers) in a range of interaction types, lead them to arrive at common interpretations for type X. (In Chapter 5 I discuss a 'markedness metric' as the cognitive faculty behind the predisposition to view linguistic choices as more or less socially marked.)

If speakers are each going their own way in type X, based only on personal choice, the results will be too fragmented to yield the common interpretations which, in fact, are found. Further, a model championing individualized interpretations has no predictive value (i.e. cannot provide generalizations across even a single interaction type). Further, a basic problem with the atheoretical nature of individualizing interactions is that this promotes individualized, *ad hoc* explanations. Such explanations often are not testable, or they are stated in a way that does not make it clear what type of data would lead to their falsification.

Recent alternative approaches to CS

I would group recent discussions of the social motivations of CS under three headings: the accidental/idiosyncratic approach, the 'better-taxonomy' approach, and the 'better-theory' approach. Only the 'better-theory' approach offers truly useful alternatives, and there are very few of these.

(1) *The accidental/idiosyncratic approach.* While there are very few practitioners espousing this approach in print today, the attitude that CS follows 'the line of least resistance' still persists (Shaffer 1977: 267). This is the lay person's typical view, of course; even some bilinguals who regularly engage in switching explain alternation in CS as 'whichever one happens to be on the tip of the tongue'. Any consideration of the empirical facts (e.g. that the amount and positioning of CS co-varies with situational and socio-pragmatic factors) makes it clear that such comments explain nothing.

Other researchers hold that when CS occurs is so much a function of individual preferences that its social motivations are not amenable to study. Of course, this is a very extreme variation on Gumperz's own position, the assumption that, while motivations can be catalogued, theoretical constructs of general applicability are not possible. Such views may even underlie some of the current enthusiasm for studying structural constraints on CS (i.e. that such study is more rewarding, since structural constraints show systematicity). For example, Lipski (1977: 261) writes:

Indeed, since the role of individual idiosyncratic factors seems to be an important aspect of code-switching, in that among groups of approximately equal bilingual abilities, some code-switch more than others, a complete determination of the sufficient conditions for code-switching probably lies beyond the reach of the behavioral sciences. With regard to the linguistic constraints, however, the path toward an eventual model seems more clearly indicated.

(2) *The 'better-taxonomy' approach*. Many analyses have been presented under this general rubric. Most of them are cast in the same mold as Gumperz's work and many use either the 1972 or 1982 article as a starting-point. A favourite method of presentation is to use an open-ended listing of 'functions' with examples, with a final disclaimer to the effect that 'there are many other functions as well'. The best of these approaches do not use the listing format, but concentrate on a few functions. These often provide excellent insights into motivations for CS. But all of them stop short of organizing any listings or insights into a coherent and comprehensive theoretical framework. Many of the articles on Spanish/English CS in the 1970s fall into this category (e.g. the collection of papers in Duran 1981).

In giving currency to the term *code-mixing*, Kachru's work (e.g. 1978; 1983) on CS between Indian languages and English offers an alternative way to classify the structural types and social motivations of CS. Kachru and his associates (e.g. Sridhar and Sridhar 1980; Bokamba 1988; Kamwangamalu 1989) argue for the recognition of *code-mixing* (CM) as distinct from *code-switching* (CS). Kachru differentiates CM and CS on the basis of social motivations. For Kachru, what he calls CS seems to be similar to Blom and Gumperz's 'situational CS' (and what I will call 'CS as a sequence of unmarked choices'), since it depends on 'the function, the situation, and the participants' (1978: 108). CM is not defined so succinctly. First, Kachru refers to its structural characteristics, implying that it is generally intrasentential: 'Code-Mixing . . . entails transferring linguistic units from one code into another. Such a transfer [mixing] results in developing a new restricted or not so restricted code of linguistic interaction' (1978: 108). Later, he suggests some social attributes/motivations of CM (pp. 113–14),

Code-mixing with English is pan-South Asian. In attitudinal and functional terms it ranks highest and cuts across language boundaries, religious boundaries, and the caste barriers. It is a marker of modernization, socioeconomic position, and membership in an elite group. In stylistic terms, it marks deliberate style. The widest register range is associated with code-mixing in English. It continues to be used in those contexts where one would like to demonstrate authority, power, and identity with the establishment. One finds evidence for this attitude in various social contexts, in parents' language preferences for their children, and in choice of preferred language in the colleges.

Kachru offers numerous vivid examples as illustrations of CM. I will show in Chapter 5 how his description of CM can be subsumed under a discussion of 'CS as the unmarked choice'.

Another work dealing with Indian bilingualism (Southworth 1980) also offers some excellent insights into the motivations for CS, again in a descriptive, interpretative framework. Southworth's main interest is in characterizing CS when there are no changes in situational factors, and when it is intrasentential as well as intersentential. From a structural point of view, he sees CS (p. 140) as an important addition to the Indian's linguistic repertoire because it goes 'beyond the style-switching of monolinguals and allows the individual a flexibility of expression that could not be obtained in a single system'. From the point of view of the sociolinguistic uses of CS, Southworth suggests (p. 139) that 'the use of the switching style relates to, and in fact signals, the social variables of (absolute) status, relative status of speaker and hearer, and social solidarity'. As did Kachru in referring to code-mixing, Southworth seems to have in mind the type of ingroup language use which I will refer to as 'CS as the unmarked choice'.

Textbook treatments of CS tend to favour the taxonomic approach to providing motivations for CS. For example, Appel and Muysken (1987) offer a taxonomy of five functions of CS. First, it serves a *referential* function, in that 'it often involves lack of knowledge of one language or lack of facility in that language on a certain subject' (p. 118). Second, it serves a *directive* function, in involving the hearer, either by excluding or including him/her. Third, they cite Poplack (1980) for stressing that CS has an *expressive* function, in that speakers emphasize a mixed identity through CS. Fourth, CS 'serves to indicate a change in tone of the conversation and hence a *phatic* function' (p. 119). Fifth, they refer to the *metalinguistic* function of CS 'when it is used to comment directly or indirectly on the languages involved' (p. 120). While no one would deny CS has these five functions, Appel and Muysken's 'linear' presentation generates a number of unanswered questions. Are not such functions as 'expressive' and 'phatic' so vague as to be vacuous? How are the two of them to be distinguished? Is the listing intended to be exhaustive? Are all functions equally important? (For example, surely the 'referential' and 'metalinguistic' functions of CS are not as important as the others.) Are they related to each other? Finally, how were they arrived at (i.e. what is their motivation)?

The same comments could be made about other taxonomic approaches to CS; Grosjean (1982) offers a similar discussion, also including seven self-reports by bilinguals as to why they use CS.

Romaine's (1989) discussion of what she calls the 'pragmatics of code-switching as a discourse mode' (p. 147) offers an interpretation more than a taxonomy. She is at pains to make clear her modest goals, writing (p. 159), 'The pragmatic approach does not generate a predictive model. Unlike formal grammatical analysis which produces rules, the pragmatic approach is interpretative.' In building her interpretation, Romaine emphasizes especially parts of the approaches of several writers, notably Gumperz (1982) and McConvell (1988).

Her organizing metaphor in approaching the motivations of CS is Goffman's (1981) term, 'footing' (Auer (1988: 199) also so discusses *footing*). Romaine writes (1995: 172), 'A change in footing implies a change in the alignment we take up to ourselves and others present, as expressed in the way the production or reception of an utterance is managed. A change in footing is another way of talking about a change in the frame of an event.'

(3) *The 'better-theory' approach*. There is not a sharp line between some of the studies to be mentioned here and those discussed above under taxonomies. The difference is that the following studies more explicitly use abstract constructs as organizing devices, and have explanation within some larger framework as a clearer goal.

Parkin (1974c) presents a transactional-game model to explain quick-witted CS in Nairobi across ethnic lines. He draws on Barth (1966) and Hymes (1962) to argue that conversations containing CS are a form of 'transaction' or 'prestation' of ethnic and socio-economic values between the participants. While his model remains sketchy, Parkin seems to see CS largely as a micro-level means to express macro-level tensions (1974c: 211):

Transactional conversations are those in which there seems to be a progressive unravelling of a repertoire of different languages (or codes) by each of the two speakers. The two processes of unravelling are seen to be triggered off by each other in a to-and-fro fashion. This reciprocal stimulus–response mechanism may take the form of challenges, counter-challenges, and concessions.

Parkin gives an example in which 'language use . . . is viewed as part of a contest' (pp. 194–5). In this interaction between a Kikuyu female stallholder in the city market and a Luo male customer, linguistic abilities figure as evidence of knowledge of other ethnic groups (ability to use Luo) and perhaps also as evidence of educational or socio-economic status (ability to use English). In this example, Luo is italicized, English is printed in small capitals, and Swahili appears in normal text type. One word (*ati*) is in Kikuyu.

KIKUYU STALLHOLDER. *Omer, nadi!*
'How are you, brother?'
LUO CUSTOMER. *Maber.*
'Fine.'
K. Ati— (Kikuyu, 'what') Nini?
'What?'

L. Ya nini kusema lugha ambao huelewi mama?
'Why [try] to speak a language you don't know, Mum?'
K. I KNOW—KIJALUO—VERY WELL!
L. Wapi! YOU DO NOT KNOW IT AT ALL. Wacha haya, nipe mayai mbili.
'Go on! You don't know it at all. Anyway, let's leave the matter, and give me a couple of eggs.'
K. Unataka mayai—*ariyo, omera,* haya ni *tongolo*—tatu.
'Two eggs, brother, OK, that will be thirty cents.'

Howard Giles and his associates have used speech accommodation theory (SAT) only in a limited sense to explain the social motivations for CS. But while they offer no comprehensive model of CS, it is not difficult to see how at least certain instances of CS could be explained under the general SAT model. SAT is concerned with explaining why people shift their speech in different interactions with others. Giles suggests that, in many social interactions, speakers desire their listeners' social approval, and use modification of their speech towards the listeners' code as a tactic to get this approval. This is called speech *accommodation* or *convergence*. But in other situations, speakers may wish to disassociate themselves from listeners; they do this by accentuating their linguistic differences. This is called speech *divergence*.

In an experimental study, Bourhis, Giles, Leyens, and Tajfel (1979) tested the divergence aspect of the theory by applying it to CS in Belgium, a nation showing ethnic tension between Flemish and French speakers. In a language laboratory situation, the reaction of Flemish-speaking university students to perceptions of ethnic threat by French-speaking Belgians were studied. The researchers found that a CS to Flemish was one means of expressing disagreement (the authors use the euphemism 'psycholinguistic distinctiveness') with the French speakers.

The effects on evaluations (along such scales as 'intelligent', 'kind', etc.) of a supposed salesman and male customer who choose to codeswitch or not are the subject of two experimental studies by Genesee and Bourhis (1982; 1988) in different settings in francophone Canada. What is methodologically distinctive about these studies is that evaluations are measured on a turn-by-turn basis, so the effect of CS in a specific turn becomes obvious. The finding of most interest here is that speakers are judged more favourably when they narrow social distance via CS; however, the 1988 study in particular shows that, if a speaker has accommodated to the addressee by switching in an early turn, he can switch back (to his own first language) in a later turn without being downgraded for divergence at this point. Also, the results show that the situational norm that 'the customer is always right' also seems to affect evaluations. However, while the effects of both societal norms and interpersonal negotiations are noted, no overall explanation is attempted—beyond what SAT already offers.

Gibbons (1987), one of the few CS studies which attempts to come up with a truly comprehensive model, includes tenets from SAT. Gibbons bases his model on empirical studies of CS between Cantonese and English among Hong Kong university students, and on the attitudes of his subjects toward this type of CS. Gibbons's study has many virtues, its main one being that he considers, in turn, the explanatory value for his data of a number of different approaches to linguistic variation. Specifically in regard to CS he considers, among others, Blom and Gumperz (1972), Scotton and Ury (1977), and Scotton (1983*a*).

The result, however, is perhaps more a set of explanatory factors than a theory; that is, the model does not include unifying abstract constructs which are sufficiently overarching to subsume (and organize) the profusion of factors and thereby offer explanatory power. Yet Gibbons is to be singled out for recognizing (as do Genesee and Bourhis) that *both* macro-level situational factors and micro-level attitudinal factors must be included in any comprehensive model. He emphasizes that choices are made against the backdrop of long-term attitudes and current psychological state, as well as the influence of the social situation and of the identities of participants on the social relationships. But he then stresses that code choice itself 'can accentuate or play down these influences because of associations between codes and elements of these factors' (1987: 133).

A modification of my own early model in Scotton and Ury (1977) is the basis of a model presented by McConvell (1988). The Scotton and Ury model depicts CS as a means to effect a redefinition of the interaction. The model argues that CS is an attempt to move an interaction from one of three social arenas to another. These arenas are the identity arena (stressing solidarity to some degree), the power arena (stressing a power differential), and the transactional arena (stressing neither solidarity nor power).

I later modified this model extensively when formulating the markedness model of Scotton (1983*a*; 1988*a*). In turn, these versions were revised to produce the current version of the model in Chapter 5. The problems with the Scotton and Ury model, as I see it, are these. First, the model requires CS to be seen always as a redefinition of relationships; CS data gathered later showed that this was not always so: what I now call 'CS itself as the unmarked choice' does not result in a change in (i.e. redefinition of) relationships (see Chapter 5). Second, the model identifies three 'arenas' as the 'locales' of all linguistic choices: an identity arena, a transactional arena, and a power arena. This tripartite division implies that all interactions can be unambiguously associated with a single arena and that there is never an interaction including elements from more than one arena. In addition, the fact that interactions are moved (via CS) from one arena to another (rather than, perhaps, along a continuum) implies too much ridigity. Third, the third arena, the transactional arena, seems poorly motivated, since it implies that relationships may be neutral in regard to both personal affinity and relative power. For example, while it is true in certain public interactions that personal affinities or even socio-economically-based statuses such as education may not be salient, there is never absolute neutrality between the participants. For example, in service encounters (at least in many cultures) a power differential exists based on the norms of the encounter itself (i.e. the maxim 'the customer is always right').

Still, McConvell prefers the model of Scotton and Ury (1977) to others. That the model does highlight the possibility of movement from one arena to another seems to be the most valuable concept in the model for him. McConvell seeks to explain data on CS among Gurindji Aborigines of the Northern Territory of Australia. His revision of the Scotton and Ury model becomes very complex; for example, he refers to eight basic ways in which the 'SPR triangle' (Speaker–Participant–Referent) can fit into a two–tier configuration (the Standard Eastern Gurundji community as one tier and the local–origin group community as the second tier).

A model is implicity offered in Gardner-Chloros (1985; 1991) in that her work tests a situationally based model of CS, and finds it wanting. The 1985 article reports on a study conducted in department stores in Strasbourg, France, a city where both French and Alsatian are spoken. The study tests hypotheses which predicted more French in department stores of higher prestige, more Alsatian and less French among older than younger customers, and variation according to topic (e.g. more Alsatian in stores selling necessities such as food and more French in stores selling luxuries). (She was able to observe interactions closely enough to know which language was being used.)

In general, Gardner-Chloros found that situationally based hypotheses could not explain the incidence of CS. For example, while the selection of the choices 'French only' or 'Alsatian only' provides support for the original hypotheses, the choice of CS does not: switching is most prevalent in the highest and lowest prestige stores. Also, in regard to age, while choice to speak French occurs in the order young–middle–old, and Alsatian in the order old–middle–young, the order for CS seems to be an inexplicable law unto itself: old–young–middle.

To explain the CS patterns she found, Gardner-Chloros suggests a set of motivations for CS having to do generally with accommodation to various elements: to the environment, to external pressures (i.e. social expectations or situational norms), and to the addressee. For example, she notes (1985: 129), 'The highest rate of switching (25%) is found among the youngest group of shoppers, who are also the most French-speaking, when they are in Jung, that is the most Alsatian-speaking store.' Also, older customers switch more with young salespersons than do young customers with older salespersons, indicating that the customer's variety is more often imposed on the sales-person than vice versa (i.e. older prefer Alsatian, young prefer French). In regard to accommodation of the addressee, Gardner-Chloros notes (p. 132) that most switching occurs when the salesperson is in the *middle* age group. She suggests that this betrays uncertainty about the linguistic preferences of the salesperson.

In her book-length study of language-use patterns in Strasbourg (1991), Gardner-Chloros discusses a 'complexity of motivations' for linguistic choices, rather than trying to present a model for which to claim general applicability. While she indicates that she is attracted to the tenets of the markedness model (Scotton 1983a; 1988a), in the last analysis she may be more in tune with LePage (1978). That is, she prefers to see CS primarily as an expression of individuality, with speakers switching in order to align themselves with the groups with which they wish—from time to time—to be identified. She writes (1991: 190):

It is a well-recognized danger of the sociolinguistic approach that it disguises im-portant intra-individual variation in seeking to provide a picture of the group. This danger should make us particularly wary of very broad concepts . . .

Rather than present an explanatory model of CS, Gardner-Chloros con-cludes by presenting her views on the major factors or functions involved in CS, comparing them with those listed by others such as Gumperz. She includes a category 'deeper reasons', and it is no surprise that she includes 'individual characteristics'.

In another study of sales person versus client choices, Van den Berg (1986) found that salespeople, whether in markets or department stores, converged more than clients to their addressees. Van den Berg studied language use in Taiwan. He uses both speech accommodation theory and the markedness model in explaining his results.

In addition to their discussion of the social motivations of CS within Gumperz's taxonomy of functions, Hill and Hill (1986: 387–401) provide another approach within the theoretical framework of the Russian literary scholar M. M. Bakhtin (1980 [1935]). Translators of Bakhtin's work refer to it as part of the discipline of 'translinguistics'; the identification of 'voices' and the theoretical possibilities for the juxtaposition of voices concern Bakhtin and his followers. Within this framework, Hill and Hill (1986: 396) oppose the idea that CS will be a fundamentally 'orderly' phenomenon:

> Linguists wish to emphasize that multilingualism is a type of competence, which is as orderly in its own way as monolingual competence. But a view of multilingualism which admits only order cannot address the fact that different languages bring with them different world views or ideologies, which may engage in battle, an engagement in which rules can be broken in order for one voice or another to achieve domination of the dialogue and impose its own point of view. When rules are broken, there can be disorganization and incoherence, and Bakhtin's translinguistic theory admits such a possibility.

As will become clearer from my discussion, in Chapters 4 and 5, of a normative framework, my comment on Bakhtin (as represented in Hill and Hill's interpretation) must be that the 'breaking' of rules is only possible in an 'orderly' system; how does one arrive at the interpretation that rules are broken except through comparisons with instances of the following of rules? Clearly, however, Bakhtin's idea of different 'voices' is very similar to the idea I develop of different 'choices'.

Several studies concern themselves only with single motivations for CS, without claiming that all CS is so motivated or that they are producing comprehensive models. For example, Scotton (1976*a*) and Heller (1988*b*) both present evidence that speakers engage in CS to avoid committing themselves to single identities.

In Scotton (1976*b*) I refer to such CS as a 'strategy of neutrality', citing evidence from workplace encounters among peers in three African cities (Lagos, Nigeria; Kampala, Uganda; and Nairobi, Kenya). While English is the main official language in all three cities, in inter-ethnic work situations, those workers who had enough competence in English to speak it all the time with co-workers preferred to use English in a CS pattern of (or alternating with) English and an indigenous lingua franca (Swahili in Kampala and Nairobi and Pidgin English in Lagos).

I argue that a CS pattern, in this particular interaction type, is a 'best' strategy: the efficacy of using any one linguistic variety is not clear because this is an 'uncertain situation'. Interactions with peers in the workplace constitute an uncertain situation; conflicting norms apply. Will a speaker be more favourably perceived by workmates for stressing his/her education (by speaking English in this case) or for stressing his/her 'homely' qualities (by speaking the indigenous lingua franca)? I also argue that a CS pattern is a 'best' strategy here because of the particular attributes of the languages used in CS which are salient in this interaction-type.

This argument is supported by extensive observational study in all three cities, as well as by quantitative data from orally administered questionnaires in Lagos and Kampala (my own research) and by Parkin's (1974*a*) study of self-reports in Nairobi. Here, a brief discussion of the Lagos and Kampala quantitative findings is included.

In Lagos, level of education was established, via a statistical test, as the sociological variable studied which is the best predictor of language-use patterns (Scotton 1976*a*: 926). For those workers in inter-ethnic situations with more than primary-school education (N = 99), some form of CS is clearly the unmarked choice. True, English on its own is a main choice (50 per cent, or 50). But 30 per cent (30) report they use English/Pidgin English; and another 16 per cent (16) say they use English in combination with an indigenous ethnic-group language.

That these mainly white-collar workers are willing to report using Pidgin English alongside their 'standard' English is worth comment. At the time of the study (and, still today, to an extent), Pidgin was hardly considered a language (it was referred to by the name 'Broken'). Further, its use was associated mainly with illiterates. For these reasons, it seems likely that the workers' use of Pidgin, as long as it is combined with English, may be even higher than they were willing to report. Certainly, however, they use it very little on its own, with only 1 per cent (one person!) with more than primary-school education claiming that Pidgin was his main medium with multi-ethnic fellow workers.

In Kampala, 'English competence' was the sociological variable studied which statistical tests indicate is the best predictor of language use (Scotton 1976*b*: 927). ('English competence' was established by assessing the respondent's ability to answer a set of questions in English; 'Swahili competence' was established in a similar way.) Among the English competents (N = 127) in the Kampala sample, a CS pattern of English/Swahili was clearly the main choice, with 43 per cent (55) reporting this. English or Swahili on its own were reported by half as many (21 per cent or 27 for English and 20 per cent or 25 for Swahili).

If one looks at the language-use patterns only of those English competents who are *also* Swahili competents, then the amount of Swahili used on its own goes up. Still, the CS combination of English/Swahili remains the main choice, with 51 per cent (36) reporting this. Swahili on its own is reported by 28 per cent (20) and English on its own is reported by 10 per cent (7).

Scotton (1976*b*: 937) argues that the concept that each linguistic variety contains more than one attribute, not all of which are equally salient in a given situation, is important in explaining these data. In the work situation, the most salient attribute of English is without a doubt 'plus education', especially in those white-collar jobs where expertise acquired via education is at a premium. Any worker would be glad to index his or her expertise via use of English. But the problem is that English has other attributes which may or may not be equally salient when the qualification 'interactions with peers' is added to 'work situation'. English has the additional attributes of 'plus authority' (through its association with anglophone Africa's colonial heritage as well as through the language-use patterns of those Africans who are now in authority). It also has the attribute 'plus formal' (via its use in public and/or formal settings or for formal topics). These other attributes mark English as a device for increasing social distance among participants, or emphasizing a power differential. The typical worker who knows English well does not want to give up the image of being well-educated, but neither does he or she wish to appear distant or pretentious with peers.

Use of Pidgin or Swahili says little about a speaker's education, since neither language is normally entirely learned in school. Pidgin is acquired almost exclusively via informal means. Swahili is now taught in the schools as a subject; but many urban children acquire it as well from multi-ethnic playmates; at the time of this study, most adult workers acquired either Pidgin or Swahili entirely informally. In addition, both Pidgin and Swahili have a certain neutrality in regard to the attribute 'high socio-economic status'. Most urban dwellers use some Pidgin (in Lagos) or Swahili (in Kampala or Nairobi) every day (e.g. in the market, in informal non-work settings), no matter what their socio-economic status. But still, near-exclusive use of either Pidgin or Swahili, *at least in the white-collar setting*, makes salient the attribute 'minus high socio-economic status', since heavy use of both is associated with workers on the lower rungs of the occupational ladder.

Yet both Pidgin and Swahili have an attribute 'plus communality', thanks to their perception as distinctively African. (For example, in Kenya, while both English and Swahili are official languages, only Swahili is awarded the title 'the national language'.) When a speaker is in the type of long-term relationship with peers which is common in workplaces, the promotion of communality is obviously desirable.

What to do? Many urban African workers take the middle course and use combinations of linguistic varieties in such an interaction type; i.e. they engage in a switching pattern between the variety which makes their expertise salient and a variety which indexes high solidarity. Such an analysis explains the relatively high use of the low-status languages, Pidgin or Swahili, in combination with English, by educated respondents. (The fact that both varieties are relatively neutral in regard to the attribute 'ethnicity' is of much additional importance.)

Unsure of the relative salience in this uncertain situation of the attributes of each linguistic variety, and therefore unsure of the balance of costs and rewards involved in using a single variety on its own, speakers choose the neutral strategy of CS. Scotton (1976*b*: 940) states this idea as a hypothesis for testing:

In an uncertain situation, a speaker will use neutrality as his prime strategy of language choice. He will choose a linguistic variety which is neutral in reference to any attribute which he perceives as salient in the situation. If, as is likely, the saliency of other attributes is unclear, he will alternate among linguistic varieties available to him, attempting to use to his advantage favorable aspects of potentially salient attributes of each variety.

Presenting oneself as occupying a neutral position may be the motivation underlying any of the three main strategies which make up the markedness model, as will become clear in Chapter 5. For example, speakers who must habitually interact in situations for which the norms seem inherently unclear or ambiguous may make CS their main way of speaking; in such cases, CS itself becomes the unmarked choice.

Heller (1988*b*: 82) takes a similar line in explaining at least some use of CS as a neutral strategy. She argues that CS as a 'strategic ambiguity' not only may neutralize conflict but may also create neutrality. The conditions necessary for CS to take on such meanings do not occur everywhere, she points out; however, in Canada, at least in the 1980s, they existed among speakers of French and English in private enterprise in Montreal and among seventh- and eighth-grade students in Toronto. She comments (1988*b*: 92):

In each of these cases . . . it is possible to predict where code-switching occurs on the basis of an understanding of the nature and dynamic of the language boundary involved. There are going to be certain people structurally involved at the boundary who are likely to be bilingual and for whom the creation of ambiguity through code-switching is likely to be a useful thing . . .

For example, in regard to anglophones in a Montreal business, Heller claims (p. 86):

[CS with French] enables a speaker to do things he or she would otherwise not be able to do: in the case of this company gain access to situations in which the criterion of access is ability to speak French without actually having to be French. By the same token it is possible to avoid some of the responsibilities of categorical language choice through this kind of code-switching.

The school in anglophone Toronto was established for the purpose of teaching francophone children. But the children do not always speak French by any means; and in the presence of teacher(s) *and* classmates, usually in the classroom, they will engage in CS. Heller remarks (p. 92):

It seems that code-switching here is a refusal to commit oneself to all the obligations of being French, while maintaining one's right to be at this school. It is a way of mediating the conflicting pressures felt by these students from different parts of their social network, and of maintaining access to both.

Finally, the work of Georges Lüdi (e.g. 1987; 1990) is building toward a model of the match or mismatch between psycholinguistic motivations and perceptions of motivations for CS. Lüdi observes that the psycholinguistic and socio-pragmatic status of contact phenomena need not coincide. That is, analysts cannot assume that there is always a match between a speaker's motivation and the addressee's interpretation in bilingual discourse. Lüdi introduces the construct *marques transcodiques* as a neutral term covering all kinds of language-contact phenomenon (borrowing, CS, interference in learner languages) detected by linguists independently of their sociolinguistic and/or psycholinguistic states. For example, an utterance with morphemes from two languages may well be an interference of L1 from the speaker's point of view (its psycholinguistic status), but hearers may consider it a CS utterance (its sociolinguistic status).

Conclusion

This chapter has surveyed research in the 1970s and 1980s relating to the social motivations of CS. The major theme developed has been the tremendous influence of the work of John Gumperz. His main positive contribution has been to persuade others working within a socio-pragmatic framework that CS is an example *par excellence* of skilled performance. Following his lead, others have taken up the appellation 'strategy' for CS, and have detailed the ways in which CS functions to convey social significance. The goal of this work, at its best, is to treat CS within some larger framework from which its social functions can be derived. Such a framework would also offer ways to view the individual socially motivated uses of CS as part of more general, even universal, discourse strategies. In Chapters 4 and 5, I attempt to provide such a framework in a revised version of my markedness model.

4

Motivations for the Markedness Model

THIS chapter presents a number of themes which motivate the markedness model and which are current in research areas concerned with language in use. This model is an explanation accounting for speakers' socio-psychological motivations when they engage in CS. It incorporates themes from a variety of disciplines, from the sociology of language (the 'allocation paradigm') to pragmatics (implicatures and intentional meaning) to social anthropology (transactions/negotiations) to linguistic anthropology (communicative competence). A common thread in all of these approaches is that participants 'know' (at some level) that they enter into conversation with similar expectations, whether about unmarked code choices or about unmarked communicative intentions. In addition, all approaches (with the possible exception of the 'allocation paradigm') have another common motif: they emphasize the speaker as a creative actor. They also all see linguistic choices as *accomplishing* more than the conveying of referential meaning.

Nine themes are discussed: communicative competence, markedness, the role of the social context, indexicality of linguistic codes, the allocation paradigm, the interactional/strategies paradigm, language as 'doing things', communicative intention, and the speaker as a rational actor.

The markedness model

The theory behind the markedness model proposes that speakers have a sense of markedness regarding available linguistic codes for any interaction, but choose their codes based on the persona and/or relation with others which they wish to have in place. This markedness has a normative basis within the community, and speakers also know the consequences of making marked or unexpected choices. Because the unmarked choice is 'safer' (i.e. it conveys no suprises because it indexes an expected interpersonal relationship), speakers generally make this choice. But not always. Speakers assess the potential costs and rewards of all alternative choices, and make their decisions, typically unconsciously.

I begin with an example of the type of data to be considered, a slightly abbreviated rendition of a naturally occurring conversation audio-recorded at a bus stop in Nairobi.

[1] (Nairobi No. 11)

(Setting: A car park. There are many people around waiting for vehicles. The people involved in the example are a somewhat shaggy-looking young man (M) about 20 years old and two young women in their late teens, apparently his sisters (S1 and S2). They are members of the Kikuyu ethnic group; their educational level is unknown. They look frightened because they are being interrogated by two uniformed policemen (P1 and P2). Two male bystanders (B1 and B2) also have something to say. The conversation is mainly in Swahili, with English italicized and Kikuyu indicated when it is used.)

M (to police). Hii *recorder* apana ya kuimba,[1] bwana, ni ya *brother* yangu ambaye ninamplelekea hapo—huko Thika—Aliniashia wakati alitutembelea hapo nyumbani.

'This recorder isn't stolen, mister. It belongs to my brother to whom I'm taking it there in Thika—He left it with me when he came to visit us at home.'

P1. Mimi sitaki hadithi. Lakini wapi *licensi* ya hiyo *record-player?* Ni watu kama wewe ambao wanawasumbua wale wananchi wengine wakiimba mali yao kila siku. Lete *licensi* ya hii kitu.

'I don't want any stories. But where is the licence of this record player? It's people like you who are giving citizens a hard time stealing from them every day [night?]. Produce the licence of this thing.'

M. Bwana, mimi nakuambia hii kitu si yangu, ni ya yule *brother* yangu.

'Mister, I'm telling you this thing is not mine; it belongs to that brother of mine.'

S1. Huu ni ukweli, bwana. Hii *player* si wa wizi. Tunamletea *our brother* wa Thika.

'That's the truth, mister. This player isn't stolen property. We are taking it to our brother in Thika.'

P2. Unasema nini, *sister?* Na hata Kiswahili chenyewe hujui? (laughter from crowd). (To M) Unafanya kazi wapi?

'What are you saying, sister. And you don't even know Swahili itself? (To M) Where do you work?'

M. Nilikuwa nikifanya kazi na *East African Power and Lighting* hivi majuzi, lakini leo sina kazi.

'I was working with East African Power and Lighting, but now I don't have a job.'

P1. Najua tu—ati—wewe ulivutwa juu ya wizi.

'I just know—what—you were sacked because of stealing.'

S2. Huyu apana mwizi—

'He's not a thief—'

---

[1] The Swahili appearing in the examples in this chapter and the following ones is not necessarily from the standard dialect: e.g. here native speakers of Kikuyu are adding a homorganic nasal, and rendering Standard Swahili *ku-iba* 'to steal' as *ku-imba.*

P2. Nyamaza! Naongea na huyu kijana. (To M) Wapi kipande chako?
'Shut your mouth! I'm talking to this youth. (To M) Where is your identity card?'
B1 (first in Kikuyu). Uyu kai ari mukigu?
'Why didn't he carry his licence along?' (Switch to Swahili and English)
Anaonekana kama ni mtu *innocent. I don't believe he has stolen that thing.*
'He looks like he is innocent. I don't believe he has stolen that thing.'
B2. *You never know.* Nafikiri hii mali ni ya *loot.* Watu kama hawa ambao hawana
kazi—wengi wao ni wezi—Gasia! *There are so many things around. The other day
friend* yangu aliimbiwa *radio* nzuri sana. Sijui askari wanafanya kazi gani kila siku.
'You never know. I think this property [the radio] is [from] [stolen] loot. People
like him who are jobless—many of them are thieves—vermin! There are so many
things around. The other day my friend had his very nice radio stolen. I don't
know what the police do each day.'
P1 (has overheard this and speaks to the crowd). *And do you suppose policemen are
gods? How else can we restrain people from stealing except this punishment?* Wewe si
mtu wa kutuambia vile tutafanya kazi—tuna sheria yetu.
'And do you suppose policemen are gods? How else can we restrain people from
stealing except this punishment? You are not a person to tell us how to do our
work—we have got the law.'
B2. Lakini usiimbe mali ya wananchi *in the name of the law.*
'But don't steal people's property in the name of the law.'
M (handing his identity card to the policeman). Hiki ndicho kipande changu. Sisi
apana watu wabaya. (To his sister in Kikuyu) Njeri! Ndumuiguithie.
'This is my identity card. We are not bad people. Njeri! Please convince him.'
P2. Hatuwezi kujua kama ninyi ni watu wabaya au wazuri ikiwa hamtatuonyesha
licence ya hiyo *player.*
'We can't know whether you are good or bad people if you will not show us the
licence of this player.'
P1 (somewhat with sympathy). *Now why did you carry that record player* namna
hii *without a licence*—na mnajua *very well that it's dangerous.* Sisi waaskari hatuwezi
kujua kama ninyi ni wezi . . .
'Now why did you carry that record player in this way without a licence—and
you know very well that it's dangerous. We policemen can't know whether you
are thieves or not . . .'
P2. Sikia, kijana—unasikia—wewe tutakupeleka Kamkunji—ulale hapo mpaka
ulete huyo ndugu yako ambaye unasema ati ako Thika. Na ni huyo ndugu yako
atanipatia *licensi* ya *record player* hii.
'Listen, young man—are you listening? We will take you to Kamkunji [police
station]—you sleep there until you bring that brother of yours whom you say is
in Thika. And he's the one [who] will bring to me the licence of that player.'
(Pulls at the young man)
S1 (to S2) (in Kikuyu). Ngai tugwika atia? Riu Mureithi witu niekuoherwo kindu
gutari. Tugwika uu ii umwe witu atengere Thika ere Ng'ang'a ati nitwonire thina
nigetha oke naarua.

'God! Now what shall we do? Now Murithi will be jailed for something that he hasn't done. This is what we shall do, one of us will go to Thika to tell Nganga that we are in trouble so that he may come quickly.'

PI (to SI and S2). Ninyi dada wa mtu huu? Kweli mnasikia Kiswahili? Ninyi watatu mlitoka wapi?

'Are you sisters of this man? Really, do you two understand Swahili? Where do the three of you come from?'

SI. Tunakaa Makandara Estate.

'We live in Makandara Estate.'

PI. Na mnaenda wapi sasa?

'And where are you going now?'

S2. Tunaenda kumtembelea kaka wetu huko Thika. Hii *recorder* ni yake—tunampelekea.

'We're going to visit our brother in Thika. This recorder is his—we're taking [it] to him.'

PI. (lectures the suspects in Swahili, then calls to P2) . . . *Let us free them. I don't think they have stolen this player* . . .

'. . . Let us free them. I don't think they have stolen this player . . .'

P2. Nendeni! (To the three) Na siku nyingine msifanye hivyo. Wakati mwingine mtalala *police station* nyote.

'Go! And don't do this again. Next time you will sleep in the police station—all of you.'

As can be seen, three different languages, Swahili, English, and Kikuyu, are used in this conversation. Swahili is spoken the most and, on the basis of a large data set of naturally occurring conversations recorded in Nairobi and extensive observation, one can confidently claim that Swahili is the most usual language for such public transactions between strangers (quantitative data in Parkin 1974a and Scotton 1982b support this claim). In the parlance of the markedness model, Swahili on its own is the most unmarked choice for this interaction type. But why, then, is there switching to both English and Kikuyu? Some of the English lexemes are obviously cultural loan-words (e.g. *radio*, *record-player*, and *licence*). A case can even be made that *brother* is a loan-word.[2] But still much English and all of the Kikuyu remain. The goal of the theory presented in Chapter 5 will be to explain such variation as the CS exemplified here.

---

[2] *Brother* qualifies as a loan-word (borrowing), based on its relative frequency of occurrence when the concept for 'male sibling/close male relative' comes up in a text. When the 40 conversations in the Nairobi corpus are studied via a concordance program, *brother* is used over 50% of the time when this concept comes up. It is interesting that, in this conversation, when the sister uses *brother*, the policeman chides her for not knowing Swahili. Later in the conversation, she uses the Swahili lexeme for 'brother', *kaka*. But, as a whole, *kaka* does not occur more than twice, if the larger corpus of 40 conversations is considered.

Communicative competence

Hymes (1972*b*) can be credited with providing linguists with the concept of 'communicative competence'. Underlying this concept is the recognition that competent speakers of a language have tacit knowledge of more than just *grammaticality*, i.e. what is a well-formed sentence in their language and what is not. In addition they are able to judge the *acceptability* of a given well-formed sentence in a given social context. Hymes has little to say about where communicative competence 'comes from'; but an obvious conclusion is that, if grammatical competence depends on a universally present, innate human language faculty, communicative competence must have the same basis.

In making his argument, Hymes was offering an alternative to Chomsky's (1965) narrow definition of the 'competent' speaker/listener in terms of grammaticality judgements only.

To Hymes (1972*b*: 281), competent speakers 'know' the answers to four questions:

1. Whether (and to what degree) something is formally *possible*;
2. Whether (and to what degree) something is *feasible* . . .
3. Whether (and to what degree) something is *appropriate* (adequate, happy, successful) in relation to a context in which it is used and evaluated;
4. Whether (and to what degree) something is in fact done, actually *performed*, and what its doing entails.

The scope which Hymes adds to the concept of linguistic competence has important consequences. However, I would add yet another item to Hymes's list of what competent speakers know and consider:

Whether (and to what degree) a linguistic choice is marked *and how it is to be interpreted* in the context in which it occurs.

This addition is perhaps no more than an addition of detail to Hymes's statement about the importance of 'whether (and to what degree) something is *appropriate* (adequate, happy, successful)'. However, such details will figure prominently in the markedness model.

A markedness metric

The markedness model also depends on the addition of a speaker's 'markedness metric' to an enlarged conception of linguistic competence.[3] This metric is part of the innate cognitive faculty of all humans. It enables speakers to assess all code choices as more or less *unmarked* or *marked* for the exchange type in which they occur.

A critical distinction is that, while the metric is a cognitive structure and therefore universal, it underlies an ability which is particular. The ability, consisting of the actual assignment of readings of markedness to codes, is only developed in reference to a specific community through social experience in interactions there. Thus, while it is a universal feature of language use that all choices are interpreted in terms of their markedness, one can speak of the markedness of a particular code choice *only* in reference to a specific speech event in a specific community.

Markedness

The use of unmarked versus marked to refer to code choices is based on the precedence within structural linguistics of using markedness both as a theory and as an organizational device to explain how linguistic systems are structured. Such discussions go back to the first half of the twentieth century and the Prague School of Linguistics, especially in the works of Roman Jakobson and Nikolai Trubetzkoy.

The principle of markedness is a recognition of various polarities within the different systems of language, from the lexicon to its sound-system. The unmarked member of a polar opposition is generally simpler. For example, within a phonological pair, the unmarked member requires fewer distinctive features in its description than the marked member; in some ways, the marked member may be thought of as the unmarked member *plus* additional specifications. Also, the unmarked member typically occurs more frequently; for example, consider the opposition between the masculine and feminine forms of singular pronouns in English. The masculine *he* occurs more frequently and also—at least in the past—may stand for both male and female persons. This is called a privative opposition because the opposition

---

[3] In Chomsky's 1980 formulation, he refers to both grammatical competence *and* pragmatic competence, seeing these two universally present states as underlying the ability to develop grammars. These competences prefigure, but are distinct from, actual linguistic proficiency in a specific language. Within his terminology, a speaker's markedness metric, of course, would be under pragmatic competence. Another way to view the markedness metric is as part of a *larger* cognitive system. That is, it is possible that, in an overall theory of innate linguistic competence, there is a specialized component of innate linguistic knowledge (whatever counts as universal grammar) and another component comprising processing/learning mechanisms. This 2nd component would be part of general cognitive capacities rather than being purely linguistic; this is where the markedness metric would be found. I thank Kate Wolfe for a useful discussion of these ideas.

is between *the presence of a property and its absence*, that is, *A* and not *A*, with 'not *A*' as the simpler and more general and therefore the unmarked member (e.g. *he*).

In reference to privative oppositions, Battistella (1990: 3–4) points out that the marked member is always defined *with respect to* the unmarked member of a pair. Also, the unmarked member even often *includes* the marked member.

Battistella uses the example of present versus past tense. The marked member, past tense, specifically signals past time, while present tense is unspecified and can be used to stand for present, past or future time (e.g. *I leave tomorrow for Europe; He shoots and misses!*). Thus, the marked member is distinguished as conveying more specific information; while it seems initially incongruous, it is in this sense that the marked member represents the absence of the unmarked member (i.e. information with less scope is more specific).

While markedness has its origins in the study of privative oppositions, the concept is also applied to equipollent oppositions. As Battistella puts it (1990: 16), this is an opposition between two opposite, but positive, features. Thus, the terms are oppositions of *A* versus *B* (where *A* = not *B* and *B* = not *A*). The best examples of equipollent oppositions may come from sound systems; e.g. /p/ and /b/ represent an equipollent opposition, opposed to each other in terms of vocal-cord vibration. Basically, it is this type of contingency relation (i.e. an equipollent opposition) which holds between the two types of choice considered in the markedness model.

However, it turns out that the neat distinction between privative and equipollent oppositions does not hold when applied to linguistic varieties; at least two features of privative oppositions apply to oppositions in reference to linguistic varieties. First, the unmarked-code choice shows the greater frequency/generality of the unmarked member in privative oppositions. Second, the unmarked choice is definitely the reference point for the marked choice. That is, the marked choice takes on much of its significance as being *not* the unmarked choice. But, as in equipollent oppositions, the marked choice is a referent in its own right as well. In contrast with the relationship in privative oppositions, the marked choice is not the *absence* of the unmarked choice. And the unmarked choice never stands for, or includes, the marked choice.

Markedness in reference to code choices

Using the concept of markedness implies that code choice is viewed as a system of oppositions. This follows from the fact that markedness is a property of oppositions. But there is no need to assume that oppositions are necessarily categorial. It is important to stress early in this discussion that markedness is used in the markedness model in a gradient sense. That is, code choices fall along a continuum as more or less unmarked. There need not be a single unmarked or a single marked choice, although there is often a dominant unmarked choice, especially within a relatively conventionalized interaction type.

The use of the terms 'unmarked' and 'marked' in reference to code choices will be discussed extensively below and in Chapter 5. For the moment, example [2] illustrates what would constitute an unmarked versus marked choice of codes in a conversation involving CS.

[2] (Scotton 1983a: 128)

(Setting: a rural bar in Western Kenya. Everyone present is a speaker of a variety in the Luyia cluster; most speak Lwidakho, the indigenous variety of the immediate area. The first speaker is a local farmer, who speaks Lwidakho and also, perhaps, a bit of Swahili. The second speaker is a local person who is now employed in an urban centre outside the area; he is home to visit his wife and children. Such an arrangement is common in much of Africa. Rather predictably, the farmer is asking the salaried man for money. It is important to note that almost the entire conversation has been in Lwidakho up to this point. Swahili and English are both indicated; otherwise Lwidakho is used.)

FARMER (Lwidakho). Khu inzi khuli menyi hanu inzala—
'As I live here, I have hunger—'
WORKER (interrupting) (Swahili). *Njaa gani?*
'What kind of hunger?'
FARMER. Yenya khunzirila hanu—
'It wants to kill me here—'
WORKER (interrupting again, with more force) (Swahili).
Njaa gani?
'What kind of hunger?'
FARMER. Vana veru—
'our children—' (said as appeal to others as brothers)
WORKER (Swahili). *Nakuuliza, njaa gani?*
'I ask you, what kind of hunger?'
FARMER. Inzala ya mapesa, kambuli.
'Hunger for money; I don't have any.'
WORKER (English). *You have got a land.*
(Swahili) *Una shamba.*
'You have land [farm].'
(Lwidakho) Uli nu mulimi.
'You have land [farm].'

FARMER. . . . Mwana mweru—
'. . . My brother—'
WORKER. . . . Mbula tsisendi.
'I don't have money.'
(English) *Can't you see how I am heavily loaded?'*

The salaried worker no doubt uses Swahili and English because of their associations with authority and with those interactions where solidarity is not salient. But within this theory, what is more important than their own intentionality is that Swahili and English are marked choices for the occasion at hand. Thus, the use of Swahili and then even English has a shock value based *not just* on their own attributes, but on the fact such usage is a *departure from the unmarked choice, from the expected*. In this case, Lwidakho (or another first-language Luyia variety) is clearly the unmarked choice for conversations in this bar in the heart of Luyialand. For the salaried worker to use Swahili is a marked choice. Even though it is widely known in Kenya, it is definitely not expected for informal talk between persons sharing the same first language and who were raised on neighbouring farms. More than anything else, Swahili is the language of outgroup encounters, the language of the multi-ethnic city. This makes its use in a monolingual village stand out. English is even more marked (less expected) in this setting, and connotes authority and formality in this case, as well as 'outgroupness'. (The statuses of Swahili and English are social facts, evinced by the large-scale empirical studies of language use in Kenya discussed in Chapter 2.)

In some communities a pattern of switching between two (or more) codes (rather than using one variety continuously) could be an unmarked choice, a pattern which will receive considerable discussion in Chapter 5 as 'CS itself as the unmarked choice'. As already indicated in Chapter 2, CS in such a pattern is the unmarked choice for many educated Zimbabweans living in Harare. Shona may be their first language, but Shona/English is their unmarked choice for all but the most formal interaction types or conversations in which ethnic solidarity must be especially established (by using Shona on its own):

[3] (Shona/English; Crawhall, unpublished data)

(The setting is a home in a Harare suburb. Two 20-year-old female student teachers are discussing marriage.)
FIRST. Mukaita ve-*age*, imwe chete munogara muchinetsana.
'If you are the same age, you will not live in peace.'
SECOND. Ende futi *better* kuroorwa nemurume anenge aguta *pleasure*.
'And then it is better to be married with a husband who is tired of pleasure.'

FIRST. Ava kuziva zvose.
'Who knows everything.'
SECOND. Ee, *because* mukadzi unogona kukasika kuzviita *adjust*, kuziva kuti yaa,
I am somebody's wife.
'Yes, because a woman can easily adjust, to know that yes, I am somebody's wife.'

The social context

Here, themes which turn on factors inherent in the context are considered. An important argument of the markedness model is that code choices are understood as indexing rights-and-obligations sets (RO sets) between participants in a given interaction type. The unmarked RO set is derived from whatever situational features are salient for the community for that interaction type. Note that I do not attempt in this theory to specify what those situational features are; to my mind, one of the shortcomings of many earlier approaches is the attempt to specify these features in some exhaustive sense. Another, related shortcoming is to assume that such a specification, such a taxonomy, has any explanatory value on its own.

The reason why such a listing achieves little is that relevant situational features will vary from community to community, and even from interaction type to type, within the same community. True, one can with some degree of confidence assert that some factors (e.g. the main social identity features of participants, as well as topic and setting) will figure in most determinations of the unmarked RO set for an interaction. But not all. For example, the social identities of customers are rarely relevant in minor service encounters (e.g. buying a newspaper or a carton of milk) in most societies.

The dynamic quality of salience

There are at least four factors of dynamic variability to consider here. First, the relative prominence or salience of factors is open to variability *across communities*; for example, differences in age among participants may be highly salient in one community and much less so elsewhere. Second, the salience of one factor will vary *across interactions* in a single community; sex, for example, has low salience in most service encounters, but high salience in social encounters. Third, the relative salience of one factor *compared to that of another* also will vary; for example, the potency of socio-economic status may be greater in a job situation in Nairobi than the salience of ethnic group; but their relative salience may be otherwise in an interaction in a bar, even though both features have salience in both interactions. Finally, as will become clear, making any linguistic choice is ultimately a *negotiation of the salience* of situational factors. That is, since the markedness model presents linguistic choices as negotiations of RO sets, and since the model derives RO sets from situational factors, these processes establish the link between a linguistic choice and the negotiation of situational-factor salience.

This is as far as I will discuss the situational factors from which is derived the unmarked RO balance for a specific speech event.

Linguistic choices as indexical

'Indexicality' is a concept figuring in the theory which is closely related to the assessment of situational factors. Below, it will be related also to such themes as 'language as social work' and 'the speaker as rational actor'.

Within this theory, indexicality is a property of linguistic varieties, in the sense proposed by the philosopher Charles Peirce (1955). He notes that there are three types of relationship between linguistic signs and their referents—symbolic, indexical, and iconic. For Peirce, indexicality seems to be a less concrete relationship than iconicity, but also less abstract than a symbolic relationship. Rather than standing for their referents (symbolic signs) or producing pictures of them (iconic signs), indexical signs 'point to' them. An example of an indexical sign is smoke coming out the windows of a house as pointing to an uncontrolled fire within.

I argue that all linguistic varieties are indexical in this way. (For another use of Peirce's concept of indexicality, see Givón 1989.) The use of each variety in a community's repertoire points to a somewhat different RO set within the interaction, and therefore to a different persona for the speaker and a different relationship with the addressee. As noted above, an RO set is an abstract construct, derived from situational factors, standing for the attitudes and expectations of participants towards one another.

The possibility of this indexicality derives from the fact that the different linguistic varieties in a community's repertoire are linked with particular types of relationships, because they are regularly used in conversations involving such types. Through this type of accumulation, a code comes to index an RO set. For example, in the Nairobi community, speaking English in a white-collar office setting implicates an RO set in which higher education and authority have special salience in the way a speaker conducts himself or herself toward the addressee and in how he or she expects to be treated in return. These associations arise through the history of the uses of English in this specific community. Speaking one's ethnic language in the same interaction type indexes a different RO set, one in which the speaker's rights and obligations are based on ethnic solidarity, and perhaps specifically to the socio–culture values and accomplishments of that ethnic group.

Salience and indexicality

Further, as discussed in Scotton (1976*b*) and reviewed in Chapter 3, the salience of the various attributes which a linguistic variety has come to index in a given community varies from interaction type to type. That is, the salience of indexicality is a dynamic concept. For example, speaking English fluently in Nairobi may be indexical of any of a set of attributes, including most prominently 'plus high educational level/socio–economic status', 'plus authority', 'plus formality', and 'plus official'. In [1] above, which involves switches to English by the police interrogating the three young people about the radio/recorder, such attributes as 'high educational level' and 'formality' have very low salience. Rather, what is salient, given that this is a confrontation which takes place in a parking lot, and with the police on the offensive, are the attributes 'authority' and 'official'. In this interaction, therefore, the fact that English has the potential to index 'high educational level' is relatively irrelevant. If the policeman were interacting with unknown fellow officers in a short course, for example, then the indexical quality of English for 'educational level' would be more salient.

What makes code choices indexical rather than symbolic is that they have more than an arbitrary relationship with the RO sets with which they are identified. Just as smoke is a frequent companion of fire, English in Kenya or Zimbabwe, for example, is not only associated with the unmarked RO set in a white-collar office encounter, but is also associated with the means by which the high-level participants achieved their status. Its mastery is linked to the educational system. Just as Swahili is indexical in Kenya of the unmarked RO set between strangers meeting in Nairobi, it brings with it a heritage as the African language promoted by colonials for their inter–ethnic encounters with Africans (i.e. strangers). (This indexicality has coloured Swahili indelibly in some undesirable ways; while it may be championed today as 'our national language', one of its main functions is still as the language spoken in a downward fashion by a superior to the *wananchi* 'the masses', or to any subordinate individual.)

Exemplifying how codes index RO sets

Example [4] illustrates how a code is linked with an RO set. A guard addresses a visitor at a Nairobi business. He views this as an encounter typifying his job, an encounter for which the unmarked RO set renders the guard as (helpful) gatekeeper and the visitor as (polite) enquirer. With no other information than the visitor's appearance, the most salient factor determining the guard's selection of an unmarked choice for enacting this encounter is whether the visitor appears to be a Kenyan African. The guard decides this is the visitor's identity and so he speaks Swahili, the unmarked choice for the unmarked RO set between two Kenyan Africans in their respective roles. In such interactions in many societies, simple efficiency is the major goal. Using a linguistic variety which is neutral in as many senses as possible, and which is also likely to be known, helps achieve this goal. Had the visitor been a *Mzungu* 'European', the guard would have tried English. But with Africans, Swahili has a number of attributes which make it the ideal candidate in Nairobi. First, it is widely spoken; in fact, I estimate that nearly 100 per cent of Africans living in Nairobi speak at least a few sentences in Swahili every day. Second, it is relatively ethnically neutral because, as noted in Chapter 2, the relatively few mother-tongue speakers of Swahili in Kenya live on the coast, some 300 or more kilometres away, and they are not numerous in Nairobi. Third, as just indicated, Swahili has a long history as a lingua franca between strangers in East Africa, making its continued use the status quo. Since the guard's apparent motivation is to convey nothing more than 'business as usual' and a very neutral RO set between himself and the visitor, Swahili is his choice to open the conversation. Recall that the policemen interrogating the young people with the radio in [1] expected their addressees to speak Swahili with them.

But when the visitor asks to see a man whom the guard knows to be from a Luyia ethnic subgroup, the guard assumes that the visitor also is a Luyia. Since the guard himself is a Luyia, if he makes this fact known, then at this point the unmarked RO set between the two of them changes. The interaction will become one between ethnic brethren, not simple strangers, and in Nairobi the unmarked RO set for intra-ethnic-group encounters is generally different from that for inter-ethnic encounters. As long as others are not present who would be excluded, the unmarked code to index this new RO set is their shared ethnic language. By switching from Swahili to Luyia, the guard acknowledges (and makes salient) their shared ethnic-group membership. But when a second visitor appears, the guard addresses him in Swahili, indexing again the more neutral RO set for such encounters.

[4] (Scotton 1988*a*: 154)

(Setting: entrance to the IBM Nairobi head office. The visitor, from the Luyia area of western Kenya, approaches and is addressed by the security guard. Luyia is italicized; otherwise Swahili is used.)

GUARD. Unataka kumwona nani?

'Whom do you want to see?'

VISITOR. Ningependa kumwona Solomon I—.

'I would like to see Solomon I—.'

GUARD. Unamjua kweli? Tunaye Solomon A—. Nadhani ndio yule.

'Do you really know him? We have a Solomon A—. I think that's the one [you mean].'

VISITOR. Yule anayetoka Tiriki—yaani Mluyia.

'That one who comes from Tiriki—that is, a Luyia person.'

GUARD. *Solomon menuyu wakhumanya vulahi?*

'Will Solomon know you?'

VISITOR. *Yivi mulole umuvolere ndi Shem L— venyanga khukhulola.*

'You see him and tell him Shem L— wants to see you.'

GUARD. *Yikhala yalia ulindi.*

'Sit here and wait.'

ANOTHER VISITOR (just appearing). Bwana K— yuko hapa?

'Is Mr K— here?'

GUARD (to this visitor). Ndio yuko—anafanya kazi saa hii. Hawezi kuiacha mpaka iwe imekwisha. Kwa hivyo utaketi hapa mpaka aje. Utangoja kwa dakika kama kumi tano hivi.

'Yes, he's here—he is doing something right now. He can't leave until he finishes. Therefore you will wait here until he comes. You will wait about five or ten minutes.'

(Guard goes to look for Solomon A—.)

How specific readings of indexicality develop

As speakers come to recognize the different RO sets possible in their community, they develop a sense of indexicality of code choices for these RO sets. Indexicality is a universal ability derived from the markedness metric in their cognitive faculty discussed above. However, of course, specific readings of indexicality only emerge when speakers experience language in use in their own community. But because everyone starts with the same equipment (the markedness metric) and has relatively similar experiences, a consensus emerges within the same community. This is the point made by Davis (1948: 89) quoted by Cicourel (1974: 20).

An individual carries his social position around in his head, so to speak and puts it into action when the appropriate occasion arises. Not only does he carry it in his head but others also carry it in theirs, because social positions are matters of reciprocal expectations and must be publicly and commonly conceived by everyone in the group . . .

Mehan (1979) makes a similar suggestion, specifically in reference to linguistic behaviour. He speaks of a 'reciprocity of perspectives', writing (p. 3) that this reciprocity 'does the work of sustaining the assumption that each of us would have the same experiences if we were to change places, had the same biography, perspective, and purposes at hand'. Of course, this is another way of stating that unmarked choices have psychological reality.

A vivid example of our sense of the unmarked indexicality of one linguistic variety, but not another, for a given RO set is offered by Fantini (1977) in his documentation of his son's acquisition of Spanish and English bilingualism. Fantini relates that, at age 2 years 8 months, Mario (his son) met a little girl of about the same age in the USA. At this point, Mario's Spanish was much more developed than his English, but even at this early age Mario recognized that the interaction was in an English-speaking environment. Fantini states that Mario's English was so limited he was only able to say (in English) *look, watch, come*, and *water*. 'Yet he judiciously avoided Spanish which he could have used with so much more facility', Fantini (1977: 5) notes.

As I hope is becoming clear, the unmarked choice as a vehicle for a given RO set in a specific exchange type is the linguistic variety which is the most expected, while the marked choice is most unusual.[4] The theory predicts that an unmarked choice for a given RO set in an interaction type can be identified empirically.

The Unmarked-Choice Hypothesis would be:

A continuum of relative frequencies of occurrence exists so that one linguistic variety can be identified as the most unmarked index of a specific RO set in a specific interaction type, in comparison to other varieties also in use.

Note that the hypothesis must be stated in relative terms, since it is possible that no single variety will stand out categorically as the unmarked choice. This greater frequency of one type of linguistic choice over others has been demonstrated empirically; in these cases, however, the unmarkedness of a

---

[4] Similar views of markedness appear elsewhere, of course: e.g. in characterizing discourse structure, Givón (1979: 88) writes: 'one may define discourse markedness as "the degree to which a discourse phenomenon constitutes a *surprise*, a break from the communicative norm"'.

specific (set of) linguistic structure(s) is indicated, not that of an entire variety. For example, Scotton and Bernsten (1988) show that there is an unmarked set of discourse units and their sequencing in direction-giving in American English. The unmarkedness of these discourse structures is supported by quantitative data across several different naturalistic experimental conditions. Across a number of independent variables, the same set of discourse units appeared in the directions of the majority of direction-givers. Neither the sex of direction-seeker or direction-giver nor other variables, such as apparent age of the direction-seeker or apparent status as student or mature stranger, were significantly associated with the production of distinctive discourse structures.

Also, unmarked choices stand out in cross-cultural (although self-reporting) studies of requests and apologies (Blum-Kulka, House, and Kasper 1989). In addition, a quantitative study (Kite 1989) of American elementary-school-teacher directives in the classroom provided significant results that an unmarked choice exists (the bald imperative) across teachers studied, with a particular marked directive (the hint directive) appearing for marked situations (i.e. disruptions).

I want to reiterate two points before moving on. First, I use unmarked versus marked choice in the singular *only* for convenience; in fact, the theory sees markedness of linguistic choices as a continuum, as indicated above. Second, markedness is very much a property related to specific RO sets in specific interaction types; that is, there is nothing universal about which codes are marked or unmarked. What *is* universal is the capacity of speakers to perceive linguistic choices as marked or unmarked relative to RO sets.

Conventionalized exchanges

How interaction types are conventionalized (i.e. the details of the behaviour, linguistic and otherwise, which is expected) and which conversations are more conventionalized than others are community-specific details. But in the more conventionalized exchanges, an unmarked code is apparent. It is the expected medium, the index of the unmarked RO set. And it is expected just because it has already appeared often in the community in concert with this RO set. I have just indicated above some of those speech acts which are relatively conventionalized across many communities (e.g. direction-giving, requests, directives), where a limited set of unmarked choices has been established empirically.

In all communities, of course, some exchanges are relatively unconventionalized; they are the ones in which norms are unclear or conflict with one another; the result is that the unmarked RO set is not clear. For example, when one's good friend becomes one's boss, what is the unmarked RO set? Such situations may be handled linguistically by using CS as an exploratory choice, I will argue in Chapter 5. Also, using CS itself as the unmarked choice is a likely strategy in uncertain situations; this has been discussed as a 'strategy of neutrality' in Chapter 3 (cf. Scotton 1976*b*). However, this is as much as I will have to say about conventionalization itself.

Speech communities and social networks

There is not strict uniformity across a community in the evaluations speakers make about indexicality or their use patterns. Early in the development of sociolinguistics, researchers did espouse the view that members of the same speech community shared norms of evaluation, even while not sharing exactly the same linguistic repertoires (e.g. Labov 1972). But later research makes clear that, for example, while some speakers positively identify only with a dialect approaching the standard, others award 'covert prestige' to non-standard dialectal variants (cf. Trudgill 1972). Other research (Genesee and Bourhis 1988) shows fragmentation of norms; in this case, not all subjects studied necessarily expect a speaker in a public-service encounter to use the variety which has been normatively/officially sanctioned (French, for example, in the case of their study in Quebec City in Canada). Certainly, the further speakers are removed from their own highly focused networks (Milroy 1982), the less their judgements and performances will be of one voice. A full discussion of the issue of the reality of speech communities is outside the scope of this volume.

The markedness model is based on the premiss that there is sufficient uniformity in markedness judgements across a community for speakers to trust that their communicative intentions are, in general, received as intended. This premiss is supported by those empirical studies (admittedly few to date) which indicate the reality of unmarked choices. This is clearly an area in which the markedness model needs more empirical support. Further, one cannot deny that misunderstandings arise, or that ambiguity regarding intent (sometimes *intended* ambiguity: cf. Scotton and Zhu 1983) is always a possible outcome.

The markedness model and the 'allocation paradigm'

Both the 'allocation paradigm' and the 'interactional paradigm' or 'strategies approach' (to be discussed in the next section) turn to the social context to explain which linguistic forms or varieties occur; however, they operate on different premisses.

The allocation paradigm views linguistic variation as the product of macro–elements in the social situation itself, and the speaker as a rather passive participant. The strong form of the allocation paradigm states that, for a certain type of speaker in any situation X in community Y, one can predict a linguistic variety Z (i.e. allocated by an unspoken community consensus) to that situation.

In contrast, the interactional paradigm downplays the effects of societal norms. Rather, the use and effects of variation are more to be explained within particularized social contexts. It is only by viewing variation within the very context of its occurrence that variation can be seen as a device which the speaker, as actor, uses *strategically* to influence the outcome of interpersonal interactions. As was indicated in Chapter 3, of course, the simple fact that CS exists at all negates the strong form of the allocation paradigm. Further, even if (for example) in situation X, variety Z *does* appear as much as 90 per cent of the time, the allocation paradigm does not address the issue of alternate usage in the remaining 10 per cent.

Still, I accept many premisses of the allocation paradigm; its basic principle that 'habitual language choice in multilingual speech communities or speech networks is far from being a random matter of momentary inclination' (Fishman 1972: 437) is a foundation-stone of the markedness model developed here. The premiss that an RO set is indexed in an unmarked sense by one code choice rather than another depends on viewing codes and their associations within the same normative framework as the allocation paradigm uses.

But the allocation paradigm does not account for all the variation; equally important, it is silent on what the association of a particular code with a set of situational factors *accomplishes*. Its model of linguistic choice is basically deterministic: it leads to the logical conclusion that speakers make the choices they do because they are constrained to do so by a societal system.

The markedness model differs in several minor, but ultimately important, ways. First, it links a code *with the unmarked RO set* for certain types of participant in an interaction, *not* with the interaction itself. This may not appear to be a major modification, but it is important, because it implies that code choices are more directly linked with interpersonal relationships than with the situational frame. A basic tenet of the markedness model is that code choices are modifiable or dynamic, depending on the circumstances. There is no rationale in making choices dynamic if they are spent only in bouncing off the sides of rather static frames. In linking them with relationships, which themselves are more open to change than the frames in which they occur, code choices are more 'empowered' to effect change. Second, this model attempts to encompass all variation in its explanation, not just the dominant choices. That is, it claims to explain both unmarked *and* marked choices. Third, it attempts to answer the implied question of what linguistic variation accomplishes in an interactional sense. Fourth, it implies a model of society more akin to a conflict model than an equilibrium model, in that it provides for the case that not every member of the same social group makes the same linguistic choices at all times. Finally, the markedness model views all choices as speaker-motivated. These points will become clearer later in this chapter and in the next.

The interactional paradigm/strategies approach

The original research question regarding variation was: 'How is it that a community member speaks different linguistic varieties at different times?' The answer has been sought via survey/interview methodologies by Fishman and Labov and associates who study demographic factors as the independent variables; it has been sought via finely tuned observations of situational factors and consideration of societal values and norms under the observational approach of Hymes and associates and their 'ethnography of speaking'. Still, neither approach entirely answers the question. This has led some researchers to consider additional factors. Their revised research question became: 'In addition to/instead of the frame set by situational variables and cultural norms/values, what else motivates speakers to vary their language use patterns?'

Some researchers today answer this restated question by suggesting that some psychological or 'expressive' factors might be considered as well. Much earlier, the most influential researchers to hint at this idea were Roger Brown and Albert Gilman (1960; repr. 1972) in their model of pronominal usage in European languages. It is probably no accident that they are psychologists, more concerned with motivations than perhaps others were.

Brown and Gilman offer a model specifically designed to account for variation in second-person pronominal usage in modern European languages (i.e. when the most 'intimate' second-personal singular form is used as against the second-person plural form). They account for variation in terms of how situational factors place an interpersonal relationship along two dimensions, naming the dimensions with the abstract constructs of 'power' and 'solidarity'. Other researchers were quick to recognize the heuristic value of these constructs for other types of linguistic variation, so that today the use of 'power' and 'solidarity' to label the motivational poles of an inter- action is commonplace. But what is of interest here is that, while Brown and Gilman predominately explain relationships only in terms of stable, situational factors (age, status, etc.), they also speak briefly of more dynamic factors (i.e. factors subject or amenable to change, such as 'like-mindedness').

Even more important, Brown and Gilman recognize that speakers may not only *present* their relationships through pronominal choices, but may sometimes actually use choices to *negotiate* relationships. Even though it is almost as an afterthought, they do acknowledge that choices sometimes violate the very co-occurrence restrictions based on static factors which it is their main purpose to explicate (1972: 277):

Sometimes the choice of a pronoun clearly violates a group norm and perhaps also the customary practice of the speaker. Then the meaning of the act will be sought in some attitude or emotion of the speaker... The general meaning of an un- expected pronoun choice is simply that the speaker, for the moment, views his relationship as one that calls for the pronoun used... These variations are not consistent personal styles but departures from one's own custom and the customs of the group in response to a mood.

Of course, as argued at length in Chapter 3, in recognizing metaphorical switching in addition to situational switching, Blom and Gumperz (1972) gave wide endorsement to the idea that linguistic choices might be personal strategies. Later (Gumperz 1982), the idea was added that metaphorical choices might receive (some of) their meanings from their violations of situational norms. Marked choices under the markedness model are, of course, such violations.

Others also were beginning to consider dynamic factors as motivating linguistic choices, although often only in passing. For example, Friedrich (1972: 276) lists ten components symbolized by Russian pronominal use. They include such static factors as 'context of the speech event'. But the last factor is a dynamic one: 'emotional solidarity—the sympathy and antipathy between the two speakers'.

Often it is the case that the dynamic factors and the purposes they serve are not clearly articulated; for example, the 'interpretative' value of choices may be mentioned, or purposes labelled as 'expressive' or 'stylistic'. Yet this line of explanation for the forces behind variation opens the door for con- sidering linguistic choices as ultimately *more than skilled performance*. Now, such variation could also be considered *a strategy for accomplishing some- thing*. This new way of looking at linguistic variation is reflected in the language researchers use to refer to their studies. For example, Gumperz's 1982 book is titled *Discourse Strategies*; and, of course, my 1976*b* article is titled 'Strategies of Neutrality', a title echoed as a chapter heading in Appel and Muysken (1987). Also, Heller (1982; 1988*b*) uses similar phrasing.

Conversation as interactive behaviour

The insistence of 'interactive' sociolinguists, and in particular of conversation analysts, that speech can only be interpreted by taking account of its interactive setting, also needs mention. Of course, in Chapter 3 I criticized these approaches for what I consider their overemphasis on the individual interaction at the cost of neglecting the interaction type and societal norms. However, three notions important to the markedness model are key themes in such work.

First is the idea that each conversational turn is best considered as a *presentation*, what I will often call a *negotiation*. That is, only through successive turns can one determine whether an earlier turn succeeded in its negotiation concerning the interpersonal relationship. (Some conversation analysts might even say that an earlier turn only achieves its interactional meaning on the basis of later turns; but I find this position too extreme.[5]) This idea is derived from (but is not the same as) Erving Goffman's well-known insight that one's conversational contribution is basically a 'presentation of self' (1959).

A second important premiss is that conversation is a co-operative enterprise (an idea also found in Grice's 'Co-operative Principle' to be discussed shortly). That is, whether a speaker's strategy is achieved depends largely on the addressee's response. (Sperber and Wilson (1986) and supporters of their 'relevance theory' might go so far as to say that even conveying referential meaning cannot be accomplished without the participation of the addressee, as will be discussed below.)

Third is the general emphasis within conversation analysis of looking at conversation as a *sequential enterprise* (cf. Goodwin 1981; Auer 1991). Applying this idea to CS, what I especially have in mind is that a switch is, after all, only a switch *if it contrasts* with what has come before and what

---

[5] It seems that participants make ongoing interpretations of what is going on and evaluations of other participants; e.g. Genesee and Bourhis's studies of language accommodation between salesmen and customers (1982; 1988) found that subjects, when called upon to do so by the experimental conditions, could make evaluations of the speakers on a turn-by-turn basis. Further, these evaluations for a specific turn sometimes changed if the speaker used a different language in a later turn than he had previously used.

follows it. If the code-choice patterning contained in a switch is similar to other choices in the discourse in which it is embedded, then the particular code choice has little communicative intention on its own, as I will argue when I discuss 'CS itself as the unmarked choice'. In contrast, for example, in the conversation presented in [5] below, the housewife's code choices with the house servant take on significance just because they contrast with her choices with the others present.

Language as accomplishing a goal

Quite naturally, the discussion now turns to the idea that language is used to communicate much more than referential meanings. This idea has its modern basis in the writings of the philosopher J. L. Austin (1962). He developed the idea that language could be used *to accomplish something*. Austin was explicit, titling his well-known volume *How To Do Things With Words*. What he had in mind to explain specifically were the functions of performative verbs, of promising, denying, etc. Before Austin, contemporary philosophers (and linguists) concentrated on the referential functions of language, referring to locutionary meaning—the sense and reference of an utterance, i.e. judgements of true vs. false. (For example, if I say *It is raining*, it is possible to question the truth value of this statement.) But Austin was concerned with the performative functions of language which give rise to illocutionary meaning. Such meanings are not subject to truth judgements (e.g. if I say *I promise to telephone you*, and do not do so, the promise is not false). One can see, therefore, that the kinds of meaning which the referential and performative aspects of an utterance convey are different. And Austin's major contribution is to highlight the idea that there are indeed performative aspects of meaning. The term 'speech act' is used to refer to utterances with such performative aspects of meaning which show illocutionary force.

Austin himself did not stress the suggestion that to produce an utterance is to engage in a certain kind of social interaction. Yet others make this interpretation. For example, Lyons (1977: 725) writes, 'One of the most attractive features of the theory of speech-acts . . . is that it gives explicit recognition to the social or interpersonal dimension of language-behavior'. The important insight is not just that Austin views at least some language use as social behaviour, but rather that he portrays language use as *accomplishing an end*. What he has in mind are such ends as committing oneself to a position (e.g. to deny) or performing an action (e.g. to launch a ship), it is true; but his ideas can be extended to include other goals such as negotiating relative position in an interpersonal relationship.

Communicative intention

Austin's work stimulated other philosophers to explore further the ways in which language communicates messages, and what those messages contain in addition to referential meanings.

Grice's co-operative principle

Ideas that speakers should be clear and co-operative in their participation in conversation go back to Aristotle, and have been stated often throughout the history of rhetoric. In 1975 the philosopher H. P. Grice gave these ideas a new twist by using them to discuss the intentional meaning of utterances. Grice introduces the verb *implicate* and its related noun *implicature*. He points out that some implicatures are conventional. Consider this utterance: *He is an Englishman; he is, therefore, brave*. Grice claims that the speaker has committed himself, by virtue of the meaning of his words, to its being the case that, as a consequence of a person's being an Englishman, that person is brave. To Grice, what is conventionally implicated is bravery to an Englishman.

But Grice's main concern is not with conventional implicatures, but with conversational implicatures: 'a conversational implicatum will be a condition that is not included in the original specification of the expression's conventional force' (1975: 58). He says further that these conversational implicatures are connected with certain general features of discourse, and he provides a set of insights about some of these features.

The most important of his insights is the 'co-operative principle' (p. 45):

Make your conversational contribution such as is required, at the stage at which it occurs, by the accepted purpose or direction of the talk exchange in which you are engaged.

He provides four maxims which set out principles of conversational conduct: maxims of quantity (e.g. 'make your contribution as informative as is required'), of quality (e.g. 'do not say what you believe to be false'), of relation ('be relevant, or make your contributions relate to the ongoing exchange or talk'), and manner ('avoid obscurity of expression, avoid ambiguity, be brief, and be orderly').

An especially important part of Grice's ideas for the markedness model
is that he discusses how conversational implicatures can arise when a speaker
'flouts' a maxim. The normal course of events is this. The speaker has said
p; there is no reason to suppose that he/she is not observing a maxim (or at
least the co-operative principle); therefore, he/she intends me to think/is
willing that I think *q*; therefore, the speaker has implicated *q*.

But a speaker may *not* observe the maxims. Grice gives this example of
a flouting of the maxim of quantity (failing to be brief or succinct). He
writes (1975: 55):

Compare the remarks:
(a) Miss X sang 'Home sweet home'.
(b) Miss X produced a series of sounds that corresponded closely with the score of
     'Home sweet home'.

Grice continues (p. 56), 'The most obvious supposition [based on (b)] is
that Miss X's performance suffered from some hideous defect.'

Grice's co-operative principle captures the notion that when participants
in conversation interpret the utterances of other participants, they make use
of the implicit assurance that all participants are co-operating with each other,
in the sense that they try to say things which will be to the point as well as
true. Because of this assurance, when looking for messages in utterances,
addressees can look for meanings of an intentional as well as a referential
nature.

The concept used here, 'communicative intention', comes from Levelt's
(1989) interpretation of Grice's insight. What makes communicative intentions special is that the listener must recognize that *the way* the utterance is
phrased has its purpose. For Grice, 'the way' tends to refer to the content
(or possibly the choice of lexical items and syntactic patterns for conveying
content); in the markedness model I extend Grice's approach to argue that
'the way' may also mean the choice of code. To make intention communicative, to account for success in CS, an adequate model must provide the
mechanism by which the addressee interprets the intention.

Levelt elaborates (1989: 59) on communicative intention in this way, but
does not really provide a mechanism:

For a speech act to be effective, the addressee must be able not only to understand
the utterance but also to recognize the speaker's intention to communicate this
information. In other words, a speaker's communicative intention involves more
than the intention to convey a thought, a wish, or whatever. In addition it involves
the intention that the utterance makes it possible for the addressee to recognize the

speaker's purpose to convey just this thought, wish or whatever. Communicative intention always involves this purpose of *intention recognition* by the addressee.

In their own model of communicative intent, Sperber and Wilson (1981; 1986) revise Grice's formulation in a more extensive way. In their earlier work, they are at pains to argue that there is no distinction between saying and implicating. Rather, they say (1981: 155) that 'the hearer uses Grice's maxims not only in deciding what has been implicated, but also in deciding what proposition has actually been expressed'.

Their basic argument, that listeners interpret messages assuming a guarantee of relevance, makes the point that speakers produce messages with communicative intention from the other side, that of the addressee. They make two related proposals which offer something of a mechanism for arriving at communicative intention: (1) that Grice's maxims may be reduced to a single principle, that of relevance, and (2) that speaker and addressee communicate on the basis of sharing a 'mutually manifest' cognitive environment; in interpreting an utterance, the addressee does so with a 'guarantee of relevance'— that whatever has been made mutually manifest is relevant, and is therefore intended for attention in arriving at the message as communicated.

One attractive aspect of Sperber and Wilson's model is that it allows for ambiguity and even lack of success in conveying communicative intention. They reject the idea of mutual knowledge as too powerful, replacing 'knowledge' with 'assumptions' (and, accordingly with 'mutually manifest environment'). An individual's cognitive environment is a set of assumptions available to him or her. 'We will argue that when you communicate, your intention is to alter the cognitive environment of your addressee' (1986: 46). Further, 'Inferential communication and ostension are one and the same process, but seen from two different points of view: that of the communicator who is involved in ostension and that of the audience who is involved in inference' (p. 54).

Grice's ideas about implicit co-operation in conversation and maxims leading to conversational implicatures, coupled with Sperber and Wilson's view of utterances as having a guarantee of relevance, have been influential in the field of pragmatics, the study of the uses of language. Their insistence that utterances have intentional as well as referential meaning (and, in Sperber and Wilson's case, that the two may be inseparable) has given a new research agenda to pragmatics. The value of these ideas to CS research is that they offer a way to rise above vagueness in discussing how it might be that a switch in code could convey important meanings over and above the referential meanings.

Code choices as 'doing social work'

An obvious question is this: what does the indexicality of codes accomplish? But what I hope is becoming equally obvious is that a code which indexes a particular RO set is 'doing social work' and can be considered in the same tradition as that of Austin's performative verbs, Grice's co-operative principle, and Sperber and Wilson's relevance theory. Speakers do their own 'social work' by using the indexical property of linguistic choices in their negotiation of their own identities and their rights and obligations with others.

An obviously related concept is that speakers act with goals, and this brings up the concept of the 'speaker as rational actor'. And, of course, viewing linguistic choices in this way is related to the interactional paradigm discussed above which sees conversation *as strategy*.

The speaker as rational actor

A number of researchers who are interested in speaker motivations have contributed to this approach. Early researchers were John Thibaut and Harold Kelley (1959) and George Homans (1966). More recently, this approach is represented in the work of Giles and his associates (e.g. Thakerar, Giles, and Cheshire 1982) and Brown and Levinson (1978; 1987).

Thibaut and Kelley, as well as Homans, who are all social psychologists, propose an overall framework which sees social interaction as a process of *exchange*. They use economic metaphors in their models of social behaviour. Participants assess the relative costs and rewards of the positions in the interaction which are open to them, with each participant striving to receive 'the best return' possible. In Scotton (1972) I apply these ideas to the choice of linguistic varieties. That is, I argue that a major motivation for using one variety rather than another as a medium of an interaction is the extent to which this choice minimizes costs and maximizes rewards for the speaker. This idea will figure prominently in the markedness model as well.

Motivations for using politeness strategies are the subject of Penelope Brown and Stephen Levinson. Their starting-point is the observation that Grice's co-operative principle incorrectly predicts the actual facts of conversation: if speakers were maximally co-operative, they would be maximally efficient in their utterances, and this is not the case. Instead, speakers use (among other things) a good deal of indirectness. To explain the cross-linguistic prevalence of structures involving indirectness, Brown and Levinson argue that speakers are rational actors who, at times, use certain structural strategies to mitigate potentially 'face-threatening acts' which they wish to perform. That is, the strategies are means of making the face-threatening act more palatable. While the markedness model does not draw on politeness theory, it shares with that theory the premiss that explaining speakers' code selections is successful only if the analyst begins by assuming that speakers are rational actors.

The notion of the speaker as a rational actor is also implicit in speech accommodation theory. This becomes clear when one considers the motivations for linguistic variation under this model. That is, if speakers want to associate with addressees, the theory predicts that they will modify their speech to make it more like that of the addressees; if speakers want to disassociate themselves, they will produce speech which diverges from that of their addressees. These motivations and their realization in CS practices as a form of accommodation/divergence are considered in the markedness model. Accommodation occurs in the case of some marked choices (i.e. those which negotiate the narrowing of social distance between participants) and under the 'deference maxim'; divergence occurs with those marked choices which negotiate the increasing of the social distance.

In general, the idea that speakers act purposefully, if often unconsciously, figures prominently in the markedness model. Of course, it follows from the tenet that speakers are more than vehicles carrying societal values, that the more stable situational factors alone cannot account for all linguistic variation across talk exchanges. That is, if one assumes that speakers are capable of asking, and regularly do ask, themselves (at some level) such questions as, Is this a long-term or a short-term relationship? What will be the costs in this conversation of switching to a linguistic variety indexing authority?, then certain other assumptions follow. For a speaker to be able to ask such questions and to take account of the nuances of difference between talk exchanges, a model must accord speakers the ability to assess the effects of code choices, and act accordingly.

Example [5] illustrates some of the ways in which code choice does social work for the goal-directed actor. This conversation was recorded in a middle-class Kikuyu home in the Buruburu area of Nairobi. The most prominent speaker is the lady of the house, Wanjiru (s). She is 28 years old and the sister of the research assistant making the recording (a university student who is only a listener in this conversation). s is a teacher and, with the equivalent of a high-school degree, relatively well-educated by Kenyan standards. Another speaker is Mariamu (M), the 19-year-old house servant, who comes from a different ethnic group (Kisii), and has a lower-level, elementary-school education. Important additional participants (who are the main subjects of conversation) are the children. These include Wangu (w), Wanjiru's first-born daughter, who is five-and-a-half years old and in standard 1 at school; Njoki (N), Wanjiru's second daughter, who is four; and Wangu's friend, Gertrude (G), a neighbour child, who comes from another ethnic group (Luo) and is in standard 3. The conversation is in Swahili, except for English, which is italicized, and Kikuyu, which is indicated where it occurs.

[5] (Nairobi No. 39)

s. Wangu! Wangu!
(Calling Wangu, the elder daughter, but no response.)
s. Hawa watoto, wataniona! Mariamu! (Calling to the house servant)
'These children, they will see me! Mariamu!'
w. Niko hapa.
'I am here.'
s. Hawa watoto wanakwenda barabara tena. Sijui ni watoto wa namna gani. Si nimewapiga *about ten minutes ago*? Hawa watoto hata nikiwanafanya nini hawawezi kuniogopa (running out with a stick) . . . Wangu, mnafanya nini?
'These children have gone back to the road. I don't know what kind of children they are. Didn't I beat them about ten minutes ago? These children, even if I do [I don't know] what, they can't fear me . . . Wangu, what are you doing?'
w. Tunacheza na hawa. Niko na viatu. Hata Njoki. Na hatunachezea kwa *gate*.
'We are playing with them [other children]. I am in my shoes. Even Njoki [has her shoes]. And we are not playing with the gate.'
s (going into street). Huyo ni nani? (Talking to another child.)
'Who is this?'
G. Naitwa Gertrude.
'I am called Gertrude.'
w. Mami, huyu ndiye *friend* wangu. Anasomea Buruburu Two School.
'Mother, she's my friend. She is schooling at Burburu Two School.'
s. Uko *class* gani, Gertrude?
'Which class are you in, Gertrude?'
G. Niko *class three*.
'I'm in standard three.'
s (to her children). Nataka muende nyumbani haraka! . . .
'I want you to go in the house quickly! . . .
w (to Gertrude who is standing in the door). Gertrude, umekuja kufanya nini?
'Gertrude, what have you come to do?'
s (to her sister, the research assistant). *Wangu has no manners*. (To Wangu in Kikuyu) Wangu, ukera mugeni uguo? Ii ingithii kwo wirwo uguo?
'Wangu, and you dare tell a visitor that. What if when you go to their house you're told that?'
(The children play. Njoki says something in Kikuyu.)
G. Njoki anasema nini?

'What does Njoki say?'

w. Wachana na Njoki. Njoki hajui Kiswahili. Njoki anachanganya Kikuyu na Kiswahili. Njoki ni kadogo—kako *nursery school* . . . Tom anajua Kiswahili?[6]

'Leave Njoki alone. She doesn't know Swahili. She mixes Kikuyu and Kiswahili. She is little—she's at nursery school . . . Does Tom know Swahili?' (Tom is Gertrude's younger brother.)

G. Ndio. Tom kako *standard one*—kama wewe.

'Yes. Tom is in standard one—like you.'

w. Kalikuwa *number* gapi? Mimi nilikuwa *number eight*.

'Which number was he? I was number eight.'

G. kalikuwa *number eighteen*. Ni ka-*foolish* . . .

'He was number eighteen. He's foolish . . .'

M (the house servant enters and says to Wanjiru). . . . Siku ile ulienda *town*, Wangu alitupa paka kwa *toilet*.

. . . That day [when] you went to town, Wangu threw the cat in the toilet.'

s. Ati nini?

'What's that?'

M. Alitupa paka *toilet* na a-ka-i-*flush*. Nilisikia wakicheka na wakati nilienda kuangalia nikakuta paka huko ndani ya *toilet*. Huko kwa maji.

Note.
a-	-ka-	-i-	-*flush*
3S	CONSEC	OBJ	flush

'She threw the cat into the toilet and flushed it. I heard them laughing and when I went to look I found the cat inside the toilet. In the water.'

s. Unasema nini? Kumbe ni Wangu alifanya hivyo . . . Hiyo paka. (To her sister) *Poor thing*. Wangu kama kijana kabisa . . .

'What are you saying? That cat. Poor thing. Wangu behaves just like a boy . . .'

M. Nasikia huruma kwa paka hii. Wakati nilitoa ilisikia baridi nikaisafisha na maji moto, halafu ni-ka-i-*rub* na kitambaa . . .

Note.
ni-	-ka-	-i-	-*rub*
IS	CONSEC	OBJ	rub

'I sympathize with this cat. When I took it out it was feeling cold and I washed it with hot water and then dried it with a cloth.'

s (to Mariamu some minutes later). Hii masikio yako ni maua au nini? Hujasikia vile nimekuambia, Mariamu. Sijui siku hizi umekuwa namna gani. Ukiwa hutaki kazi, sema hivyo. Nimemaliza kutengeneza vitanda ni-ka-*wash all the clothing* na wewe bado maliza na *kitchen*. Ni nini unafanyia hapo?

---

[6] The use of *ka-* as a noun-class prefix in the Swahili of these children and some other 2nd-language speakers of Swahili is worth comment. This prefix is the singular member of Bantu classes 12/13, which often carry a meaning of 'diminutive'. Both these classes were lost in Swahili at some point in its development, although they are still maintained in many other Bantu languages. What is happening in Nairobi (and elsewhere), it seems, is that some speakers are *borrowing back* into Swahili this class prefix from their own 1st languages; its use signifies 'smallness'. To date, *ka-* is definitely not part of standard Swahili.

Note. ni-   -ka-   -wash
      IS   CONSEC   wash

'Are your ears flowers or what? You haven't yet heard what I told you, Mariamu.
I don't know what's become of you these days. If you don't want work, say so.
I have finished making the beds and I washed all the clothes and you haven't yet
finished with the kitchen. What are you doing in there?'

s (later, to Wangu in Kikuyu). Muuma ku?
'Where were you?'

w. Barabara kucheza na *friends.*
'In the road playing with friends.'

s. Na sasa mnataka nini?
'And what do you want now?'

w. Chakula.
'Food.'

w (to Mariamu). Kwanza wapeleke *upstairs*, Mariamu, uwavae nguo nzuri—
wameharibu hizi. (To sister) *They are so dirty.* Hawa watoto ni *untidy.* (In Kikuyu)
Nyagiko! . . . (Swahili again) Wangu ndiye *extreme.* (In Kikuyu) Wangu, utukitie
uu?
'First take them upstairs, Mariamu. Dress them in nice clothes—they have
spoiled these. They are so dirty. These children are untidy. So untidy! Wangu is
extreme. Wangu, who do you take after?'
(Swahili again to children and Mariamu) Kwenda juu mvae nguo nzuri.
'Go upstairs and put on nice clothes.'

w (to sister after house girl has gone in Kikuyu). Nii uyu muiritu—
'This girl—'
(In Swahili) Hana masikio
'She has no ears.'
(In Kikuyu) Nii ndiroigite ningumubuta ndirariguo ngurula ungi ku.
'I even said that I would sack her but then I didn't know where I would get
another maid.'

The children, but especially their mother, Wanjiru (s), index simultaneous
identities and participation in several different RO sets in a few lines. No
doubt Wanjiru views her membership in the Kikuyu ethnic group positively,
since it is a numerically dominant group in Nairobi, as well as perhaps the
largest group in Kenya as a whole. Also, many of its members are known to
enjoy a relatively high socio-economic level and are proud of this reputa-
tion. Wanjiru speaks Kikuyu to her sister and also to Wangu.

But, as a resident of Nairobi, Wanjiru also indicates her urban identity by
making heavy use of Swahili. She even speaks Swahili to her children most
of the time (at least here, Kikuyu is used mainly to reprimand them). She
also tries Swahili, not English or Kikuyu, with the unknown child, Gertrude.

And Swahili seems to be a main language of informal encounters for the children, even with their mother. For them, Swahili seems to have a certain *authenticity* as a language one acquires at school and play and shares with other children.

And everyone in the conversation has an identity associated with English (the house girl to a lesser extent). The children, who sprinkle their Swahili with English, are studying English in school and their language indicates they are making their way up the educational ladder. The two adult Kikuyu sisters have already achieved a high standard of education. They are proto-typical educated urban dwellers in Africa, aligning themselves both with their own ethnic group and with other speakers of English, no matter what the ethnic background.

But in relation to the concept of 'doing social work', Wanjiru's language use with the house girl, Mariamu, is most obviously instructive. Note that Wanjiru speaks to Mariamu almost entirely in Swahili. One might well argue that the RO set she is negotiating with Mariamu is one designed to keep Mariamu at a social distance. And her comments to Mariamu, and then later to her sister about Mariamu, indicate a clear coolness towards her.

As already noted, Swahili is associated with a variety of 'transactional' RO sets in Nairobi. For some of these transactions (such as service encounters) socio-economic status is not salient, and Swahili use reveals no special status. But socio-economic status is clearly salient in work situations, and it is Swahili which is the vehicle of downward directives (i.e. employer to subordinate). And this is part of the social work (that the communication *is* downward) which Wanjiru's use of Swahili to Mariamu performs.

In using Swahili almost exclusively with her, Wanjiru does not extend Kikuyu ethnic identity to Mariamu (by expecting her to understand Kikuyu) nor does she acknowledge any educated status to her (by speaking to her in as much English as she uses with her sister, although she finds it hard to finish a sentence to anyone without some English). It is clear from Mariamu's speech that she knows some English.

Of course, example [5] also illustrates the concept of the speaker as rational actor. It is important to stress that this concept does not imply either that the speaker is necessarily making linguistic choices consciously, or that the speaker is rational in the logical sense of 'manifesting reason'. Rather, the primary implication of viewing the speaker as rational actor is simply that at some level speakers are goal-directed.

The following CS example is taken from Goyvaerts and Zembele's research in Bukavu, Zaire. They themselves refer to this example as an instance of 'the unmarked choice type'. They write (p. 79):

... this kind of codeswitching is typical for some interactions among peers who use shifting to signal their mutually multiple identities. Thus speakers are boasting, symbolically as it were, of the range of their identities. One should not forget that in Bukavu, where the largest part of the population is to be situated within the 10–25 age group, youngsters in the shanty town lack any financial or material means to procure status symbols. However, status can be obtained through language use and at no cost at all for that matter!

In this example French is in small capitals and Lingala is in italics; otherwise Swahili is used.

[6]   (French / Lingala / Swahili; Goyvaerts and Zembele 1992: 74–5)

(Setting: At home, a group of young people are watching TV.)

A. DIS *omonaki* MATCH *wana*? . . . EN TOUT CAS *po na ngai*, IL FALLAIT *kaka* ARBITRE *abimisa* JOUEUR *wana* . . . PARCE QUE TANTOT ni kucheza mubaya, TANTOT ni kuPROVOQUER benzake . . . *Kobeta* BALLE *ango ayebi ata kobeta malamu te.*

'Hey you! Did you watch that soccer game? Anyway, as far as I am concerned, it was necessary for the referee to send off that player . . . he plays awfully, then he provokes his partners . . . Playing like this; he doesn't even know how to play.'

B. *Ya solo! Ye azalaki na* MISSION SPECIALE: *ko*MARQUER SON VIS-À-VIS, C'EST TOUT. IL EST PROFESSIONNEL TU SAIS.

'Right! He had a special mission: to closely watch his adversary, that's all. He is a professional you know.'

C. Muache kwanza shie tusikie MATCH. Ile COMMENTAIRES mutaifanya nyuma. LE MATCH EST PLUS IMPORTANT QUE CETTE BLAGUE' LÀ.

'Be quiet, let us first listen to the match. You'd better leave those comments until later. The match is more important than that joke.'

D. *Bino bozalaka ndenge mini?* Si muache fujo!

'How are you behaving? Please, stop the noise!'

Empirical support for 'social work' in codeswitching

Two different experimental studies indicate that speakers are, indeed, making linguistic choices with social goals in mind (Scotton and Ury 1977; Scotton 1982*a*). These articles report on similar studies. For the 1977 study, facsimile audio-recordings, using local persons as actors, were made of four actual conversations involving CS which had taken place in Kenya. The recordings were played to 70 subjects living in western Kenya, who were asked this question about each conversation: 'From just listening to these people talk, what can you tell me about what is happening in the conversation?' No mention was made of language switching, or even of language, in the question.

No attempt was made to channel responses. Most subjects did spontaneously connect the switching with an attempt on the part of one or more speakers to redefine their relationship (i.e. negotiate a different RO set) with the other participant(s). That is, for three of the four conversations, a statistical test (Fisher's exact test) showed that the distribution of responses was significant ($p < .01$), with the majority of subjects mentioning both that switching took place and that there was some attempt to redefine the relationship between participants. For example, in one conversation, when one of the participants (who all come from the same ethnic group and who have been speaking their mother tongue) disagrees with the leader, the leader switches to English to make his point again. Fully 77 per cent (54 out of 70 subjects) commented on the change to English. All of these stated that the change indicated the topic's importance to the speaker; some (27 per cent) also said the speaker was stressing his own importance.

Scotton (1982a) reported a similar study, but this time the subjects were asked to select one of the possible answers 'about the relationship of the persons speaking' from a set of five choices on a questionnaire which they could examine. The facsimile conversations played took place in western Kenya. The subjects ($N = 35$), who worked in Nairobi but who visited families in Western Kenya regularly, were similar in type to the persons involved in the recordings, or knew such persons. Three recorded conversations were played to these subjects. They overwhelmingly chose those possible responses which referred to the relationship of the speaker to the other participants. In one case, for example, a petty official switches to Swahili at a local meeting which has been conducted in Lwidakho up to this point. Out of 35 subjects, 34 chose this response: 'He wanted to show that he was official and not just an ordinary Luyia person.' What was particularly telling in this study was that subjects did *not* choose those responses which are often put forward as folk explanations of CS, such as 'He switched to Swahili because he could express himself better in that language', or 'He was more used to speaking Swahili', or 'Swahili is the national language and we should use it'.

[7] (Scotton 1982a: 438–9)

(Meeting of a location development committee. Twice during the meeting, the location chief, who is chairing the meeting, responds forcefully in Swahili, although Lwidakho, with some English switching, has been the medium of the meeting. All present are first-language speakers of Lwidakho. The chief, a relatively minor official in the local-government system, is moderately well educated and does speak some English. But he may well choose Swahili to make his authoritative argument because he does not want to take the chance of making any mistakes in English in front of the various members who are more educated than he is, especially the teachers.)

TEACHER (Lwidakho). Tsi shilinji tsya *Local Rate* tsyamenya T— yi tsi ligavulwa lyatsyo shilili lilahi muno tawe. Mwahana khu tsi *project* tsindala tsinyishi nendio shivuli vulahi tawe. Genyekhanenga khu-*revise* ligavula yili.

'Money for the "local rate", which is in T—, wasn't properly shared out to the projects we have so that some have been granted more money than others and this is not good. This committee should have been the one to portion out the money. The whole breakdown should be revised.'

CHIEF (Swahili). Mimi kama *chief*. Naweza kuamua na ni lazima mkubaliane nami, mpende, msipende.

'I'm the chief. I can decide and it's necessary that you agree with me, whether you like it or not.'

Awareness that language is a tool

That speakers 'know' at an unconscious level that certain choices are unmarked affirmations of the expected and others implicate 'something else' is clear from the conscious remarks they sometimes make about linguistic choices. For example, in [8] two teachers are conversing, in the staffroom at a teachers' college in western Kenya, about the problems of buying charcoal (for cooking fuel).

[8] (Myers-Scotton, unpublished data)

TEACHER I. 'Just before I went to Machakos, I bought some charcoal from that man. He only gave me half a bag and told me one day I could get the other half. To this day, I have not got it. I gave him, plus my *gunia* [Swahili = sack]. He has eaten my money, eaten my gunia, eaten my charcoal. He is a man who dresses in blue. He talks a lot of English. And he thinks he is better than other charcoal sellers. He has a big qualification.'

TEACHER II. 'You see, whether he knows English he is not better than the one who speaks Swahili, and he [the Swahili-speaker] is a gentlemen. Whether he speaks broken Luyia and I communicate with a pleasant person who sells me charcoal, it is better than somebody who speaks King's English.'

And in example [9] a Nairobi bus conductor overtly comments negatively on the use of English by a cheeky passenger on a crowded bus when Swahili is the unmarked index of the unmarked RO set for such an exchange.

[9] (Myers-Scotton, unpublished data)

CONDUCTOR (to a smartly dressed young man who is standing): Umesha lipa nauli?

'Have you already paid the fare?'

YOUNG MAN. *Don't you see that I am in a position in which I can't take something from my pocket?*

'Don't you see that I'm not in a position to take anything from my pocket?'

SAME YOUNG MAN (adding in Swahili). Ninyi mnachaza [for *mnajaza*] watu kwenye gari na hamna viti vya kutosha.

'You people fill the bus with people and you don't have enough seats.'

CONDUCTOR. Hii ni mali ya mwenyewe au serikali. Si mali yako uifanyie huo mchezo wako mbaya. Wako humu dani waliojua Kiengereza, lakini wanatuheshimu.

'This is the property of the owner or the government. It isn't your property so that you should make your bad play [comment]. There are people within [the bus] who know English, but they show us respect.'

These two examples show not only that speakers are aware of linguistic choices but that they do not always make the unmarked choice. (If they did, there would be no variation to explain except in terms of situational factors. And CS itself would only occur as the unmarked choice.)

What motivates speaker choices?

Up to this point, I have tried to explicate those themes or theoretical approaches which figure in the markedness model. Let me now put them together in a theory of the social motivations for CS.

Markedness and the normative framework

Speaking of choices as marked or not assumes that they take place in a normative framework. As indicated above, while speakers are innately equipped with a markedness metric, they only make actual readings of markedness through experience with language use in a community. They then view the codes in their community's repertoire as more unmarked or more marked, according to community norms, as the index of the unmarked RO set between certain participants in a given talk exchange. This argument implies that conversations are more or less conventionalized, that speakers have some sense of the unmarked 'script' or 'schema' for them. Assuming that speakers have this sense of what is normative does not mean that all speakers in the community must think the prevailing scripts/schemas are legitimate, or that they all must have access to the linguistic repertoire enabling them to participate fully in all interactions.

As I hope is clear by now, I argue that it would not be possible for a speaker to assume that his or her messages, whether the choice is unmarked or marked, have communicative intentions (i.e. as unmarked or marked) unless an underlying normative framework existed, with readings of markedness for the potential code choices. That is, the normative framework is necessary for speakers to be able to interpret code choices.

For this reason, even though I see the markedness model as presenting a dynamic view of the code choices themselves, I cannot agree with those researchers who see the social meaning of choices as largely generated by the dynamics of the interaction itself. It is true that a part of the social meaning does develop in the actual turn-taking of a conversation; but most of the interpretation depends on the framework of markedness which is provided by societal norms. That is, community patterns of use, not the individual conversation, ought to be the most primitive unit in analysis.

Speakers as goal-directed actors

Having put in place the normative framework, I must now stress that the markedness model does not view the actual choices themselves as arising from norms. How does this match what appears directly above? While norms largely determine the interpretations of choices, speakers, not norms, make choices. Speakers weigh the costs and rewards of alternative choices and make their decisions. And, since all have identical markedness metrics, enabling them to abstract markedness judgements based on language use in their community, they make similar interpretations of the intended indexicality of a given code choice for an RO set in a given exchange. With a sense of the markedness ratings of potential code choices and of the consequences of making one choice rather than another, speakers proceed.

Note the limited role the model gives to situational factors as such. Speakers work out what is going to be the unmarked code choice for them in a given exchange by deriving from whatever situational factors are salient the unmarked RO set and a code as its unmarked index. While it is useful in a descriptive sense to know which factors apply in a given situation, a listing of such features has no value in explaining actual choices. Speakers need situational factors as input—as signposts of markedness. But speaker motivations, not social factors, direct choices.

The heart of this model, therefore, is the claim that the range of linguistic choices for any specific talk exchange can be explained by speaker motivations based on readings of markedness *and calculations of the consequences of a given choice*. When speakers engage in CS, it means they perceive the interaction—either initially or as it progresses—as one in which they can best maximize their rewards (taking account of the specific community context) by using two or more linguistic varieties. So conceived, the model can account for the majority of choices which follow the normative patterns of the allocation paradigm; but it can also explain as equally well-motivated the choices which that paradigm has to view as aberrant.

Summary

This chapter has introduced a set of themes or theoretical approaches (along with mention of their major proponents) which motivate the markedness model. I hope to have conveyed the idea that a major motivation for variety in linguistic choices in a given community is the possibility of social-identity negotiations.

That is, a meta-message of conversational moves is that the medium is a comment[7] on speakers' perceptions of themselves and their relations with others. I use the term 'negotiate' for this process in the sense defined by the dictionary as treating with another or with others in order to come to terms or reach an agreement. A negotiation is a dynamic enterprise, with at least two sides, but without a foregone conclusion or even a prescribed route to a conclusion.

The models discussed in this chapter offer the addressee varying degrees of prominence in influencing the interaction (although some have little to say about this at all). Even in those approaches which give prominence to the speaker as a rational actor, the addressee/audience may be seen as such a major factor in influencing choice that the model is, in fact, an audience-centred model. This is the case both with speech accommodation theory

---

[7] The 'comment' message of choosing one linguistic variety rather than another is best thought of as a 'weak' versus 'strong' implicature, following the usage of Sperber and Wilson (1986) regarding types of implicatures. Grice (1975), of course, coined the term 'implicature'. In arguing for the recognition that weak as well as strong implicatures figure in the scope of pragmatics, Sperber and Wilson (1986: 197) write: 'An act of communication merely makes manifest which assumptions the communicator intends to make manifest ... It does not necessarily make the audience actually entertain all the assumptions communicated. This is true of implicatures too. Implicatures are merely made manifest by the act of communication ... Some implicatures are made so strongly manifest that the hearer can scarcely avoid recovering them. Others are made less strongly manifest. It is enough that the hearer should pay attention to some of these weaker implicatures for the relevance of the intended interpretation to become manifest.' They go on to say (p. 200): 'Clearly, the weaker the implicatures, the less confidence the hearer can have that the particular premises or conclusions he supplies will reflect the speaker's thoughts, and this is where the indeterminacy lies. However, people may entertain different thoughts and come to have different beliefs on the basis of the same cognitive environment. The aim of communication in general is to increase the mutuality of cognitive environments rather than guarantee an impossible duplication of thoughts.'

and with politeness theory, at least in my view. They both stress the speaker as absorbed with the addressee's perceptions and acting based on those perceptions. In contrast, the markedness model is predominantly a speaker-centred model. No model of conversation can ignore the effect of the addressee (and of the audience, too, for that matter) on speaker choice. But in the markedness model, speakers make choices primarily based on enhancing their own positions, or at least communicating their own perceptions. This central idea will become clearer, I hope, in Chapter 5.

5

A Markedness Model of Codeswitching

THE previous chapter discussed the theory to account for code choices in general and its antecedents. Here the markedness model in relation to CS is presented. The model consists of a set of general maxims applying to any code choice. This chapter discusses their application to CS, and provides examples illustrating their realization.

By using a single concept, markedness, as an organizing device, this model's approach to the social functions of CS is different from those of other researchers. The markedness model involves an explicit set of constructs which are linked together in such a way as to give special significance to certain concepts and variables. In this way, it accounts for all types of CS and their social motivations as one of four complementary types. Relating the types to one another in this unified way contrasts with producing an open-ended taxonomy of functions.

The negotiation principle

Modelled after Grice's 'co-operative principle' (1975), a 'negotiation principle' is seen as underlying all code choices:

Choose the *form* of your conversation contribution such that it indexes the set of rights and obligations which you wish to be in force between speaker and addressee for the current exchange.

This principle embodies the strongest and central claim of the theory presented here: that all code choices can ultimately be explained in terms of such speaker motivations.

The markedness model of CS rests on this principle, and on the maxims following from the principle. These are: (1) the 'unmarked-choice maxim', (2) the 'marked-choice maxim', and (3) the 'exploratory-choice maxim'. There are also two auxiliary maxims to the unmarked-choice maxim, the 'virtuosity maxim' and the 'deference maxim', both directing the speaker toward seemingly marked choices. How they are appropriately considered under the unmarked-choice maxim will be discussed below. In following these maxims, speakers engage in CS resulting in one of these four related types: (1) CS as a sequence of unmarked choices; (2) CS itself as the un-marked choice; (3) CS as a marked choice; and (4) CS as an exploratory choice.

CS as an unmarked choice

The unmarked-choice maxim directs speakers as follows:

Make your code choice the unmarked index of the unmarked RO set in talk exchanges when you wish to establish or affirm that RO set.

Following this maxim results either in CS as a sequence of unmarked choices (hereafter sequential unmarked CS) or as CS *itself* as the unmarked choice (hereafter unmarked CS). The two types of unmarked CS occur under different circumstances, but ultimately have related motivations: sequential unmarked CS is triggered by a change in the situational factors during a talk exchange. Situational factors remain more or less the same during the course of the exchange when unmarked CS occurs. Instead, its presence depends more on the participants' attitudes—toward themselves and the social attributes which the codes and their alternation index. But in either case, CS is the unmarked choice for the unmarked RO set, given the participants and other situational factors.

Sequential unmarked CS

When one or more of the situational factors change *within the course of a conversation*, the unmarked RO set may change. For example, in [4] in Chapter 4, when the security guard discovers that the enquirer comes from his own ethnic group, the content of the factor 'ethnicity' changes from 'unknown' to 'shared', and the unmarked RO set changes from that holding between strangers to that between ethnic brethren. In many cases, the unmarked RO set changes when the participant makeup of a conversation changes (i.e. someone comes or goes) or when the topic is shifted.

Whenever the unmarked RO set is altered by such factors, the speaker will switch codes if he or she wishes to index the new unmarked RO set. By making the unmarked choice the speaker is accepting the status quo and acknowledging the indexical quality of the unmarked code.[1]

---

[1] An example of the sense of the unmarkedness of different linguistic varieties for certain pur-poses from the ancient world is found in Brosnahan (1963: 46–7). Brosnahan cites Lewis (1950) about the position of Turkish as the official language of administration in the Near and Middle

That speakers generally will choose to accept or negotiate the new un-marked RO set is predicted by the model. This prediction is motivated by a number of factors, but especially the costs/rewards model discussed in Chapter 4 (cf. Thibaut and Kelley 1959). The rewards of following societal norms by indexing the unmarked RO set are calculable: speakers need only consider the consequences they have witnessed or experienced many times already in their community when the unmarked choice has been made. The costs of this choice are that no change in the predicted RO set between the speaker and other participants is likely to result; in contrast, it is likely that the exact rewards possible through negotiating a change in the RO set are unknown. Unless accepting the unmarked RO set is especially onerous, the speaker will take the 'safe' course and make the unmarked choice.

While the change in the markedness of RO sets which triggers sequential unmarked CS is external to the speaker, I want to emphasize that it is still the speaker who has the choice to respond to this change. The unmarked response is to switch codes to the index of the new, unmarked RO set, an indication of the speaker's acceptance of that set for the remainder of the conversation. Blom and Gumperz (1972) identify such CS as situational switching; but I prefer to label this CS in such a way as to indicate that the change in codes is speaker-motivated, not driven by the situation. No matter what the situational factors, it remains up to the speaker to make the choice to act upon them.

Example [1] shows how sequential unmarked CS choices are realized, based on a change in addressee. In this conversation, Edward M. is visiting his relative, John M., who is an executive in a soft-drink bottling company in Nairobi. The two have greeted each other in their shared mother tongue, but then—partly because of the topic and setting, partly because other persons are present or arrive on the scene—they speak mainly English, which, along with Swahili, constitutes the unmarked realization of most of the interactions John M. has in his office. Note that John M. switches from one language to another as the addressee changes. He speaks English to his white-collar subordinate, but when he calls to the receptionist to get a soft drink for Edward M., he switches to Swahili. Then he switches back to English again to lecture a salesman. While John might speak in either Swahili or English to his higher-level staff members, in this conversation the topic calls for him to express his authority; English is the more unmarked

East: 'So deep-rooted was the feeling that only Turks were equipped by nature to govern that in the fourteenth century we find a Mameluke secretary of Syrian birth addressing the Arabs in Turkish through an interpreter rather than in his mother tongue, for fear lest he should lose face by speaking the despised language of the subject people.'

choice for this purpose. Edward also switches from speaking English to the subordinate to speaking Swahili to the receptionist. Swahili is italicized.

[1] (Myers-Scotton, unpublished data)

SUBORDINATE (entering John M.'s office and speaking to Edward M. just after John M. has stepped out for a minute). Where has this guy gone to?

EDWARD. He's just gone out. He will soon be back.

JOHN (to subordinate when he returns). Why did you change the plan of our stand at the showground? Who recommended the change? . . .

SUBORDINATE (looking guilty). Nobody told me.

JOHN. Go and change it according to our previous plan. Also make sure that the painting is done properly.

JOHN (to Edward when subordinate has left). I've told this man how to build our stand, but he went and did a different thing. *Ni mtu mjeuri sana.* ('He's a stubborn person.') I'll make him pay for the paint he spoilt.

JOHN (calling to receptionist). *Letea mgeni soda anywe.*

'Bring the guest a soda so that he may drink.'

RECEPTIONIST (to Edward). *Nikuletee soda gani?*

'What kind of soda should I bring you?'

EDWARD. *Nipe Pepsi.*

'Give me a Pepsi.'

SALESMAN (entering). *Sikuweza kufika kwa sababu nilikuwa mgonjwa.*

'I couldn't come because I was not well.'

JOHN. Well, I wanted you to explain something about one of your receipt books . . . There's a mistake somewhere. Take it back and make the totals again.

JOHN (to Edward when salesman leaves). This one will not earn any money at the end of this month. He has a big shortage.

Example [2] illustrates how a speaker (or writer, as is the case here) can use sequential unmarked CS to indicate a change in tone, rather than a literal change in situational factors. The example involves a letter written to me by a Tanzanian friend. Although we were both living in Nairobi, the Tanzanian decided to write a letter to me. The letter began in Swahili, with an explanation of the circumstances which occasioned the request. But when he arrives at the 'delicate' subject of asking for a loan from a friend, he switches to English, as if to mark the seriousness of the subject. Also, although his English is good, it is more remote from him than Swahili, which is his first language. Therefore, the unmarked choice for him, in order to distance *himself* from the embarrassment of asking for money, is English.

[2] (Scotton 1979: 72)

. . . Nina shida ya lazima sana ya pesa kwa sasa. Naomba sana unisaide.

'I have a great need of money right now. I ask you to help me.'

(Switch to English). Well, this is the first time since I knew you, I think, to borrow money. I know money can break our friendship.

Many CS studies cite the quoting of the remarks of someone else from a previous conversation (i.e. reported speech) as a common example of CS. Such switching also exemplifies sequential unmarked CS. The code used in the reported speech is unmarked for the RO set for the earlier conversation, while the code preceding and following the quoting is unmarked for the RO set of the present conversation. Using CS for quotation, therefore, makes the narration more vivid because it makes it 'closer to the real thing'. It may be common and even predictable, but it is important to recognize that such CS is not especially remarkable.

Making unmarked choices indicates acceptance by the speakers of the role relationships which persons in their communities with their social identities typically have with one another. Recall that the key word in describing unmarked choices is 'expected'. It follows that the speaker probably devotes the least conscious attention to this type of CS, although all types generally are executed without the speaker making a conscious choice. However, level of consciousness in CS, as in most linguistic choices, is unstudied; further, how it might be studied empirically is not clear.

CS itself as the unmarked choice (unmarked CS)

Speaking two languages in the same conversation is also a way of following the unmarked-choice maxim for speakers in many bi/multilingual communities in certain types of interaction. Examples [3–8] illustrate examples from urban Africans, for whom switching between the alien official language and an indigenous language is the unmarked choice for many interaction types. Elsewhere in the world, such switching is very frequent in certain communities, but hardly present at all in other ones. Why this is so is discussed below. In this sense, unmarked CS contrasts with the other three types of CS which occur universally wherever there are bi/multilinguals. It also contrasts with the other types, in that *each* switch in unmarked CS does not necessarily have a special indexicality; rather, it is the *overall pattern* which carries the communicative intention.

In such switching, speakers engage in a continuous pattern of using two (or more) languages; often the switching is intrasentential and sometimes within the same word. The other types of switching do not show the same to-and-fro nature (unless there is an unusually complex sequence of change in situational features, as in [1]).

[3] (Crawhall, unpublished data)

(Two fragments of a conversation recorded at a shopping centre near a housing estate in Harare, Zimbabwe. The three participants are all first-language speakers of Shona. The two speakers are in their early 20s and have 'O'-level education (equivalent to a high-school diploma); one is a student teacher. The listener is an 18-year-old school-leaver. Shona is the matrix language here, with English italicized.)

SHONA 1. Unonoziva chiri kunetsa. *Time* iya *long back*, zvakange zvisinganetsa waingoenda wonotaura kuna *bursar* waona kuti ndatora vanhu vakaita *so* vakaita *so* waona kana uchida vanhu ve-*temporary* unotanga wa-*apply* ku-*Ministry of Labour* wopihwa vanhu vacho waona.

'You know the problem. A long time back, it was easy because you just got to the bursar and told him that "I take employed people so and so", you saw if you wanted people for temporary, first of all you had to apply to the Ministry of Labour, you were given your people.'

SHONA 2. Saka iye a-ka-*apply*.

'So he applied.'

SHONA 1 (later, about a trip he made). Saka ukabuda *so* mu-bhawa [*bar*] woenda *the other side* uchiona *the lake* iri pazasi *so* nenzou, ndichifamba waona. *The view is nice* waona.

'If you get out of the bar, and go to the other side you can sit down and see the lake below and elephants walking about, you see. The view is nice, you see.'

[4] (Swahili/English No. 18)

(Part of a conversation recorded at a shopping centre near a housing estate in Nairobi. The three participants come from three different ethnic groups; all are relatively well-educated young men. The Luo (L) is about 17 years old and is in form 1 (equivalent to beginning high school); the Kalenjin (K) is about 23 years old and is in form 4; and the Kamba (M) is about 24 years old, and in form 6. Swahili is the matrix language of this conversation, with English italicized.)

L. Mbona hawa *workers* wa East African Power and Lighting wakaenda *strike*, hata wengine nasikia washawekwa *cell*.

'And why on earth did those East African Power and Lighting workers strike, even I've heard some have been already put in cells [in jail].'

K. Ujue watu wengine ni *funny* sana. Wa-na-*claim* ati mishahara yao iko *low* sana. Tena wanasema eti hawapewi *housing allowance*.

'You know, some people are very funny. They are claiming that their salaries are very low. They also say—eh—they are not given housing allowances.'

M. Mimi huwa nawafikiria lakini wao huwa na *reasonable salary*.

'As for me, I used to think, but they have a reasonable salary.'

K. Hujajua watu wengi *on this world* hawawezi kutoesheka. Anasema anataka hiki akipewa a-na-*demand* kingine.

'Don't you know yet that some people on this world [*sic*] can't be satisfied. He says he wants this and when he is given [it], he demands another [thing].'
L. . . . Kwani ni ngumu sana ku-*train* wengine? Si ni kupata *lessons* kidogo tu halafu waanze kazi?
'. . . Why it is difficult to train others? Isn't it just to get a few lessons and then they should start work?'

When and where does unmarked CS occur? Certain conditions must be met for unmarked CS. First, the speakers must be bilingual peers; such switching typically does not happen when there is a socio-economic differential between speakers or when they are strangers. Second, the interaction has to be of a type in which speakers wish to symbolize the dual memberships that such CS calls up. Typically, such interactions will be informal and involve only ingroup members. Third, proficiency in the languages used in the switching is not a sufficient condition; perhaps the most important criterion is that the speakers must *positively evaluate* for their own identities in this type of interaction the indexical values of the varieties used in the switching. Fourth, while speakers must be relatively proficient in the two (or more) languages involved, the degree of proficiency is open to question, and the literature on CS to date does not give a clear answer. I myself have not studied proficiency levels systematically; my impressions, based on several different data sets from Nairobi and from Harare, are that the majority of speakers engaging in such CS are relatively proficient in all the languages.[2] But my impression is that engaging in such switching is more associated with *familiarity* with using the languages together than it is necessarily associated with high proficiency or with any social-identity factors, such as education or age. A structural argument supports the view that high proficiency is not required if the unmarked CS consists largely of singly occurring, embedded-language morphemes which are inserted into a matrix-language morphosyntactic frame. The psycholinguistic 'cost' (in terms of proficiency in the embedded language) of such an insertion operation should be relatively low (i.e. requiring little ability in the embedded language beyond knowledge of its content words).

In addition, it is important to acknowledge that not all groups need show exactly the same performance patterns in unmarked CS. However, I want to stress that I argue elsewhere (e.g. Myers-Scotton, 1992*a*; 1993), and cite extensive empirical data to support a model making the claim, that the same underlying *principles* govern the grammatical structure of CS in the same

---

[2] Certainly, I make no assumptions that speakers have *equal* proficiency in the languages which they use in unmarked CS.

general way. What may vary from community to community, or from social group to group within the same community, is whether, within the parameters of these principles, certain options are exercised. For example, it is entirely possible that different social groups (i.e. possibly based on exposure through education to one of the languages involved) within the same geographical area (i.e. in the same city) might both use the same languages in their unmarked CS, but use them to different degrees. Further, from the structural point of view, some might show more intraword switching (i.e. English verb stems with Shona or Swahili tense/aspect prefixes, as in [3] and [4]) than others. The degree of this type of switching might be a function of relative proficiency.

It is important to emphasize that unmarked CS is not just a form of 'age-grading', an ephemeral part of the expression of youth by a limited group in the community. True, in the Nairobi data set of 40 naturally occurring conversations studied here, the great majority of persons engaged in such switching are young and relatively well educated, although they are by no means among the most highly educated Kenyans nor are they members of the élite. And in a Harare corpus of 66 adult, working-class persons interviewed in the suburb of Chitungwiza, there are still many instances of conversations including such switching.[3] What is worth mentioning for the Chitungwiza data is that the users of this type of switching are generally persons holding jobs requiring a good deal of English usage. Frequently, however, the jobs are simply service positions, not jobs requiring high education.

The conditions promoting unmarked CS are met in many communities, but not in all. They are met in much of the Third World in general. Such nations are often characterized by this sociolinguistic profile:

(*a*) Ethnic-group languages are maintained and/or indigenous lingua francas (such as Swahili in Kenya) have currency.

(*b*) At the same time, a former colonial language has been institutionalized as the unmarked medium of status-raising activities such as higher education, inter-ethnic communication between the highly educated, and business and governmental interactions, especially with foreign nationals.

The following scenario lies behind unmarked CS in Africa. Formerly, locals spoke their own common first language with their ethnic peers and an indigenous lingua franca with other Africans and some colonials. The colonial language was largely reserved only for interactions between colonial

---

[3] The Chitungwiza interviews are the basis of a study of English loan-words into Shona (cf. Bernsten 1990; Myers-Scotton, 1993*b*; Bernsten and Myers-Scotton, 1993).

personnel and other foreign nationals and possibly a few Africans (the very highly educated or those working closely with colonials). With independence and the advent of more universal elementary education and more access to higher education, more locals have become proficient in the official language. This language is sometimes the medium of education even from the very first grades, and almost always the medium of the upper grades.

Further, many locals now hold the positions formerly held by the native speakers of the colonial language; they are now the highest-level civil servants, the university lecturers and educational administrators, and the second, if not the top, level of corporate executives. For example, recall John M., the executive in [1]. Following the model of the foreign nationals who previously occupied these jobs, the locals use the official language at least part of the time in these jobs. Further, some speak this language at least part of the time at home, for the instrumental reason that it gives their children some practice in the medium which is crucial to their educational advancement. This use of the alien official language even spills over to leisure activities for some.

But because their primordial group memberships are *also* salient for them in a positive sense, locals do not use the official language exclusively, even at work. Often they engage in CS which includes this language, but also at least one indigenous language. Further, the matrix language (i.e. base language) of their conversations is typically not the official language, but either a shared ethnic-group language (e.g. Shona for many in Harare or Kikuyu for some in Nairobi) or a relatively neutral lingua franca (e.g. Swahili in Nairobi, Wolof in Dakar, Senegal, or Lingala in Kinshasa, Zaïre).

Examples [3] and [4] illustrate a typical pattern of CS found in Nairobi and Harare among the more highly educated or those who use the alien official language often at work. The young men in [3] all speak the same first language, although they may speak different dialects; yet they combine English with their Shona. However, because the young men in [4] come from different ethnic groups and probably do not know each other's first languages, they must resort to a lingua franca to converse with each other.

All the young men are accustomed to using English regularly, since they have recently left school, or are still in school, and the medium of their course work is English. As Harare residents, the Zimbabwean young men have countless occasions to use Shona every day, since the majority of people in Harare are first-language speakers of a Shona dialect. Further, Shona is not a minor language; recall that it is the language of 80 per cent of Zimbabweans and one of the official languages (along with English and Ndebele). As Nairobi residents, the young men in [4] also have many occasions to use Swahili in service encounters and many inter-ethnic inter-actions. Swahili use is firmly established as a marker of urbanism in Kenya. A person not able to speak Swahili in Nairobi would be identified as a provincial, no matter how well he/she speaks other languages, including English. And Swahili has recently gained more academic prestige in Kenya (recall, for example, that it is now a required subject on the primary school-leaving examination). Further, both Shona and Swahili share an attribute important in the nationalistic climate of Africa; they are 'indigenous'.

So the question is: why don't the young men in Harare just speak Shona and those in Nairobi just speak Swahili with each other? It is because, while both Shona and Swahili have some appeal based on their associations, English has another type of cachet which they do not wish to relinquish. English remains more identified with upward social mobility than Shona or Swahili. No one could hope to hold a high-level position in government or industry without speaking English well. Also, it is the language of the international community for Zimbabweans and Kenyans; its role in the international mass media gives it added appeal, especially for younger speakers.

The young men in [3] and [4] are not satisfied with *either* the identity associated with speaking English alone *or* that associated with speaking Shona or Swahili alone when they converse with each other. Rather, they see the rewards in indexing both identities for themselves. They solve the problem of making a choice by evolving a pattern of switching between the two languages. Thus, CS itself becomes their unmarked choice for making salient simultaneously two or more positively evaluated identities.

Such examples can be multiplied many times over in the urban centres of Africa. Interestingly, speakers are often unaware that they are engaging in unmarked CS, and typically perceive their medium to be the indigenous language; this perception can be explained by recognizing that that language is the matrix language for the switching.[4] For example, in writing about Akan/English CS, Forson (1979: 127) made these comments:

participants in normal Akan–English code-switching consider themselves to be speaking Akan. The discourse usually begins in Akan, and as it progresses, the speakers freely use strands of English items of varying lengths. They normally are taken aback when their attention is drawn to the fact that they are 'mixing'. The same speakers might even protest the possibility of anybody 'speaking like this' if they came across a transcribed text with normal code-switching, probably their own utterances . . .

---

[4] I would argue that the reason speakers think they are speaking the indigenous language is that, as the matrix language, this is the language which sets the morphosyntactic frame of the structures permissible in CS sentences. The contribution of the embedded language is much more limited.

More examples will be included to give more of the flavour of unmarked CS. In [5] a Luyia man is interviewing a Luyia woman, who is a nurse in Nairobi. They come from the same home area and he is a friend of her husband. She switches from their shared mother tongue, Lwidakho, to Swahili to English. As a long-term resident of Nairobi, she now uses Swahili as her main language; but at work she also uses English, and with some fellow mother tongue speakers she speaks Lwidakho on its own. But with fellow ethnic-group members of like socio-economic background, her unmarked choice is CS, involving all three of her languages. English is italicized and Lwidakho is indicated as such; otherwise Swahili is used. In the translation, Lwidakho is italicized.

[5] (Myers-Scotton 1991*a*: 65)

INTERVIEWER. Unapenda kufanya kazi yako lini? Mchana au usiku?
'When do you like to do your work? Days or nights?'
NURSE. *As I told you, I like my job.* Sina ubaguzi wo wote kuhusu wakati ninapofanya kazi. *I enjoy working either during the day* au usiku yote ni sawa kwangu. Hata *family members* wangu wamezoea mtindo huu. *There is no quarrel at all.* (Lwidakho). Obubi bubulaho. (Swahili again). Saa zengine kazi huwa nyingi sana na *there are other times when we just have light duty.* (Lwidakho). Walwale vanji, *more work*; (Lwidakho). valwale vadi, (Swahili again). kazi kidogo.
'As I told you, I like my job. I have no difficulty at all regarding when I do work. I enjoy working either during the day or at night; all is OK as far as I'm concerned. Even my family members have got used to this plan. There is no quarrel at all. *There is no badness.* Sometimes there is a lot of work and there are other times when we just have light duty. *More patients*, more work; *fewer patients*, little work.'

(Note intrasentential switching in *family members wangu* 'my family members' ('family members' + 'my', with *wangu* showing noun–class agreement for the plural class containing people).)

In [6] two schoolteachers, who are native speakers of Shona, are conversing about the relative progress of boys and girls in school. English is italicized; otherwise Shona is used and is the matrix language.

[6] (Myers-Scotton 1993*a*)

TEACHER. Manje zvakafanana nekuti kana uri kuita *grade one* manje saka vana vazhinji vechisikana ku-*primary* vanogona sitereki.[5] Vanokasika ku-*absorb* zvinhu.

---

[5] I thank Hazel Carter for drawing my attention to the presence of *sitereki* here. The lexeme *sitereki* is not Shona, but comes from Fanagalo/Chilapalapa, a Zulu-based pidgin much used as a lingua franca in the South African mines. It was also used by white farmers to their African workers in former southern Rhodesia before Zimbabwe became independent.

But as time goes on vana kuenda ku-*grade five, six, seven, form one* vanonoka kuita catch-up mu-ma-*lessons. But once they catch up they go ahead.*

'Now, for example, it is the same when you are in grade one now so that many of the girls [understand] much better. They hurry to absorb things. But as time goes on, children go to grade five, six, seven, and form one boys are late to catch up with lessons. But once they catch up they go ahead.'

(Note the intrasentential switching, including English verb stems with Shona infinitival prefixes (e.g. *ku-absorb* 'to absorb') and also in the prepositional phrase *mu-ma-lessons* 'in lessons' with the Shona locative prefix (*mu-*) and the Shona noun-class prefix (*ma-*).)

Example [7] comes from Senegal, where French often is involved in un-marked CS. The speaker is a young man in Dakar who is a native speaker of Wolof, but also knows French well. French is the sole official language of Senegal, while Wolof is a widely known indigenous lingua franca, especially in the capital of Dakar. French is italicized; otherwise Wolof is used as the matrix language.

[7] (Swigart, 1990)

YOUNG MAN. Mësoon naa *lire* been *Jeune Afrique Magazine, non pas Jeune Afrique Magazine,* benn *Famille et Développement. Journalistes* yu *journal* boobu ñoo demoon def ay kii, *quoi, enquête* la, *je ne sais pas,* ci *prison* Sénégal. *Mais,* soo gisee, soo ko *lire*-e, dangay bëgg jooy sax, dangay wax ne *jamais, jamais* duma def loo xamene dinañu ma japp, yobu ma ci kaso bi. *Mais,* benn *article* bu *lamentable* laa ia wax! 'I once read a *Jeune Afrique Magazine,* no, not *Jeune Afrique Magazine,* [one called] *Famille et Développement.* The journalists from that paper went to do some, uh, well, it was an enquiry. I don't know, on Senegalese prisons. Well, if you saw, if you read it, you would just want to cry, you would say never, never will I do something that they will get me for and take me to prison. I'm telling you about a really pitiful article!'

Note:	mësoon		naa	*lire*		
	do–once PAST		IS	read		
	soo	gisee,	soo		ko	*lire*-e
	if-2S	saw	CONDIT-2S		it	read-2S CONDIT

Example [8] of unmarked CS comes from a conversation between two Nigerian women students studying in the USA. They are native speakers of Yoruba, the matrix language here.

[8] (Oloruntoba 1990: 2)

Emi o ma *mention* gbogbo iru ikan bi iyen, *because* mi o *feel* pe mo lati se. 'I did not mention things like that because I don't feel I have to.'

Note:	o	ma	*mention*	mi	o	*feel*
	NEG	IS	mention	IS	NEG	feel

Examples [6] and [7] especially include instances of borrowing as well as of CS. Example [6] includes a number of established loans from English into Shona (e.g. *grade one, primary, grade five, six, seven,* and *form one*) as well as true codeswitches. It is often the case that CS as an unmarked choice includes such loan-words from one of the partners in CS, typically from the language of higher socio-economic prestige. Example [7] also has at least one established loan, the noun *article*; the verb stem *-lire* 'read' is also a possible borrowing. Singly occurring lexemes/morphemes from the embedded language, whether they are CS forms or borrowings, show similar morphosyntactic integration into the matrix language (cf. Myers-Scotton, 1992*b*; 1993*b*).

Structural features.   The structural characteristics of the type of CS found under unmarked CS contrast with those of sequential unmarked CS. While the latter is typically realized by intersentential switching, unmarked CS may include alternating sentences, but may more typically include a good deal of intrasentential switching, as shown in [3–8]. This switching takes two forms: constituents composed of morphemes from both languages, or embedded language 'islands' (cf. Myers-Scotton, 1993*b*). Constituents composed of morphemes from both languages include (from [4]) *wa-na-claim ati mishahara yao iko low sana* 'they claim their salaries are very low'). Also recorded are a number of 'islands' such as the formulaic expression in [7], *je ne sais pas* 'I don't know' from French). While both CS as a marked choice and CS as an exploratory choice may be realized by intrasentential CS and therefore show these structures, intrasentential switching is especially characteristic of unmarked CS. (However, this claim needs empirical testing.)

Another structural feature of CS in general is especially evident in unmarked CS as well. This is the fact that one of the two (or more) codes involved is the main or matrix language and the other is the embedded language. The designation 'matrix language' as against 'embedded language' assumes critical importance in my discussion of structural aspects of CS (cf. Myers-Scotton, 1992*a*; 1993*b*). As can be seen from the examples cited in this volume, the matrix language supplies more of the morphemes for the discourse; more importantly, it supplies all the 'system' morphemes (i.e. inflections and function words) for intrasentential constituents with morphemes from both languages.

In some communities, the matrix language for a conversation may change from one conversation to another, depending on the socio-psychological correlates of the different conversations. For example, this is reported to be the case for some Hispanics in the USA for whom Spanish is the matrix language for some topics or some fellow Hispanics, and English is the matrix language for other topics and participants. Those conditions do not, however, seem to exist at present in African settings. At least, in all the African data sets I have studied, as well as those cited by other researchers in Africa involving an international language (English or French), it is always an indigenous language, not the international language, which is the matrix language. Some writers on African CS confirm this state of affairs, even if they do not recognize the concept of matrix language versus embedded language. For example, Agheyisi makes this point in writing about CS between Nigerian languages and English (she calls it 'interlarded speech'). She also notes that this code is most characteristically used in the ingroup interactions cited above as a defining feature of CS itself as the unmarked choice (1977: 100–2):

When it [interlarded speech, IS] is used in formal settings, it is often to relax the stiff formality normally characteristic of official transactional interactions, for which English is the usual code. However, the style of IS often used in such settings features a high proportion of English words, *though the overall speech is still perceived as a variety of the indigenous language* [my emphasis] . . . Generally, however, by far the most frequent occurrence of IS is in settings usually associated with the use of the indigenous language. This is typically in casual conversation with friends, colleagues, relatives and other acquaintances.

At the outset of this discussion of unmarked CS, I indicated that such switching does not occur in all communities. It only occurs in those communities where speakers wish to index simultaneously, and especially for their informal, ingroup interactions, the identities associated with the unmarked use of more than one code. Still, such communities are numerous; for example, unmarked CS is extremely common in India between Indian languages and English. In Chapter 3, I indicated that the type of CS which Kachru (1978; 1983) refers to as code-mixing between Hindi and English would seem to qualify as unmarked CS. This is also the case for the examples Southworth (1980: 139) cites between English and Malayalam: 'We might ask . . . why people who are fluent in English bother to use Malayalam at all. The answer seems to be that to carry on a conversation entirely in English would create an extremely formal atmosphere. Making excessive use of English is, in fact, a way of keeping a person at a distance.' Southworth goes on to cite a sentence in English spoken by a professor to a graduate student, but with a Malayalam tag, commenting: 'The effect produced was that of a speaker who wished to remind his hearer from time to time that, even though they were speaking English, they still identified with each other as Indians (and as Malayalis).'

The same general explanation applies to the switching by Marathi speakers between Marathi and either English, Hindi, or Sanskrit, as discussed by Pandharipande (1990). However, she sees the function of such switching as giving the language, not the speaker, dual identities (p. 17):

> The important point to note here is that speakers choose to mix those diverse codes (English, Hindi, Sanskrit) with Marathi rather than switching to those codes . . . the major point is that the speakers choose the appropriate codes to mix with Marathi in order to make Marathi function in the domains where those individual codes, but not Marathi, are functional. For example, English is the marker of modernity. The process of mixing Marathi with English gives the former code the color of 'modernity'.

Unmarked CS is also frequent elsewhere in south and south-east Asia; for example, Pakir (1989: 381), writing about the Baba community of Singapore where CS involves Hokkien, Malay, and English, describes the alternation as 'negotiating a collective identity', and says it suggests 'a "we-code" which draws upon some subcultural conventions inaccessible to outsiders'.

Unmarked CS is also found in most Hispanic communities in the USA where there is switching between English and Spanish. The Spanish/English examples Gumperz cites in several articles (e.g. 1970: 132–3; 1982: 81) are instances of unmarked CS, I would argue. And in writing about Puerto Ricans in New York, Poplack (1988b: 232) makes comments very reminiscent of the description of unmarked CS; for example, she states that 'bilingualism is seen to be emblematic of New York Puerto Rican identity (as compared both with Island Puerto Ricans and non-Puerto Rican anglophones . . .)'. Barker's (1947) description of language-use patterns in Tucson, Arizona, in the 1940s indicates switching between the local dialect of Spanish and Standard Spanish was the unmarked choice of those middle- and upper-middle-class persons (such as priests and physicians) with daily contacts in the lower-class neighbourhoods where the local southern Arizona dialect was the unmarked choice.

Among recent immigrants in Europe there are all the conditions which would predict the emergence of unmarked CS, since it is (as noted above) an index of dual identities, both of which have positive evaluations for the speaker. Here, as elsewhere, the simultaneous use of two languages sets immigrants apart from their fellow first-language speakers who remain behind in the homeland, or who have only recently arrived. Writing about characteristics of the language of immigrants and 'guest workers' in Europe

(from such places as Turkey and North Africa), Lüdi (1990: 130) specifically points out that, while CS can be an indication of imperfect command
of the target language, it also can be a 'la marque d'une identité linguistique
originale', a connotation potentially positive.

Where unmarked CS is not predicted. The expectation is that unmarked
CS should not occur at all in narrow diglossic communities (the Arabic-
speaking nations of the Middle East, at least, if not the other exemplars
included in Ferguson 1959). The claim is that the high (H) and low (L)
varieties in narrow diglossic communities, which are closely related genetically, hardly occur in the same interaction type. If this is the case, the H
and L varieties can never both be unmarked for any RO sets in the same
interaction type, even for different individuals. Therefore, it is difficult
(although perhaps not impossible) to see how using the H and L varieties in
an unmarked CS mode could develop in such communities, at least between
H and L varieties as Ferguson conceived them (cf. Scotton 1986). Empirical
studies of current usage patterns are called for.

However, if an alien variety enters the equation—for example, a former
colonial language such as French in North Africa—then the prediction
would be that CS as the unmarked choice is just as likely here as in other
former colonial nations. And, indeed, empirical evidence indicates that this
is the case. In Morocco, for example, such CS involving French and the
Moroccan version of Modern Standard Arabic is very frequent among the
educated (Lahlou 1989; Heath 1989).

Of even more interest are those cases where *little* incidence of unmarked
CS is predicted (cf. Scotton 1988c). These are communities where the main
candidates for such switching are also symbols of present intergroup competition or conflict. The extent to which such attitudes exist is not an either
or matter, of course. Thus, it is expected that communities will not divide
sharply, but will rather fall along a continuum in terms of the incidence of
unmarked CS. Where there is a good deal of intergroup tension and this
tension is expressed by language loyalty, little unmarked CS is predicted.
To the extent that this hypothesis is supported, the incidence or non-
incidence of unmarked CS becomes an indicator of intergroup harmony or
conflict.

Thus, the hypothesis predicts that unmarked CS will be infrequent or
non-existent in such communities as Belgium, where ethnic rivalry along
language lines between Flemish and French speakers is very salient. Recall
that the experimental study by Bourhis *et al.* (1979) discussed in Chapter 3
clearly supported the claim that language is associated with ethnic identity

in Belgium. Similarly, little unmarked CS is predicted for ingroup exchanges among Catalans living in Catalonia who are bilingual in Catalan and Castilian Spanish. Findings in Calsamiglia and Tuson (1984) on language use in Barcelona support this prediction.[6] The same applies to French/English CS among French Canadians in Quebec Province. Many of these francophones are bilingual in English, of course, and use it daily. They even make positive evaluations of English for some purposes. But the point is that they do not positively evaluate English as the unmarked index of the individual persona or role relationships which they wish for their ingroup interactions with fellow francophones. That these francophones differ in their CS patterns from those living in Ontario Province is clearly shown in the massive study of CS and borrowing within various Ottawa (Ontario) versus Hull (Quebec) neighbourhoods which is reported in Poplack, Sankoff, and Miller (1988), Poplack (1988a), and Poplack (1988b). Based on my formulation of the conditions necessary for unmarked CS to be favoured, such CS would be predicted as more prevalent among francophones in Ottawa (Ontario), than in Hull (Quebec). (One would not expect startling differences, however, since the two communities are only on opposite sides of a provincial border, not geographically distant entities.)

Unfortunately for me, however, these authors do not make the same divisions between CS and borrowing which I propose, making an explicit test of this prediction difficult. The major sticking-point is that Poplack and associates exclude from their discussion of CS what they call 'nonce borrowings', generally singly occurring English lexemes showing both morphological and syntactic integration into French. They agree that these forms may occur only once, but they still call them borrowings. At least in these papers, Poplack and associates prefer to reserve the term 'code-switching' for 'multiword sequences, which remain lexically, syntactically, and morphologically unadapted to recipient language patterns' (Poplack 1988b: 97). (Examples of such a 'true' CS would be the phrase *but as time goes on*, or the

---

[6] Comments by Calsamiglia and Tuson (1984: 117–19) indicate that the type of CS used by Catalan speakers is hardly ever CS itself as an unmarked choice; rather, it seems to be CS as a sequence of unmarked choices and/or CS in line with the virtuosity maxim (switching because of the interlocutor) or CS as a marked choice (for expressive effect). 'In all of the groups where there are speakers of both languages, we find that the Catalan speakers switch to Castilian primarily as a function of interlocutor. None the less, we can see that in groups where there is a high percentage of Catalan speakers ... an additional type of code switching occurs, and Castilian is used as an expressive resource. In these cases the use of Castilian has a symbolic value since it is associated with spheres of activity such as school, government, etc. which represent domains where Castilian has been the only language used for many years ... In a situation where Castilian is not required they use it, breaking the conventional norm in order to accentuate a particular aspect. In all of these cases, expressive effects are achieved: distancing, objectivity, irony, etc.'

sentence *But once they catch up they go ahead* in [4] above.) But the forms they call 'nonce borrowings' are what I would call single-morpheme/lexeme switches. The ramifications of this disagreement become clear when one looks at examples of unmarked CS. Singly occurring embedded-language forms are perhaps the most distinctive feature of this type of CS. For example, recall such single forms as *-demand* in *a-na-demand* 'he demands' in [4]: *Anasema anataka hiki akipewa anademand kingine* 'He says he wants one thing and if he is given [it] he demands another.'

Since such forms are grouped with borrowings in the analysis of Poplack *et al.*, it is difficult to test my claim that unmarked CS (including such intrasentential CS) is more likely to be the norm in the Ottawa communities than in the Hull communities. Still, the statistics of Poplack *et al.* on the number of nonce borrowings (they are more frequent in Ottawa) and the amount of CS of any type (much greater in Ottawa) lends support to my prediction. For example, Poplack (1988*b*: 110) includes statistics showing that, in the three Ottawa neighbourhoods studied, nonce borrowings account for a minimum of 12.1 per cent of all borrowings, while in the two Hull communities the figures are 6.9 and 5.6 per cent. That is, there are many more indicators of unmarked CS in the Ottawa communities, at least according to the criteria I follow. And the concluding remarks in Poplack, Sankoff, and Miller (1988) indicate clearly that they found community norms to be most predictive of both CS and borrowing patterns. Their extensive analysis also shows that the factor of social class has no real explanatory power regarding the proportion of nonce borrowings (to total borrowings) nor does bilingual proficiency. They state their findings in this way (97–8):

But although individual bilingual proficiency does appear to have a systematic effect, because the most proficient English speakers are able to access their greater knowledge of L2 for nonce and idiosyncratic borrowings, the environmental influence is paramount. The norms of the community override individual abilities.

And they conclude by explicitly linking nonce borrowing and CS in this way (p. 98):

Our results indicate that borrowing, especially nonce borrowing, resembles code switching in that it must be a community MODE (Poplack 1980) in order to gain any real currency. An individual's personal ability is operative but is mediated by the norms of his speech community.

My characterization of unmarked CS is entirely in line with their conclusions: the distinctive features of such CS are, in fact, *both* what they call 'nonce borrowings' *and* what they call CS; therefore, that the same type of speaker uses both is no surprise. Also, of course, the very possibility of such CS occurring frequently is very sensitive to community norms, as I hope my discussion above has indicated; therefore, their finding of the differences between the Ontario (Ottawa) and Quebec (Hull) communities is supportive of my prediction.

CS as a marked choice

In cases of CS as a marked choice, the speaker simply dis-identifies with the expected RO set. The conversation takes place in a relatively conventionalized interaction, for which an unmarked code choice to index the unmarked RO set between participants is relatively clear. But, rather than follow the unmarked choice maxim, the speaker takes a different path, the marked-choice maxim. This maxim directs speakers to:

Make a marked code choice which is not the unmarked index of the unmarked RO set in an interaction when you wish to establish a new RO set as unmarked for the current exchange.

In making a marked choice, the speaker is saying in effect, 'Put aside any presumptions you have based on societal norms for these circumstances. I want your view of me, or of our relationship, to be otherwise.' Thus, a marked choice derives its meaning from two sources: first, since it is *not* the unmarked choice, it is a negotiation against the unmarked RO set; and second, as 'something else', the marked choice is a call for *another* RO set in its place, that for which the speaker's choice is the unmarked index.

This should make it clear that marked choices show relativity in two senses. Their very recognition and interpretation depends on their contrast with the unmarked choice and their indexicality of the RO sets for which they would be the unmarked choice. Ervin-Tripp (1976: 61) makes this point in detailing directives in American English:

If the speaker wishes to add nuances to meaning, it is necessary to shift code, dialect, or language, or use a nickname or honorific which is not obligatory. The embroidery added to imperatives, such as address terms, 'sir', rising pitch, and 'please' was also found with imbedded imperatives and even question directives. (Do you have any more cookies, please?) These forms were available to add optional marking to indicate deference or ingratiation, but since they also appeared in cases of greater difficulty or distance, and to set off discourse-imbedded utterances as directives, *their social interpretation depends on what the normal, unmarked form would be in that context.* If the normal form in a farewell between adults is 'good-night', then 'nighty-night' carries an affective nuance derived from its use to children.

Also, whether a choice is marked is strictly relative. For example, in a study of language choice in Liberia, Breitborde (1977) has substantial empirical support showing that Kru, the first language in the community he was studying, is normally the unmarked choice of neighbourhood interactions. However, he discusses a neighbourhood political meeting in which Kru is a marked choice (p. 416):

In this social situation, the principal aspect of actors' identities relative to interaction was their unquestionable *kwi* [= 'civilized'] political status as TWP [*a contemporary political party*] members. Here, English is the ordinary, expectable language. Judge Nimley makes his remark in Kru, expressing an attribute ('Kru'? 'Interior Kru'?) that ordinarily would be eclipsed by his *kwi* posture in this social situation. Thus, *Kru is the marked language with reference to the internal structure of this social situation.* [My emphasis.]

Unity among marked choices. I want to emphasize that there is a single, general motivation for making marked choices, even though a number of specific effects may result, depending on the context. Others have noted that speakers engage in what is here called marked CS to indicate a range of emotions from anger to affection, and to negotiate outcomes ranging from demonstrations of authority or of superior educational status to assertions of ethnic identity. All these, however, can be subsumed under one general effect: to negotiate a change in the expected social distance holding between participants, either increasing or decreasing it.

The preceding chapters have already included many examples of marked choices, although they have not been identified as such. Making marked choices may be the most universal use to which CS is put because such CS occurs in all communities and at all linguistic levels.[7] For example, what is labelled 'foregrounding' in the stylistic analysis of literary works would count as 'making the marked choice' under this model. And I would argue that most irony is conveyed by making a marked choice, whether in content, in structure, or both.

Use of marked CS to increase the social distance via authority/anger. One of the most common uses of marked CS is to express authority, along with anger

[7] It is true that there are probably *more morphemes involved in CS utterances* when CS itself as the unmarked choice occurs. But, as pointed out, this type of switching is not found in every community.

or annoyance. It is important to recognize that one can rarely attribute just a single purpose to marked CS. It can be argued, of course, that those who have the luxury of expressing anger are often those who also have authority. Example [7] in Chapter 4 illustrates a marked CS combining authority and anger when the local chief switches to Swahili in a meeting where the local language is the unmarked choice. Examples [9–13] below, from Kenya and Zimbabwe, show how, in these nations with their anglophone colonial heritage, English is often the medium of a marked CS switch to express an authoritative/angry stance.

[9] (Scotton and Ury 1977: 16–17)

(A passenger on a bus in Nairobi and a bus conductor (a person who collects fares, not the driver) enter into an interaction. The conductor asks the passenger where he is going in order to determine his fare. English is italicized; the rest of the interaction is carried out in Swahili, the unmarked choice for such a transaction.)
PASSENGER. Nataka kwenda Posta.
'I want to go to the post office.'
CONDUCTOR. Kutoka hapa mpaka posta nauli ni senti hamsini.
'From here to the post office, the fare is 50 cents.'
(Passenger gives the conductor a shilling, from which he should get 50 cents in change.)
CONDUCTOR. Ngojea *change* yako.
'Wait for your change.'
(Passenger says nothing until some minutes have passed and the bus is nearing the post office where the passenger plans to get off.)
PASSENGER. Nataka *change* yangu.
'I want my change.'
CONDUCTOR. *Change* utapata, Bwana.
'You'll get your change.'
PASSENGER. *I am nearing my destination.*
CONDUCTOR. *Do you think I could run away with your change?*

Clearly, the passenger switches to English to reinforce his annoyance at not having received his change. He is indicating that he has the necessary education to have a position of authority. But the conductor, by replying in English, asserts his own position as the passenger's equal.

Two more 'bus' examples from Nairobi also show the use of English in marked CS to negotiate authority. In [10] the conductor's goal in switching to English is to impress the passenger with his authority. He is speaking to a well-dressed young man who, he can assume, will understand English. The conductor begins in Swahili, the unmarked choice, as he is passing down the aisle, collecting fares.

[10] (Myers-Scotton 1990*a*: 99)

CONDUCTOR. Umelipa nauli ya basi?
'Have you paid the bus fare?'
YOUNG MAN. (No response.)
CONDUCTOR. Unaenda wapi?
'Where are you going?'
YOUNG MAN. Nafika Jerusalem.
'I'm going to Jerusalem [housing estate].'
CONDUCTOR. *You must always say clearly and loudly where you are going to alight.*
OK?

In (11) a passenger addresses a busy conductor in English on a hot and crowded bus. While the referential message no doubt annoys the conductor, the fact that the passenger presents it in English makes it doubly annoying. This does not seem to be a marked choice which succeeds! The conductor clearly understands what the passenger has said, but he responds in Swahili.

[11] (Myers-Scotton 1990*a*: 99)

CONDUCTOR (shouting in Swahili). Fugueni madirisha!
'Open the windows!'
WELL-DRESSED PASSENGER. *That is your job.*
CONDUCTOR. Wewe mjinga sana. Kama wewe unaketi karibu na dirisha, mbona unataka mimi nije hapo kufungua hili dirisha?
'You are a real fool! If you are seated near the window, why on earth do you want me to come to open this window?'

Anger, authority, and exclusion are all conveyed through a marked CS to English in example [12]. Five Luyia men are talking in their western-Kenya home area about setting up a business. The first speaker, who is the informal chairman of the group, has been doing most of the speaking up to this point. Their shared first language (Lwidakho) is the unmarked choice; English is italicized.

[12] (Scotton and Ury 1977: 18)

CHAIRMAN. Galolekhanga ndi genyekhanga kuranje vyashara yivi mu mweli gwa Januari.
'We should start this business in January.'
1ST MEMBER. Suviranga yeyo ningangani indahi.
'I think it's a good idea.'
CHAIRMAN. Khushili khutoshitsa makhuva ga mapesa geru tawe. Nikhwenyi khuve vulahi, gadukhananga khuve ni tsishilingi tsielefu tsivili. Lwa khuli varanu ndi, vuli mundu alavuliza tsishilingi tsimya tsine.

'We haven't arranged about our money. If we want to be all right, we should have two thousand shillings altogether. Since we're five, each one will pay 400 shillings.'

1ST MEMBER. Ah, tsefu tsivili? Yezo ni tsinyishi muno. Unyala khuva nu murialo kurio nivi?

'Ah, two thousand? That's too much. Who can afford that much?'

CHAIRMAN. Mumanye khwenya mapesa manyisi.

'You know we need a lot of money.' (Switches to English) *Two thousand shilllings should be a minimum. Anyone who can't contribute four hundred shillings shouldn't be part of this group. He should get out.*

1ST MEMBER (not understanding English). Uvoli shi? Shimbulili vulahi tawe.

'What have you said? I haven't understood properly.'

2ND MEMBER. *Yes, four hundred shillings is reasonable.* (Switches to Lwidakho) Gadukhnananga sha mundu ahana tsishilingi tsimye tsine ni khwenyi khuranjitsi vyashara yivi.

'It's probable that each person should contribute four hundred shillings if we want to start this business.'

The switch to English gives some weight of authority to the chairman's comment, since use of English is associated with persons of authority. While it is also designed to exclude the disagreeing member (surely the chairman knew he did not understand English), it also signals to him that he is 'out of step' with the rest of the group (i.e. if he doesn't know English, perhaps he doesn't have enough money to participate).

Finally, in [13] a Zimbabwean university student is refusing to give a fellow student money. He has already refused once in their shared mother tongue, the Ndau dialect of Shona. But the other student persists. Finally, the speaker switches to English.

[13] (Scotton 1988a: 170)

STUDENT. *I said, 'Andidi'. I don't want!*

Marked CS as an ethnically-based exclusion strategy. In the multi-ethnic cities of Africa, people are very much aware of their own ethnic-group member-ship and that of others. Sometimes far from their homeland, people turn to those they can identify as sharing the same language in an attempt to ease the strains of urban anonymity. There is an instrumental value in keeping ethnicity salient, of course: fellow ethnic-group members can help a person get a job or a place to live. But for this very reason, outgroup members suspect members of the same ethnic group of gross favouritism. One result is that people are generally careful to avoid overt displays of ethnicity, such as using one's own ethnic languages in multi-ethnic settings. This is a main reason why the 'public' languages in Africa are generally relatively ethnically neutral varieties.

Yet, in a variety of circumstances, speakers take a gamble and use their ethnic languages in front of others as marked CS. Invariably, those participants who are excluded are also offended; but, again, such a choice is a matter of weighing the costs and rewards. And some speakers decide the rewards are great enough to make the marked choice.

In [14] two University of Nairobi female students from the Kamba group switch to their own language, Kamba, in front of the two male students from the Kalenjin ethnic group with whom they have been talking. Swahili/ English has been their main medium, a typical unmarked choice for such an interaction. Kamba is italicized and English is indicated; otherwise, Swahili is used.

[14] (Myers-Scotton, unpublished data)

KALENJIN 1. Leo nitatoka kazini mapema sana. Nimewaacha wageni nyumbani.
'Today I'll leave work very early. I've left [some] visitors at home.'
KAMBA 1. Wageni gani hao?
'What sort of visitors?'
KALENJIN 1. (English) You don't know them. (Swahili again) Wanatoka nyumbani.
'You don't know them. They come from home.'
KALENJIN 2. Ni wale niliwaacha huko jana ama ni wengine?
'Are they those I left there yesterday or others?'
KAMBA 2 (turning to other Kamba woman). *Jane, too unaiva iyoo? Ndineekwona kanisani.*
'Jane, where were you yesterday? I didn't see you at church.'
KAMBA 1. *Ninaendia utembea musyi. Ona mdinasyoka nginya kwakya kuu.*
'I went home. I didn't even return until this morning.'
KAMBA 2. *Niki nduneendavya uithi kwo. Ninai ndonya ukunenga valua umatwaie . . .*
'Why didn't you say you were going there? I would have sent a letter to them . . .'
KALENJIN 1. Meschack, wacha sisi twende. Naona Judith na Mary wameanza kuongea kinyumbani ili tusisikie.
'Meshack, let's leave. I see that Judith and Mary have begun to speak "at home" [i.e. their mother tongue] so that we can't understand.'
KALENJIN 2. Hata ndio mimi naona. Nadharau mtu kutumia lugha yake wakati kama huu. Wacha niende kuona kama Kamau ako huko kwake. Si tuende!
'Even I've noticed. I scorn [having] a person to use his/her own language at a time like this. Leave [it], let me go to see if Kamau is at his place. Shouldn't we go?'
KAMBA 1. Mbona mnatoroka? Sijaongea na ninyi vile nilitaka.
'Why on earth are you running off? I haven't yet talked with you as I wanted to.'
KALENJIN 2. Maliza yenu kwanza. Tatarudi saa nyingine.
'Finish your [business] first. We'll come back at another time.'

While the switch to Kamba as a marked choice narrows the social distance between the two women, making salient their shared ethnic identity, it alienates the two men, who come from another ethnic group and do not understand Kamba. The Kamba women protest that they do not understand why the men are upset. It seems they had expected to 'get away' with a sub-conversation in front of the men, but the men feel insulted; once more, they respond by leaving.

Certainly, it is probably the case that persons from more powerful groups can engage in such CS with more impunity than others. However, it also happens, depending on the sociolinguistic character of the community, that persons from groups *with little power* can and do exploit CS to exclude. For example, in Malawi, most (educated) persons speak Chewa, which is an official language alongside English and the first language of the majority of the population. Thus, by switching to Chewa, the ethnic Chewa hardly can exclude anyone. But relatively few individuals outside other, minority ethnic groups speak those groups' languages. By switching to their own language, the members of such minority groups gain interactional, if not lasting, power by demonstrating that they have the ability to exclude others.[8]

It is no surprise that any CS which excludes never seems to be liked by those it excludes, even if there are no overt objections. Often, the persons shut out of the conversation complain; that is, they see the use of an ethnically marked language which excludes them as an unacceptable choice. In other words, this is a marked choice which is rejected by at least those who are shut out. Recall that, in Chapter 2, example [6] presented three secretaries chatting in an office. Because the two Luo secretaries spoke to each other in Luo, the Kikuyu secretary objected to the type of relationship such a practice was negotiating; that is, she felt she was only spoken to (in Swahili) when the Luos wanted something from her.

In example [15], alienation results from a marked choice in Lagos, Nigeria. The following example is the narration of an incident by a young educated Yoruba man.

[15] (Scotton 1975: 86)

I was invited out recently by a friend, who is also a Yoruba, who had just returned from five years in one of the northern states [where he had learned Hausa]. We visited a relation of his on Lagos Island. On the way back, we stopped to see some of my friend's acquaintances in Ebute Metta. When we got there, we met two Hausamen, *and I totally became a stranger in their company* [my emphasis]. The language of discussion had changed to Hausa. I had to watch their mouths

---

[8] I thank Sylvester Ron Simango for bringing this to my attention (based on his own experiences in Malawi).

and guess what they said by their actions. Whenever I wanted to talk to my friend, we spoke either English or Yoruba, at which time the other gentlemen felt cheated and embarrassed. Finally I became so uneasy . . . I had to leave alone.

Exactly the opposite situation is shown in [16], where a Hausa man is excluded by the use of Yoruba. Using Yoruba in this case also seems to index ethnic-group solidarity in Lagos, which is in the Yoruba heartland, in opposition to the Hausa soldier, who is an outsider in southern Nigeria. This example was related to me by my Yoruba research assistant.

[16] (Scotton 1975: 87)

One evening a policeman arrested a Yoruba lady who is a co-tenant [for selling food goods which had entered Nigeria illegally, a rather common offence]. He was a Hausa man who could speak no Yoruba at all. I was among the other people who tried to persuade the policeman, using English, not to take the lady to the station because it was such a minor offence. But he insisted on going, and we all followed him. At the station, the desk sergeant was a Yoruba, *so there and then the matter was settled in the Yoruba language* [my emphasis] to the disgrace of the Hausa man, and the lady was therefore allowed to go home.

The message is the medium.   While a marked choice often complements its referential message (e.g. anger is the message of the speaker's words and the marked-code choice is associated with authority), it can stand on its own in its indexical function regarding RO sets. That is, the fact a marked choice is used *at all* has a message of its own. This is obvious in at least two ways. First, when a marked choice carries a repetition or referential content, this content is redundant, so the 'real' message lies with the change in social distance which the marked choice is negotiating. Second, a marked choice's referential message does not have to be 'understood' for its social message of communicative intent to succeed. This is clear in [17]. The conversation takes place in the medical dispensary of Jericho housing estate in Nairobi, a housing development for lower-middle- and lower-class workers. What sparked the exchange was that a woman (who turns out to be a Luyia) had gone—by mistake—into the men's rest-room. The exchange begins while she is still inside and then continues when she comes out. Swahili is the unmarked choice in such a setting, but the woman switches to her own Luyia variety (italicized).

[17] (Scotton 1982a: 432–3)

MAN (to another woman outside). Mbona hamukumwambia aende kwa choo wanaume?
'Why on earth didn't you tell her not to go into the men's rest-room?'

WOMAN (emerging from the rest-room now and overhearing his comment). *Mimi apana mjinga kama unavyodhania. Ende ita mkeo mjinga, apana mimi.*
'I'm not a simpleton, as you claim. Go call your wife a simpleton, not me.'
MAN. *Ona huyu mchenzi. Ulijifunza wapi tabia [tapia] hiyo yako? Rudi risavuni ukafanyie huko hizo tapia zako za kishenzi.*
'Look at this uncivilized person! Where did you learn your manners? Go back to the reserve where you can behave in such a way.'
WOMAN (switching now to her first language, a Luyia variety). *Mindu chelea miruyi yiji chayikholelaza vindu vyosi Nairobi hanu!*
'These people with suspended ears have monopolized everything here in Nairobi!'
(Reference to Kikuyu people because the man looks like a Kikuyu.)
(Man returns insult, now speaking Kikuyu.)

In this case, it is not at all clear whether the Kikuyu man has any idea of what the Luyia woman is saying when she switches to Luyia. But her communicative intent is clear!

Marked CS for aesthetic effect. A final example of a marked choice is included because it occurs in a retelling of an incident and may or may not have occurred in the original. Therefore, its use demonstrates especially well the creativity involved in making marked choices. Here, the use of English accords authority to the policeman, who is being quoted. The conversation, which takes place in Nairobi and is between a Kisii man and two Luyia men in their 40s, none of whom have high standards of education, has been entirely in Swahili up to this point; that is, not only is Swahili the unmarked choice, but CS is not characteristic of these speakers' conversation. Then the topic switches to the police, and the Kisii man tells about having been stopped by the police recently. His retelling of the incident is entirely in Swahili up to the climax, when he reports the police as taking into custody another person, who is either unfortunately caught (unfairly) in the net or is, in fact, a thief. The police are reported as saying (in English) *let's go*, which is repeated in Swahili, *twende*. It is interesting to speculate whether the police, in fact, said *let's go* in English. Whatever the case, the use of English at the climax achieves a truly artistic effect. The story-teller evokes the authority of the police by using English. Using English in Kenya can still conjure up the colonial era; and, even today, an ability to speak English is associated with any persons of authority.

[18] (Nairobi No. 5)

(Kisii tells his story about an encounter with the police)
Juzi nilikuwa natoka huko chini, kufika hapa, sijui kwa junction wa Matumabo Road, kufika hapo nikapata mmoja yuko nyuma na mwengine yuko mbele. Basi nikaona

watu wa kundi, sikujua ni watu gani. Mimi natembea tu natoka kwa duka nikasikia,
'We, kuja.'
'The other day I was coming down there when I reached the junction of
Matumbato Road. Arriving there I found one person behind me and another in
front. Well, I saw a group of people, I didn't know what sort of people. I just
went along [and] coming from the shop I heard, 'You, come.'
Kwenda pale naambiwa, 'Kaa.' 'Unaweza kutuonyesha kitambulisho?' Nikatoka,
akanyamaza. 'Ya kazi?' Sijui ilikuwa nini, mimi sitembei na iyo vitu lakini nilikuwa
nimetembea na yote. Nikaambiwa, 'Wewe enda.'
'Going there, I was told, 'Sit.' 'Can you show us your identity card?' And I
showed [it] and he was silent. '[What about the card] of work?' I don't know what
it was, but I usually never carry these things, but I had been walking with them
all [that night]. And I was told, 'You, go.'
Jamaa mwingine akakuja na kamfuko. 'Hebu, fungua hiyo mfuko. Iko nini?'
'Ndizi.' 'Fungua.' Akafungua. 'Haya, kitambulisho?' Hakuwa nayo, hati anasema
anatoa ndizi hapa kwa duka.
'And another person came with a small bag. 'I say, open the bag. What's there?'
'Bananas.' 'Open.' And he opened [the bag]. 'OK, identity card?' He didn't have
it. He said he got the bananas here from the store.
(The story ends) Akaambiwa, 'Hapana. *Let's go.* Twende.'
'And he was told, "No. Let's go. Let's go."'

Marked choices as echoic.   Elsewhere in the CS literature there are many
examples of CS as a marked choice, although the writers do not identify
them as such. Often, such examples are explained as adding 'stylistic effect';
but the markedness model explains such choices in a more principled way.
What causes the 'effect' is the unexpectedness or markedness of the code
choice. But what gives marked choices their contextual import is that they
are echoic,[9] for they call up 'something different' from what has been presented thus far or is expected. And what makes this model principled is that
the 'something different' which a marked choice indexes is not all that
elusive. True, the exact communicative intent of a marked choice may be
more ambiguous than explicit; but the intent always depends on existing
'scripts' within the societal system for which the marked choice would be
unmarked.

Speakers as entrepreneurs.   Those who make marked choices are reminiscent
of the 'language entrepreneurs' of Minderhout (1972: 57):

---

[9] Sperber and Wilson (1982) use the term 'echoic' to refer to the effects of irony. I see marked
choices as similarly echoic, in that they refer back to another scenario (i.e. another RO set). I see
irony as essentially the effect of a marked choice.

The appropriateness of the individual's behavior is a product of enculturation. To most people these differences are social facts. To others these differences represent exploitable resources . . . The entrepreneur is an innovator, acting upon a deductive prognosis of results and taking risks where necessary in order to make a profit.

As indicated earlier, making a marked choice is clearly a gamble preceded, consciously or unconsciously, by some weighing of the relative costs and rewards of making this choice rather than an unmarked choice. In line with this calculation, a marked choice is an innovation *how and where it is used.* But it is not an innovation *in the system.* Again, as with all choices, marked choices must be 'part of the system' in order to be interpreted. Still, its user may definitely be considered an innovator in the entrepreneurial sense. The discussion in Chapter 6 will include indications of how the markedness model may be made more predictive. One prediction is that users of marked choices may be one of two types: those with status sufficiently high to allow them to take chances; and those so positioned that the possibility of achieving such status is real, and would be heightened through successful negotiations of personal/interpersonal position through marked choices. The second category surely includes entrepreneurs, and the first category might as well.

The theory of code choice presented here is more speaker-oriented than audience-oriented, in contrast with both speech accommodation theory (e.g. Giles *et al.* 1987) and politeness theory (Brown and Levinson 1987). Of course, the speaker cannot completely ignore addressees in making choices, but CS better represents the imprint which speakers wish to make for themselves on a conversational exchange than anything else. They are thinking of their own position in the RO set being negotiated. This speaker orientation is most extreme in making marked choices. Such a choice has its effect, no matter whether the addressee reciprocates in kind; in fact, true reciprocity is often not the desired response.

Structural flagging. Marked CS is often structurally flagged. This is not surprising; after all, marked choices are meant to call attention to themselves. Flagging occurs at several different levels. First, the content of a marked choice is often a repetition of what has already been said in the unmarked medium of the exchange; alternatively, the marked choice may come first, with the message repeated in the unmarked choice. Either way, the speaker makes sure that the referential content is understood (by using the unmarked medium, which other participants presumably understand); and, by using a marked choice, he/she also makes sure that his/her move away from the unmarked RO set in regard to the subject at hand registers with the addressee. Example [2] cited in Chapter 4, in which the salaried worker produces the same referential message ('You have [some] land [to farm]') in three different languages (Swahili, English, and then Lwidakho) is an example of a marked choice realized by repetition.

Second, marked choices are very typically phonologically flagged. Often a marked choice is produced with a higher pitch than surrounding utterances, or with emphasis. For example, in Chapter 4 [7], when the local chief switches to Swahili to insist upon his authority, he raises his voice as well. I will say no more about phonological flagging; but it is clearly present with perhaps most marked choices, and could be studied systematically.

CS as an exploratory choice (exploratory CS)

Finally, speakers may employ CS when they themselves are not sure of the expected or optimal communicative intent, or at least not sure which one will help achieve their social goals. In these cases, speakers follow the exploratory-choice maxim:

When an unmarked choice is not clear, use CS to make alternate exploratory choices as candidates for an unmarked choice and thereby as an index of an RO set which you favour.

Exploratory CS occurs least commonly, simply because it is not often 'needed' for this purpose since, typically, an unmarked choice is clear. That is, usually the unmarked RO set for a given speaker and other participants in a given exchange is clearly derivable from situational factors in concert with community norms. But in the least conventionalized exchanges an unmarked choice is not obvious. This happens when there is a clash of norms (e.g. when the conversation is with a former classmate who is now a university student in [19], or the conversation between a sister and a brother, but in his place of business, not at home, as in [20] below). Exploratory CS is also found when it is not clear which norms apply (e.g. when little is known about the social identities of a new acquaintance). Another reason why exploratory CS occurs is that overall societal norms are in a state of flux, possibly because of a change in language policies. This was the case in francophone Canada in the 1970s, when legislation was passed mandating that French replace English in certain contexts. Heller (1982: 112–13) gives an example collected during this period in a Quebec hospital. Clearly, the participants do not know which language is unmarked, as their extensive switching between English and French attests.

If any of these conditions prevail, speakers may use CS to propose first one code and then another. Their intent, and an intent which they expect addressees to recognize, is to propose the RO set associated with a particular code as the basis for the interaction. If the first code is not reciprocated, they propose another—or, in some cases, they persist, perhaps unsuccessfully. Because of the interactive nature of the conversation when exploratory CS is used, this type of CS best illustrates how CS is a 'true' negotiation.

Example [19] illustrates exploratory CS on the part of a local resident who is trying to show solidarity with the visitor and also impress him. It seems that the local is trying to negotiate an RO set in which he aligns himself with the visitor in worldliness and education. But the visitor does not reciprocate, seeming to find this negotiation inappropriate in the setting. The conversation takes place in a bar in a Kikuyu village in Kenya. The speakers are former classmates. The first speaker (K1) is educated to School Certificate level (high-school equivalent), but not higher, and is now an upwardly mobile businessman. The second speaker (K2) is a university student in Nairobi and is just home for a visit. Three languages are used; Kikuyu (or possibly Kikuyu/Swahili) would be the unmarked choice. English is italicized and Swahili is indicated; otherwise Kikuyu is used.

[19] (Myers-Scotton, unpublished data)

K1. *How are you, Mr Karanja?*
'How are you, Mr Karanja?'
K2 *Fine*, niguka.
'Fine, I've just arrived.'
K1. *Well, please let's take one bottle*, ga (Swahili) kuondoa *dust* wa *thought*.
'Well, please let's take one bottle, a little to remove the dust from our thoughts.'
K2 (Swahili). sawa.
'Fine.'
K1 (to bar waiter) (Swahili). Lete *scotch on the rock* [sic] hapa.
'Bring scotch on the rocks here.'
WAITER (Swahili). Nini?
'What?' (The waiter has no idea what K1 has in mind. This is a rural bar.)
K1. *Hear him! Tusker beer warm.*
'Listen to him! Some warm Tusker beer.'
K2. *How are things?*
'How are things?'
K1. Ti muno. *Why were you rioting in the Nairobi campus?*
'Not bad. Why were you rioting in the Nairobi campus?'
K2. No maundu ma kimucii.
'Just matters of home.'
K1. *Even if the country cannot do without you* gu-*stone cars* ti wega.
'Even if the country cannot do without you, to stone cars is not good.'

The reason this is analysed as an exploratory choice is that the businessman seems to be at a loss as to how to relate to his former classmate. One aspect of his exploratory CS is to use English, a marked choice in this rural bar where all the customers are locals and native speakers of Kikuyu. The other aspect is to speak some Kikuyu and even some Swahili. But he does not pay attention to how his former classmate reponds. In the end, he appears foolish because he uses English inappropriately and more often than his comrade, who, of course, is the one more used to speaking English regularly, thanks to his university studies. One cannot know, of course, why the businessman orders scotch on the rocks in a bar which stocks only unrefrigerated (warm) bottled beer; but it would seem he is only trying to let his comrade know about his worldliness. His use of English seems part of the same plan. Note that his familiarity with English is very open to question, since Kikuyu (or Swahili) is even the matrix language of his English utterances here: his utterance, *Tusker beer warm*, with the modifier following the head noun, follows Kikuyu morpheme order, not English (cf. Myers-Scotton, 1993, on the morpheme-order principle).

Example [20] from western Kenya illustrates another negotiation. Whether it is a failed negotiation depends on whose point of view is taken, the sister's or the brother's. A Luyia woman enters a grocery store owned by her brother in the provincial capital. The unmarked choice to use in business transactions is Swahili; but the unmarked choice to use with one's family is the shared mother tongue. Thus, any single choice must be an exploratory choice. Speaking Lwidakho, the mother tongue in this case, establishes solidarity as the basis of the interaction. Speaking Swahili makes it a more impersonal exchange, and also more public, since others present will understand. In this case, the sister attempts a negotiation of solidarity, partly because she wants a handout from her brother. But he switches from the shared mother tongue to Swahili, to let the sister know she is being treated as a customer, not a sister. Lwidakho is italicized; otherwise Swahili is used.

[20] (Scotton and Ury 1977: 17)
BROTHER. *Vushele muno mbotswa.*
'Good morning, sister.'
SISTER. *Vushele.*
'Good morning.'
BROTHER. *Uli mulamu?*
'Are you all right?'
SISTER. *Yee, hadi vutsa.*
'Yes, just a little.'

BROTHER. Dada, sasa leo unahitaji nini?
'Sister, now today what do you need?'
SISTER. *Nenyanga umbe munyu.*
'I want you to give me some salt.'
BROTHER. Ah, unahitaji kaisi gani?
'How much do you need?'
SISTER. *Mbe kutukha mang'ondo gasava.*
'Give me sixty cents' worth.'
BROTHER. Na kitu gani kingine?
'And what else?'
SISTER. *Nakenyi shindu shindi nawutsa mang'ondo gavula.*
'I would like something else, but I've no money.'
BROTHER. Asante sana, dada. Kwa heri.
'Thank you, sister. Goodbye.'
SISTER. *Urio. Muno ulindwi.*
'Thank you. Goodbye.'

Notice that neither brother nor sister gets the other to acquiesce to the RO set each proposes, and the sister leaves without everything she came for. Possibly the sister does not speak Swahili well enough to switch, but it is unlikely that she does not know enough Swahili to carry out this simple transaction. The brother could have maintained the shared first language, of course.

Denison (1971) also offers an especially good example of an exploratory choice which does not succeed. It comes from Sauris, a linguistic island in mountainous north-east Italy where the home language is a German variety, but where community members are also fluent in Friulian, a Romance variety. Standard Italian is also generally known. In the example he cites, a woman arrives in a bar to find her 56-year-old husband drinking with his cronies, although he had been sent out to go to the dairy with the milk. The wife upbraids her husband in German, the unmarked choice for home encounters and, therefore, domestic disputes. The husband makes a sudden switch to Friulian, which would be the unmarked choice of a friendly conversation in the bar in which others might well participate. Denison writes (1971: 172–3):

For a moment, but alas! only for a moment, his wife was thrown off balance, and was constrained to make her immediate response—an ironic echo (note that it was not mere repetition)—in Friulian also.

But then she firmly returns the conversation to German. The husband's exploratory choice has not worked. Denison (pp. 172–3) writes of this switch to Friulian as a ploy [which] failed to get him off the hook by retrieving the situation from the domain . . . of conjugal dispute and putting it back in the domain of good-natured talk in Friulian at the bar, in which all present would feel free to participate . . . Here . . . we have an instance of the way in which individuals, by skilful manipulation of diatypes, seek to steer situations—or better, perhaps—to *create* situations to their own advantage.

In describing code choice among Indonesian students in the United States in the 1960s, Tanner (1967: 24–5) gives a characterization of what I am calling exploratory CS, making especially clear its quality of negotiation:

Indonesian is a safe first choice, giving participants an opportunity to gather adequate information about each other so they can make a transition to another more appropriate code . . . the party who contemplates changing . . . often tests out the other by inserting into the discussion a few words of the code to which he wishes to shift. If the other responds in kind, the transition is usually rapidly completed. If not, the former need never acknowledge that any such change of code was even considered.

Let me conclude this discussion by citing two successful exploratory choices. In the first, a young man is asking a young woman to dance at a Nairobi hotel. He does not seem to be sure which language will help him succeed, so he begins with the most neutral choice, Swahili. But he has little success. Finally, following her lead, he proceeds to English. This satisfies her, or at least the negotiation of the RO set associated with English in this exchange wins a dance. Swahili and English are used, with English italicized.

[21] (Scotton 1988a: 177)

HE. Nisaidie na *dance*, tafadhali.
'Please give me a dance.'
SHE. Nimechoka. Pengine nyimbo ifuatayo.
'I'm tired. Maybe the following song.'
HE. Hii ndio nyimbo ninayopenda.
'This is the song which I like.'
SHE. Nimechoka!
'I'm tired!'
HE. Tafadhali—
'Please—'
SHE (interrupting). *Ah, stop bugging me.*
HE. *I'm sorry. I didn't mean to bug you, but I can't help it if I like this song.*
SHE. *OK, then, in that case, we can dance.*

The second example was recorded in a market in Lagos. A woman and a market seller have just completed a transaction in pidgin English for a bag of garri (maize meal) when she asks him if she may leave the bag there while she fetches her child from school. Now the seller looks at the woman more closely and then says that she reminds him of an Efik man he knows. At this point, the woman switches to Efik as in exploratory CS, knowing that she is an Efik by ethnic group and wondering if the seller is also. He responds in Efik, with smiles. The entire transaction is then repeated in Efik. The verbatim interaction is not given here.

CS as a strategy of neutrality

One can see that both unmarked CS and exploratory CS serve as strategies of neutrality. By avoiding speaking only one code, bilinguals avoid committing themselves to a single RO set. The speaker recognizes that the use of each of two languages has its value in terms of the costs and rewards which accrue with its use (i.e. in terms of the RO set it indexes). The speaker decides to choose a middle path regarding these costs and rewards by using two (or more) languages in a single conversation.

Unmarked CS is the ultimate middle avenue. By definition it invokes dual identities. As discussed in Chapter 3, Scotton (1976*b*) interprets the predominance of CS in work situations in three African cities (and also simply alternating between two languages as the medium of a conversation) as a strategy of neutrality.

Exploratory CS does not make duality its goal in the same way as unmarked CS, but it does employ CS as the 'safe choice' in arriving at the code with a costs–rewards balance acceptable to all participants. That is, the speaker makes use of the neutrality provided by the *process* of switching to arrive at a solution which itself may well be a single code.

CS as a deferential strategy

One of the two apparent violations of the unmarked-choice maxim is the 'deference maxim'. This maxim directs speakers:

Switch to a code which expresses deference to others when special respect is called for by circumstances.

In fact, of course, this maxim complements the unmarked-choice maxim by calling for deference where it is unmarked (i.e. when societal norms indicate it is appropriate). Thus, what appears to be a marked choice becomes unmarked.

While deference is often indicated by using honorific titles or indirect requests, a major form of showing deference is to accommodate oneself to an addressee's code. In fact, this is another way of expressing what is covered by Giles's speech accommodation theory discussed above. But other expressions of deference are possible, as in [22].

In [22], a 12-year-old Luo boy, who knows English well from his studies, declines to answer his father in English; he responds instead in their shared mother tongue, Luo. In this particular instance, he does not dare speak English. He reported that he felt he must show 'respect' by responding in Luo, since his father's tone indicated he was angry. In this case, deference is accomplished by using the language (Luo) which indexes an RO set in which his father is the acknowledged superior. English is italicized; otherwise Luo is used.

[22] (Myers-Scotton, unpublished data)

FATHER. *Where have you been?*
SON. Onyango nende adlu aora, baba.
'I've been to the river, father.'

The virtuosity maxim and CS

Whenever any participants in the conversation do not have the linguistic ability in the unmarked choice, the virtuosity maxim directs speakers:

Switch to whatever code is necessary in order to carry on the conversation/ accommodate the participation of all speakers present.

As with the deference maxim, it seems clear that this maxim complements the unmarked-choice maxim; at least, it applies in most societies where speaking a language all can understand is considered appropriate. When speakers themselves have to switch languages on account of their own lack of facility in the unmarked choice, it is interesting that they often overtly recognize the unmarked choice by apologizing for their need to speak something else.

In Africa, the virtuosity maxim often comes into play to accommodate others. Educated persons typically recognize the limited repertoire of less educated family members, especially their elders, by switching to the shared mother tongue in their presence. (This, of course, is not the only motivation for speaking the mother tongue; it is often the unmarked choice in home interactions anyway.) In [23] a Luo student at the University of Nairobi reports how he accommodates to his elderly father, even though he is speaking to his brother (with whom he normally does a good deal of switching to English and Swahili):

[23] (Myers–Scotton, unpublished data)

My brother and I have to be conscious of our words after father arrives. The talk becomes slow because we spend time choosing the words which the old man will understand and those which will not offend him. Before he arrives, we were using such sentences as *Mekosiche enough water tu chu* ['These cattle are not getting enough water nowadays']. But after his arrival we must say *Mehosiche beeh che yame tuchu*. This avoidance of our normal use of English mixed with our Luo is meant to accommodate our old father into the situation.

Conclusion

This chapter offers an explication of the markedness model as applied to CS. Many examples, drawn almost entirely from African data, support the argument. Under the model, all CS can be explained as having one of four related motivations: (1) CS as a sequence of unmarked choices (sequential unmarked CS) occurs when situational factors change within the interaction and the speaker wishes to index the new unmarked RO set in alignment with them; (2) CS itself as an unmarked choice (unmarked CS) occurs when the speaker wishes to index two identities or 'attitudes' toward the interaction (and therefore two RO sets) simultaneously; (3) CS as a marked choice (marked CS) occurs when a speaker wishes to negotiate an RO set other than the unmarked one; and (4) CS as an exploratory choice (exploratory CS) occurs when the unmarked RO set is uncertain. Markedness is the concept which unifies all four types of switching. It figures in speakers' choices to switch codes and in the implicatures these choices provide for the addressees.

Unmarked CS differs from the other three types in that here it is the *overall* pattern of CS which provides the social message, not any single individual switch. With the other CS types, it is the point of the switch itself (and what follows) which has social import. Individual switches in unmarked CS may have specific rhetorical functions within the conversational text, of course; it is just that each one does not index a new social message.

6

Conclusion

THE goal of this volume has been to provide a general theoretical treatment of the socio-psychological motivations for codeswitching (CS) as a language-contact phenomenon. The arguments have been illustrated with many naturally occurring examples from African contexts; the volume is also, therefore, a description of the types of CS which involve African languages. As such, the result is, I hope, not only an explanation of the motivations of CS, but also a view of those aspects of African life glimpsed in everyday conversations involving CS. Descriptive emphasis has been on Kenya and especially its capital, Nairobi. A number of examples from Harare, Zimbabwe, are also included. Additional examples from other areas of Africa make the case that the phenomena discussed are not localized; they come from other areas of Africa, such as the capitals of Senegal (Dakar) and Nigeria (Lagos), as well as from Zaïre and Ghana. References to CS in other areas of the world are additional evidence of the generality of the phenomenon and its motivations.

The general argument: a synthesis

The argument developed in this book is that all speakers have a 'markedness metric', an innate, internalized model which enables them to recognize that all code choices are more or less 'unmarked' or 'marked'. 'Unmarked' is used to mean that the choice of a particular linguistic variety is *expected* as the medium for a talk exchange, given the norms of the society regarding the salience of specific situational factors present (e.g. the speaker and addressee, the topic, the setting). 'Marked' choices are at the other end of a continuum; they are not usual, and in some sense they are *dis-identifications* with what is expected.

This idea is based on the premiss that speakers and addressees know (as part of their communicative competence) that choice of one linguistic variety rather than another expresses social import. This premiss is embodied in the negotiation principle, which sees code choices as identity negotiations. 'Identity' is used in a very general sense; I do not mean to imply that code choices can fashion new persons out of speakers. What they *can* do is negotiate a particular identity for the speaker *in relation to* other participants in the exchange. That is, code choices can be seen as bids to alter the rights-and-obligations set which holds between participants; it is in this limited sense that 'identity' is intended.

This argument implies that, in all communities, interaction types are more or less conventionalized, that speakers have some sense of 'script' or 'schema' for how interactions are to be conducted in an unmarked way. However, just how they are conventionalized (i.e. the details of convention-alization, including expected type of behaviour, linguistic and otherwise) and which interactions are more conventionalized than others are community-specific details. Speakers only acquire these specific details through experi-ence in their own communities.

But even though community members all possess a sense of relative markedness, and even though they have common experiences regarding markedness, not all speakers make the same choices in the same interaction types. True, many do make the unmarked or expected choices, given what they have internalized about the markedness of codes for a specific interaction; but some make a range of marked choices. Variation in the choice of linguis-tic varieties or codes results because some speakers exploit the indexicality of the available choices, including their relative markedness for the ex-change. For speakers, markedness is a tool, while for addressees it is an index of their interpersonal negotiations. One way to convey communicative intention, therefore, is through code choice.

The general argument of the markedness model proposed here is this: members of bilingual communities know that codeswitching (CS) is a strategy which is followed when speakers perceive that their own costs–rewards balance will be more favourable for the conversation at hand through engag-ing in CS than through using only a single code (whether throughout the conversation or only at a specific point).

Under the markedness model, CS has one of four motivations: (1) CS as a sequence of unmarked choices (sequential unmarked choices); (2) CS it-self as the unmarked choice (unmarked CS); (3) CS as a marked choice (marked CS); and CS as an exploratory choice (exploratory CS). These are discussed in Chapter 5, with the motivational antecedents for such a model of CS presented in Chapter 4.

Community norms represent the starting-point for the model. Speakers operate as creative, rational actors, but within a normative framework specific to their community. This framework is responsible for the interpretation of choices (i.e. where they fall on a continuum of markedness as well as what their more specific interpretations will be).

Therefore, the markedness model sees speakers as making choices, not because norms direct them to do so, but rather because they consider the consequences. That is, linguistic choices are based on readings of consequences. The model proposes that speakers weigh the costs and rewards of alternative choices; variation results because different speakers weigh the costs and rewards differently.

Predicting choices

What about the types of person who will engage in CS and their purposes, as well as the interaction types favouring CS? Six general predictions regarding CS follow from the key concepts of the theory. They also take into account the findings of sociolinguistic research into language variation across social groups.

First, when faced with choosing paths, the majority of speakers will follow the known path and make unmarked choices, thereby maintaining the status quo in the RO sets in which they participate. Thus, CS will not be a frequent choice except when it is an unmarked choice.

Second, the more linguistically conservative a group is, the more unmarked choices, in general, it will make. For example, women would generally be expected to make more unmarked choices than men. (However, if there is a change in the macro-social conditions prevailing in their community so that women see that making marked linguistic choices might facilitate their upward mobility, they will be among the major users of marked choices; see below.) Thus, if CS is examined in terms of social-group membership, most CS as a marked choice will occur among the more linguistically innovative groups.

Third, the more potential a group has for upward mobility, the more likely its members are to make marked choices in interactions allowing for status-raising. Such persons are characterized by possessing whatever social-identity factors the community sets as prerequisites for mobility, e.g. youth, high educational level, or the 'right' ethnic-group membership. Thus, it is predicted that the bulk of marked choices will come from such persons.

Fourth, the choices of persons already having high standing in the community in terms of socio-economic status or political power is more difficult to predict. One might argue, based on other studies (e.g. Labov's (1972) finding of the conservative response by the salespeople at the highest-status department store to the innovation of 'r-ful' speech in New York City), that such persons are not inclined to make marked choices of any type extensively.

It could be argued that they have already 'arrived', and have little to gain from negotiations relying on an uncertain base. However, an opposing point of view is that those persons possessing high status on one or more scales are the very persons who can *afford* to gamble in assessing costs and rewards; they may be just the persons to make the most marked choices, and therefore may be heavy users of CS.

The fifth prediction, therefore, is that these persons will favour marked choices in the form of CS. As is the case for the other predictions, more relevant empirical research is needed; however, such studies as Scotton (1985; 1988*d*), which deal with stylistic choices, suggest that high-status persons exploit marked CS as an interpersonal strategy.

Finally, a sixth prediction regarding interaction type: that more CS will occur in the least conventionalized exchanges. That is, uncertain situations, where conflicting norms seem to apply and their relative hierarchy is unclear, are prime sites for CS. Scotton (1976*b*) provides empirical evidence supporting this prediction for work situations in three African cities (Kampala, Uganda; Lagos, Nigeria; and also Nairobi).

The interaction of cognitively based and social knowledge

The markedness model is based on the crucial claim regarding communicative intentions that speakers 'know', and also operate on the premiss that their addressees 'know', relative readings of markedness for a given interaction type in their community.

The details of such knowledge, developed through exposure to language in use, is obviously social. No matter how creative speakers themselves may be in engaging in CS, their choices can be effective only if they can count on a relatively common interpretation of the intention of specific choices. That is, while choices are not determined, their interpretation is socially constrained.

Yet, the ability to exploit the switching of codes has a cognitive base. This is the universally present 'markedness metric', providing an aptitude for assessing codes (and CS) in terms of their markedness as indexical of rights-and-obligations balances. This side of code choice is stressed because it supports the claim that making readings of markedness for choices in CS and using them as indexical of communicative intentions are universal phenomena. That is, while the examples cited here are themselves not generalizable, it is claimed that the principles underlying them are generally applicable: that CS as a phenomenon can be explained within the terms of the markedness model. The model and its predictions await further testing.

References

ABDULAZIZ (MKILIFI), M. H. (1972), 'Triglossia and Swahili–English Bilingualism in Tanzania', *Language in Society*, 1: 197–213.

ABDULAZIZ, M. H. (1982), 'Patterns of Language Acquisition and Use in Kenya: Rural–Urban Differences', *International Journal of the Sociology of Language*, 34: 95–120.

AGHEYISI, R. N. (1977), 'Language Interlarding in the Speech of Nigerians', in P. F. A. Kotey, and H. Der-Houssikian (eds.), *Language and Linguistic Problems in Africa* (Columbia, SC: Hornbeam Press), 99–110.

ANGOGO, M. R. (1980), *Linguistic and Attitudinal Factors in the Maintenance of the Luyia Group Identity*, Ph.D. (Austin: Univ. of Texas, Dept. of Linguistics).

APPEL, R. and MUYSKEN, P. (1987), *Language Contact and Bilingualism* (London: Arnold).

ATKINSON, J. M., and HERITAGE, J. (eds.) (1984), *Structures of Social Action* (Cambridge: Cambridge Univ. Press).

AUER, J. C. P. (1984), 'On the Meaning of Conversational Code-Switching', in J. C. Auer and A. Di Luzio (eds.), *Interpretative Sociolinguistics: Migrants— Children—Migrant Children* (Tübingen: Niemeyer), 87–108.

—— (1988), 'A Conversation Analytic Approach to Code-Switching and Transfer', in Heller (1988*a*: 187–213).

—— (1990), 'A Discussion Paper on Code Alternation', in European Science Foundation (1990: 69–88).

—— (1991), 'Bilingualism in/as Social Action: A Sequential Approach to Code-Switching', in European Science Foundation (1991*c*: 319–52).

AUSTIN, J. L. (1962), *How to Do Things with Words* (Oxford: Oxford Univ. Press).

BAKHTIN, M. M. (1980) [1935], *The Dialogic Imagination* (Austin: Univ. of Texas Press).

BARKER, G. C. (1947), 'Social Functions of Language in a Mexican-American Community', *Acta Americana*, 5: 185–202.

BARTH, F. (1966), *Models of Social Organization*, Occasional Papers of the Royal Anthropological Institute, 23 (London).

BATTISTELLA, E. L. (1990), *Markedness: The Evaluative Superstructure of Language* (Albany, NY: State Univ. of New York Press).

BEARDSLEY, R. B., and EASTMAN C. M. (1971), 'Markers, Pauses and Code Switching in Bilingual Tanzanian Speech', *General Linguistics*, 11: 17–27.

BENDER, M. L., BOWEN, J. D., COOPER, R. L., and FERGUSON, C. A. (eds.) (1976), *Language in Ethiopia* (Oxford: Oxford Univ. Press).

BERNSTEN, J. G. (1990), 'The Integration of English Loans in Shona: Social Correlates and Linguistic Consequences', Ph.D. (East Lansing, Mich.: Michigan State Univ., Dept. of Linguistics and German, Slavic, Asian, and African Languages).

—— and MYERS-SCOTTON, C. (1993), 'English Loans in Shona: Consequences for Linguistic Systems', *International Journal of the Sociology of Language* 100/101: 125–49.

BLOM, J. P., and GUMPERZ, J. J. (1972), 'Social Meaning in Structure: Code-Switching in Norway', in Gumperz and Hymes (1972: 409–34).

BLUM-KULKA, S., HOUSE, J., and KASPER, G. (eds.) (1989), *Cross-Cultural Pragmatics: Requests and Apologies* (Norwood, NJ: Ablex).

BOKAMBA, E. (1988), 'Code-Mixing, Language Variation, and Linguistic Theory: Evidence from Bantu Languages', *Lingua*, 76: 21–62.

BOURHIS, R. G., GILES, H. H., LEYENS, J. P., and TAJFEL, H. (1979), 'Psycholinguistic Distinctiveness: Language Divergence in Belgium', in H. Giles and R. St Clair (eds.), *Language and Social Psychology* (Oxford: Blackwell), 158–85.

BREITBORDE, L. B. (1977), 'The Social Structural Basis of Language Variation in an Urban African Neighborhood', Ph.D. (Rochester, NY: Univ. of Rochester, Dept. of Anthropology).

—— (1983), 'Levels of Analysis in Sociolinguistic Explanation', *International Journal of the Sociology of Language*, 39: 5–34.

BROSNAHAN, L. F. (1963), 'Some Historical Cases of Language Imposition', in J. Spencer (ed.), *Language in Africa* (Cambridge: Cambridge Univ. Press), 7–24.

BROWN, P., and LEVINSON, S. (1978), 'Universals in Language Usage: Politeness Phenomena', in E. Goody (ed.), *Questions and Politeness*, (Cambridge: Cambridge Univ. Press), 56–289.

—— —— (1987), *Politeness: Some Universals in Language Usage* (includes Brown and Levinson (1978)) (Cambridge: Cambridge Univ. Press).

BROWN, R., and GILMAN, A. (1960), 'The Pronouns of Power and Solidarity', in T. Sebeok (ed.), *Style in Language* (Cambridge, Mass.: MIT Press), 253–76.

CALSAMIGLIA, H., and TUSON, A. (1984), 'Use of Languages and Code-Switching in Groups of Youth in a Barrio of Barcelona: Communicative Norms in Spontaneous Speech', *International Journal of the Sociology of Language*, 47: 105–21.

CARTER, H. (1991), Personal communication.

—— and KAHARI, G. P. (1972), *Kuverenga ChiShona: An Introductory Reader* (mimeo) (London: School of Oriental and African Studies).

CHOMSKY, N. (1965), *Aspects of the Theory of Syntax* (Cambridge, Mass.: MIT Press).

—— (1980), *Rules and Representation* (Oxford: Blackwell).

CICOUREL, A. V. (1974), *Cognitive Sociology: Language and Meaning in Social Interaction* (New York: Free Press).

CLYNE, M. G. (1969), 'Switching between Language Systems', *Actes du 10ème congrès internationale des linguistes*, (Bucharest: Éditions de l'Académie de la République Socialiste de Roumanie), 343–9.

—— (1972), 'Perception of Code-Switching in Bilinguals', *ITL Review of Applied Linguistics*, 16: 45–8.

—— (1982), *Multilingual Australia* (Melbourne: River Seine).

CRAWHALL, N. (1990), Shona/English unpublished data.

DAVIS, K. (1948), *Human Society* (London: Macmillan).

DENISON, N. (1971), 'Some Observations on Language Variety and Pluralism', in E. Ardener (ed.), *Social Anthropology and Language* (London: Tavistock), 157–83.

DOKE, C. M. (1931), *Report on the Unification of the Shona Dialects* (Hertford, England: Stephen Austin).

—— (1943), *Outline Grammar of Bantu* (mimeo) (Johannesburg: Univ. of the Witwatersrand).

DURAN, R. (ed.) (1981), *Latino Language and Communicative Behavior* (Norwood, NJ: Ablex).

EDWARDS, J. (1985), *Language, Society and Identity* (Oxford: Blackwell).

EDWARDS, W. F. (1983), 'Code Selection and Shifting in Guyana', *Language in Society*, 12: 295–311.

ERVIN-TRIPP, S. (1972), 'On Sociolinguistic Rules: Alternation and Co-occurrence', in Gumperz and Hymes (1972).

—— (1976), 'Is Sybil There? The Structure of Some American English Directives', *Language in Society*, 5: 25–66.

EUROPEAN SCIENCE FOUNDATION (1990), *Papers for the Workshop on Concepts, Methodology, and Data* (Basle, 1990) (Strasburg: European Science Foundation).

—— (1991*a*), *Papers for the Workshop on Constraints and Models* (London, 1990) (Strasburg: European Science Foundation).

—— (1991*b*), *Papers for the Workshop on Impact and Consequences* (Brussels 1990) (Strasburg: European Science Foundation).

—— (1991*c*), *Symposium on Code-Switching in Language Contact* (Barcelona, 1991) (Strasburg: European Science Foundation).

FABIAN, J. (1986), *Language and Colonial Power: The Appropriation of Swahili in the Former Belgian Congo 1880–1938* (Cambridge: Cambridge Univ. Press).

FANTINI, A. (1977), *Language Acquisition of a Bilingual Child* (Brattleboro, Vt.: Experiment Press).

FERGUSON, C. A. (1959), 'Diglossia', *Word*, 15: 325–40.

FISHMAN, J. A. (1968), *Advances in the Sociology of Language* (The Hague: Mouton).

—— (1972), 'The Link Between Macro- and Micro-Sociology in the Study of Who Speaks What to Whom and When', in Gumperz and Hymes (1972: 435–53).

—— COOPER, R. L., and MA, R. (1971), *Bilingualism in the Barrio* (Bloomington, Ind.: Indiana Univ. Press).

FORSON, B. (1979), *Code-Switching in Akan–English Bilingualism*, Ph.D. (Los Angeles: Univ. of California, Dept. of Linguistics).

FORTUNE, G. (1955), *An Analytic Grammar of Shona* (London: Longman Green).

—— (1957), *Elements of Shona* (Harare: Longman).

FRIEDRICH, P. (1972), 'Social Context and Semantic Features: The Russian Pronominal Usage', in Gumperz and Hymes (1972: 270–300).

GARDNER-CHLOROS, P. (1985), 'Language Selection and Switching among Strasbourg Shoppers', *International Journal of the Sociology of Language*, 54: 117–35.

GARDNER-CHLOROS, P. (1991), *Language Selection and Switching in Strasbourg* (Oxford: Oxford Univ. Press).

GELFAND, M. (1973), *The Genuine Shona* (Gwelo, Zimbabwe: Mambo Press).

GENESEE, F., and BOURHIS, R. Y. (1982), 'The Social Psychological Significance of Code-Switching in Cross-Cultural Communication', *Journal of Language and Social Psychology*, 1: 1–27.

—— —— (1988), 'Evaluative Reactions of Language Choice Strategies: Francophones and Anglophones in Quebec City', *Language and Communication*, 8: 229–50.

GIBBONS, J. (1983), 'Attitudes towards Languages and Code-Mixing in Hong Kong', *Journal of Multilingual and Multicultural Development*, 4: 129–47.

—— (1987), *Code-Mixing and Code Choice: A Hong Kong Case Study* (Clevedon, Avon: Multilingual Matters).

GILES, H., MULAC, A., BRADAC, J. J., and JOHNSON, P. (1987), 'Speech Accommodation Theory: The First Decade and Beyond', in M. L. McLaughlin (ed.), *Communication Yearbook No. 10* (Beverly Hills, Calif.: Sage), 13–48.

GIVÓN, T. (1979), *On Understanding Grammar* (New York and London: Academic Press).

—— (1989), *Mind, Code and Context: Essays in Pragmatics* (Hillsdale, NJ: Erlbaum).

GOFFMAN, E. (1959), *The Presentation of Self in Everyday Life* (New York: Doubleday).

—— (1981), 'Footing', in *Forms of Talk* (Philadelphia: Univ. of Pennsylvania Press), ch. 3.

GOODWIN, C. (1981), *Conversational Organization* (New York and London: Academic Press).

GOYVAERTS, D. L., and ZEMBELE, T. (1992), 'Codeswitching in Bukavu', *Journal of Multilingual and Multicultural Development*, 13: 71–82.

GREENBERG, J. H. (1963), *The Languages of Africa*, special supplement to *International Journal of American Linguistics*, 29/1.

—— (1971a), 'African Languages', in *Language, Culture, and Communication* (Stanford, Calif.: Stanford Univ. Press), 126–36.

—— (1971b), 'Urbanism, Migration, and Language', in *Language, Culture, and Communication* (Stanford, Calif.: Stanford Univ. Press), 198–211.

GRICE, H. P. (1975), 'Logic and Conversation', in P. Cole and J. L. Morgan (eds.), *Syntax and Semantics*, iii (New York and London: Academic Press), 41–55.

GROSJEAN, F. (1982), *Life with Two Languages: An Introduction to Bilingualism* (Cambridge, Mass.: Harvard Univ. Press).

GUMPERZ, J. J. (1967), 'Linguistic Markers of Bilingual Communication', *Journal of Social Issues*, 23: 137–53.

—— (1970), 'Verbal Strategies in Multilingual Communication', in J. E. Alatis, (ed.), *Georgetown Round Table on Language and Linguistics* (Washington, DC: Georgetown Univ. Press), 129–41.

—— (1976), 'The Sociolinguistic Significance of Conversational Code-Switching', in *Papers in Language and Context* (Berkeley, Calif.: Language Behavior Research Laboratory), 1–26.

—— (1982), 'Conversational Code-Switching', in *Discourse Strategies* (Cambridge: Cambridge Univ. Press), 55–99.

—— and HERNANDEZ-CHAVEZ, E. (1970), 'Cognitive Aspects of Bilingual Communication', in W. H. Whiteley (ed.), *Language and Social Change* (Oxford: Oxford Univ. Press), 115–25.

—— —— (1978), 'Bilingualism, Bidialectalism, and Classroom Interaction', in M. Laurie and N. Conklin (eds.), *A Pluralistic Nation* (Rowley, Mass.: Newbury House), 275–94.

—— and HYMES, D. (eds.) (1972), *Directions in Sociolinguistics* (New York: Holt, Rinehart, Winston).

GUTHRIE, M. (1967–70), *Comparative Bantu* (4 vols.) (London: Gregg Press).

HANNAN, M. (1959), *Standard Shona Dictionary* (Salisbury: Southern Rhodesia African Literature Bureau; repr. 1961, London: Macmillan).

HASSELMO, N. (1970), 'Code-Switching and Model of Speaking', in G. G. Gilbert (ed.), *Texas Studies in Bilingualism* (Berlin: de Gruyter), 179–210.

—— (1972), 'Code-Switching as Ordered Selections', in E. S. Firchow (ed.), *Studies for Einar Haugen* (The Hague: Mouton).

HEATH, J. (1989), *From Code-Switching to Borrowing: A Case Study of Moroccan Arabic* (London: Routledge & Kegan Paul).

HEINE, B. (1980), 'Language and Society', in B. Heine and W. J. G. Möhlig, (eds.), *Language and Dialect Atlas of Kenya*, i (Berlin: Reimer), 60–7.

HELLER, M. (1982), 'Negotiations of Language Choice in Montreal', in J. J. Gumperz (ed.), *Language and Social Identity* (Cambridge: Cambridge Univ. Press), 108–18.

—— (ed.) (1988a), *Code-Switching: Anthropological and Sociolinguistic Perspectives* (Berlin: Mouton de Gruyter).

—— (1988b), 'Strategic Ambiguity: Codeswitching in the Management of Conflict', in Heller (1988a: 77–96).

HILL, J. H., and HILL K. C. (1986), *Speaking Mexicano* (Tucson, Ariz.: Univ. of Arizona Press).

HOLM, J. (1989), *Pidgins and Creoles*, i, ii (Cambridge: Cambridge Univ. Press).

HOMANS, G. (1966), 'Social Behaviour as Exchange', in E. P. Hollander and R. G. Hunt (eds.), *Current Perspectives in Psychology* (Oxford: Oxford Univ. Press), 13–53.

HYMES, D. (1962), 'The Ethnography of Speaking', in T. Gladwin and W. C. Sturtevant (eds.), *Anthropology and Human Behavior* (Washington, DC: Anthropological Society of Washington), 15–53.

—— (1967), 'Models of the Interaction of Language and the Social Setting', *Journal of Social Issues*, 23/2: 8–28.

—— (1972a), 'Models of the Interaction of Language and Social Life', in Gumperz and Hymes (1972: 35–71).

—— (1972b), 'On Communicative Competence', in J. Pride and J. Holmes (eds.), *Sociolinguistics* (Harmondsworth, Middx.: Penguin), 269–93.

ITEBETE, P. A. N. (1974), 'Language Standardization in Western Kenya: Luluyia Experiment', in Whiteley (1974a: 87–114).

JACOBSON, R. (1977), 'The Social Implications of Intrasentential Codeswitching', in R. Romo and R. Paredes (eds.), *New Directions in Chicaono Scholarship* (special issue of *The New Scholar*) (San Diego, Calif.: Univ. of California), 227–56.

——— (1978a), 'Interlanguage as a Means of Ethno-cultural Identification' (Washington, DC: US Dept. of Education).

——— (1978b), 'Code-Switching in South Texas', *Journal of the Linguistic Association of the Southwest*, 3: 20–32.

——— (ed.) (1990), *Codeswitching as a Worldwide Phenomenon* (New York: Peter Lang).

JOSHI, A. (1985), 'Processing of Sentences with Intrasentential Code Switching', in D. Dowty, L. Karttunen, and A. Zwicky (eds.), *Natural Language Parsing* (Cambridge: Cambridge Univ. Press).

KACHRU, B. (1978), 'Code-Mixing as a Communicative Strategy in India', in J. E. Alatis (ed.), *International Dimensions of Bilingual Education* (Washington, DC: Georgetown Univ. Press), 107–24.

——— (1983), 'On Mixing', in B. Kachru (ed.), *The Indianization of English: The English Language in India* (New Delhi: Oxford Univ. Press), 193–207.

KAHARI, G. and CARTER, H. (1972), *A Grammatical Sketch of Shona* (vol. ii of Carter and Kahari (1972)) (London: School of Oriental and African Studies).

KAMWANGAMALU, N. (1989), *Code-Mixing across Languages: Structure, Functions, and Constraints*, Ph.D. (Urbana, Ill.: Univ. of Illinois, Dept. of Linguistics).

KAPANGA, M. (1989), 'Why Shaba Swahili Is Not a Pidgin or Creole', paper presented at annual African Linguistics conference (Univ. of Illinois, Urbana).

KARIUKI, M. (1986), *Determinants of Language Choice of Middle-Level Managers in the Kenyan Public Sector*, MA (East Lansing, Mich.: Michigan State Univ., Dept. of Communication).

KASHOKI, M. (1978), 'The Language Situation in Zambia', in Ohannesian and Kashoki (1978: 9–46).

KITE, Y. K. (1989), *One, Two, Three, a Counting Lesson in Fourth Grade? A Study of Teacher Directives*, MA (Columbia, SC: Univ. of South Carolina, Linguistics Program).

KRAPF, J. L. (1985), *Outline of the Elements of the Ki-Suaheli Language with Special Reference to the Kinika Dialect* (Tübingen: Niemeyer).

LABOV, W. (1966), *The Social Stratification of English in New York City* (Washington, DC: Center for Applied Linguistics).

——— (1972), *Sociolinguistic Patterns* (Philadelphia: Univ. of Pennsylvania Press).

LADEFOGED, P., GLICK, R., and CRIPER, C. (1971), *Language in Uganda* (Nairobi: Oxford Univ. Press).

LAHLOU, M. (1989), 'Arabic–French Codeswitching in Morocco', paper presented at annual African Linguistics conference (Univ. of Illinois, Urbana).

LANCE, D. (1970), 'The Codes of the English–Spanish Bilingual', *TESOL Quarterly*, 4: 343–51.

——— (1975), 'Spanish–English Code-Switching', in C. Hernandez-Chavez (ed.), *El Lenguaje de los Chicanos* (Arlington, Va.: Center for Applied Linguistics), 138–53.

LEPAGE, R. B. (1978), *Projection, Focussing and Diffusion*, Occasional Paper No. 9 (St Augustine, Trinidad: Society for Caribbean Linguistics). Reprinted as No. 9 in York Papers in Linguistics (University of York, 1980).

——— and TABOURET-KELLER, A. (1985), *Acts of Identity: Creole-Based Approaches to Language and Ethnicity* (Cambridge: Cambridge Univ. Press).

LEVELT, W. J. M. (1989), *Speaking* (Cambridge, Mass.: MIT Press).

LEVINSON, S. C. (1983), *Pragmatics* (Cambridge: Cambridge Univ. Press).

LEWIS, B. (1950), *The Arabs in History* (London).

LIPSKI, J. (1977), 'Code-Switching and the Problem of Bilingual Competence', in M. Paradis (ed.), *Aspects of Bilingualism* (Columbia, SC: Hornbeam Press), 250–64.

LÜDI, G. (1987), 'Les Marques transcodiques: regards nouveaux sur le bilinguisme', in G. Lüdi (ed.), *Devenir bilingue—parler bilingue* (Tübingen: Niemeyer), 1–21.

—— (1990), 'Les Migrants comme minorité linguistique en Europe', *Sociolinguistica*, 4: 113–35.

LYONS, J. (1977), *Semantics*, i, ii (Cambridge: Cambridge Univ. Press).

McCLURE, E., and McCLURE, M. (1988), 'Macro- and Micro-sociolinguistic Dimensions of Code-Switching in Vingard', in Heller (1988*a*: 25–51).

McCONVELL, P. (1988), 'MIX-IM-UP: Aboriginal Codeswitching, Old and New', in Heller (1988*a*: 97–149).

McGINLEY, K. (1987), 'The Future of English in Zimbabwe', *World Englishes*, 6: 159–64.

MAZRUI, A., and MPHANDE, L. (1990), 'How Is a Code-Mixer's Grammar Organized? Evidence from Sheng', paper presented at annual African Linguistic conference (Univ. of Georgia, Athens).

MEHAN, H. (1979), *Learning Lessons* (Cambridge, Mass.: Harvard Univ. Press).

MILROY, L. (1982), 'Social Network and Linguistic Focussing', in S. Romaine (ed.), *Sociolinguistic Variation in Speech Communities* (London: Arnold), 141–52.

—— and MUYSKEN, P. (eds.) (forthcoming 1995), *Two Languages, One Speaker: Cross-disciplinary Perspectives on Code-Switching* (Cambridge: Cambridge Univ. Press).

MINDERHOUT, D. (1972), 'The Entrepreneur's Use of Language', in D. Smith and R. Shuy (eds.), *Sociolinguistics in Cross-Cultural Analysis* (Washington, DC: Georgetown Univ. Press), 57–66.

MKANGANWI, K. (1989), 'English in Zimbabwe', seminar paper, 2 May 1989 (Univ. of Birmingham).

—— (1990), Personal communication.

MYERS-SCOTTON, C. (1990*a*), 'Code-Switching and Borrowing: Interpersonal and Macrolevel Meaning', in Jacobson (1990: 85–110).

—— (1990*b*), 'Élite Closure as Boundary Maintenance: The Evidence from Africa', in B. Weinstein (ed.), *Language Policy and Political Development* (Norwood, NJ: Ablex), 25–41.

—— (1991*a*), 'Intersections between Social Motivations and Structural Processing in Codeswitching', in European Science Foundation (1991*a*: 57–82).

—— (1991*b*), 'Whither Code-Switching? Prospects for Cross-Field Collaboration: Production-Based Models of Code-Switching', in European Science Foundation (1991*c*: 207–32).

—— (1992*a*), 'Constructing the Frame in Intrasentential Codeswitching', *Multilingua*, 11: 101–27.

—— (1992*b*), 'Comparing Codeswitching and Borrowing', *Journal of Multicultural and Multilingual Development*, 13: 19–40.

—— (1993*a*), 'Building the Frame in Codeswitching: Evidence from Africa', presented at annual African Linguistics conference (Athens, Ga., 1990), in S. Mufwene and L. Moshi (eds.), *Topics in African Linguistics* (Amsterdam: Benjamins), 253–78.

—— (1993*b*), *Duelling Languages: Grammatical Structure in Codeswitching* (Oxford: Oxford Univ. Press).

NGARA, E. A. (1982), *Bilingualism, Language Contact and Planning* (Gwelo, Zimbabwe: Mambo Press).

NURSE, D., and HINNEBUSCH, T. (1993), *Swahili and Sabaki: A Linguistic History* (Berkeley, Calif.: Univ. of California Press).

—— and PHILLIPSON, G. (1980), 'The Bantu Languages of East Africa: A Lexicostatistical Survey', in Polome and Hill (1980).

—— and SPEAR, T. (1985), *The Swahili: Reconstructing the History and Language of an African Society 800–1500* (Philadelphia: Univ. of Pennsylvania Press).

OHANNESSIAN, S. (1978), 'The Teaching of Zambian Languages and the Preparation of Teachers for Language Teaching in Primary Schools', in Ohannessian and Kashoki (1978: 292–328).

—— and KASHOKI, M. E. (eds.) (1978), *Language in Zambia* (London: International African Institute/Oxford Univ. Press).

OLORUNTOBA, Y. (1990), Personal communication.

PAKIR, A. (1989), 'Linguistic Alternates and Code Selection in Baba Malay', *World Englishes*, 8: 379–88.

PANDHARIPANDE, R. (1990), 'Formal and Functional Constraints on Code-Mixing', in Jacobson (1990: 15–32).

PARKIN, D. (1974*a*), 'Status Factors in Language Adding: Bahati Housing Estate in Nairobi', in Whiteley (1974*a*: 147–66).

—— (1974*b*), 'Language Shift and Ethnicity in Nairobi', in Whiteley (1974*a*: 167–88).

—— (1974*c*), 'Language Switching in Nairobi', in Whiteley (1974*a*: 189–216).

PEIRCE, C. S. (1955), 'Logic as Semiotic: The Theory of Signs', in *Collected Papers of Charles Sanders Peirce*, ed. C. Hartshorne and P. Weiss (Cambridge, Mass.: Harvard Univ. Press).

PLATT, J. L. (1977), 'A Model for Polyglossia and Multilingualism (with Special Reference to Singapore and Malaysia)', *Language in Society*, 6: 361–78.

POLOMÉ, E., and HILL, C. P. (eds.) (1980), *Language in Tanzania* (London: International African Institute/Oxford Univ. Press).

POPLACK, S. (1980), 'Sometimes I'll start a sentence in Spanish y terminol Español: Toward a Typology of Code-switching', *Linguistics*, 18: 581–618.

—— (1988*a*), 'Contrasting Patterns of Code-Switching in Two Communities', in Heller (1988*a*: 215–44).

—— (1988*b*), 'Language Status and Language Accommodation along a Linguistic Border', in P. Lowenberg (ed.), *Language Spread and Language Policy* (Washington, DC: Georgetown Univ. Press), 90–118.

—— Sankoff, D., and Miller, C. (1988), 'The Social Correlates and Linguistic Processes of Lexical Borrowing and Assimilation', *Linguistics*, 26: 47–104.

Pride, J. B. (1979), 'A Transactional View of Speech Functions and Codeswitching', in W. McCormack and S. Wurm (eds.), *Language and Society* (The Hague: Mouton), 27–53.

Romaine, S. (1995), *Bilingualism* (2nd edn.) (Oxford: Blackwell).

Rubin, J. (1968), *National Bilingualism in Paraguay* (The Hague: Mouton).

Sachdev, I., and Bourhis, R. (1990), 'Bilinguality and Multilinguality', in H. Giles and W. P. Robinson (eds.), *Handbook of Language and Social Psychology* (New York: Wiley), 295–308.

Sacks, H. (1967), Lecture notes (MS, Univ. of California, Irvine).

Sankoff, G. (1971), 'Language Use in Multilingual Societies: Some Alternative Approaches', in J. B. Pride and J. Holmes (eds.), *Sociolinguistics* (Harmondsworth, Middx.: Penguin), 31–51.

Schegloff, E. (1972), 'Sequencing in Conversational Openings', in Gumperz and Hymes (1972: 346–80).

Scotton, C. M. (1972), *Choosing a Lingua Franca in an African Capital* (Edmonton, Alberta: Linguistic Research).

—— (1975), *Multilingualism in Lagos: What It Means to the Social Scientist'* (Columbus: Ohio State Univ., Dept. of Linguistics), 78–90.

—— (1976a), 'The Role of Norms and Other Factors in Language Choice in Work Situations in Three African Cities', in R. Kjolseth and A. Verdoodt (eds.), *Language and Society* (Louvain: Peeters), 201–32.

—— (1976b), 'Strategies of Neutrality: Language Choice in Uncertain Situations', *Language*, 52: 919–41.

—— (1977), 'Linguistic Performance as a Socio-economic Indicator', *Journal of Social Psychology*, 102: 35–45.

—— (1978), 'Language in East Africa: Linguistic Patterns and Political Ideologies', in J. A. Fishman (ed.), *Advances in the Study of Societal Multilingualism* (The Hague: Mouton), 719–60.

—— (1979), 'Codeswitching as a "Safe Choice" in Choosing a Lingua Franca', in W. McCormack and S. Wurm (eds.), *Language and Society* (The Hague: Mouton), 71–88.

—— (1982a), 'The Possibility of Codeswitching: Motivation for Maintaining Multilingualism', *Anthropological Linguistics*, 14: 432–44.

—— (1982b), 'An Urban–Rural Comparison of Language Use among the Luyia in Kenya', *International Journal of the Sociology of Language*, 34: 121–36.

—— (1982c), 'Learning Lingua Francas and Socio-economic Integration: Evidence from Africa', in R. L. Cooper (ed.), *Language Spread* (Bloomington, Ind.: Indiana Univ. Press), 63–94.

—— (1983a), 'The Negotiation of Identities in Conversation: A Theory of Markedness and Code Choice', *International Journal of the Sociology of Language*, 44: 115–36.

SCOTTON, C. M. (1983*b*), 'Comment: Markedness and Code Choice', *International Journal of the Sociology of Language*, 39: 119–28.

—— (1985), '"What the Heck, Sir": Style Shifting and Lexical Colouring as Features of Powerful Language', in R. L. Street, Jr., and J. N. Cappella (eds.), *Sequence and Pattern in Communicative Behaviour* (London: Arnold), 103–19.

—— (1986), 'Diglossia and Codeswitching', in J. A. Fishman *et al.* (eds.), *The Fergusonian Impact*, ii (Berlin: Mouton de Gruyter), 403–15.

—— (1988*a*), 'Codeswitching as Indexical of Social Negotiation', in Heller (1988*a*: 151–86).

—— (1988*b*), 'Patterns of Bilingualism in East Africa', in C. B. Paulston (ed.), *Handbook of Bilingualism and Bilingual Education* (Westport, Conn.: Greenwood), 203–24.

—— (1988*c*), 'Codeswitching and Types of Multilingual Communities', in P. Lowenberg (ed.), *Language Spread and Language Policy* (Washington, DC: Georgetown Univ. Press), 61–82.

—— (1988*d*), 'Self-Enhancing Codeswitching as Interactional Power', *Language and Communication*, 8: 199–211.

—— and BERNSTEN, J. (1988), 'Natural Conversation as a Model for Textbook Dialogue', *Applied Linguistics*, 9: 372–84.

—— and URY, W. (1977), 'Bilingual Strategies: The Social Function of Code-Switching', *International Journal of the Sociology of Language*, 13: 5–20.

—— and ZHU, W. (1983), '*Tóngzhi* in Chinese: Conversational Consequences of Language Change', *Language in Society*, 12: 477–94.

SHAFFER, D. (1977), 'The Place of Code-Switching in Linguistic Contacts', in M. Paradis (ed.), *Aspects of Bilingualism* (Columbia, SC: Hornbeam Press), 265–74.

SINGH, R. (1983), 'A Note on Code-Switching and Stratification in North India', *Language in Society*, 12/1: 71–3.

SOUTHWORTH, F. C. (1980), 'Indian Bilingualism: Some Educational and Linguistic Implications', *Proceedings of the New York Academy of Sciences*, 345: 121–46.

SPERBER, D., and WILSON, D. (1981), 'Irony and the Use–Mention Distinction', in P. Cole (ed.), *Radical Pragmatics* (New York and London: Academic Press), 295–318.

—— —— (1982), 'Mutual Knowledge and Relevance in Theories of Comprehension', in N. Smith (ed.), *Mutual Knowledge* (New York and London: Academic Press), 61–131.

—— —— (1986), *Relevance: Communication and Cognition* (Cambridge, Mass.: Harvard Univ. Press).

SRIDHAR, S. N., and SRIDHAR, K. (1980), 'The Syntax and Psycholinguistics of Bilingual Code-Mixing', *Canadian Journal of Psychology*, 34: 407–16.

STEERE, E. (1870), *A Handbook of the Swahili Language, as Spoken at Zanzibar* (London: SPCK).

STEWART, W. (1968), 'The Functional Distribution of Creole and French in Haiti', in R. O'Brien (ed.), *Georgetown University Round Table Selected Papers on Linguistics 1961–65* (Washington, DC: Georgetown Univ. Press), 460–70.

SWIGART, L. (1990), Personal communication.

TANNER, N. (1967), 'Speech and Society among the Indonesian Élite: A Case Study of a Multilingual Community', *Anthropological Linguistics*, 9: 15–39.

THAKERAR, J. N., GILES, H., and CHESHIRE, J. (1982), 'Psychological and Linguistic Parameters of Speech Accommodation Theory', in C. Fraser and K. Scherer (eds.), *Advances in Social Psychology of Language* (Cambridge: Cambridge Univ. Press), 205–55.

THIBAUT, J., and KELLEY, H. (1959), *The Social Psychology of Groups* (New York: Wiley).

TRUDGILL, P. (1972), 'Sex, Covert Prestige, and Linguistic Change in the Urban British English of Norwich', *Language in Society*, 1: 179–95.

——— (1974), *The Social Differentiation of English in Norwich* (Cambridge: Cambridge Univ. Press).

VALDES-FALLIS, G. (1976), 'Social Interaction and Code-Switching Patterns: A Case of Spanish–English Alternation', in G. Keller, R. Tescher, and S. Viera (eds.), *Bilingualism in Bicentennial and Beyond* (New York: Bilingual Press), 54–85.

VAN DEN BERG, M. (1986), 'Language Planning and Language Use in Taiwan: Social Identity, Language Accommodation, and Language Choice Behavior', *International Journal of the Sociology of Language*, 59: 97–115.

WEINREICH, U. (1953), *Languages in Contact*, repr. 1967 (The Hague: Mouton).

WHITELEY, W. H. (1969), *Swahili, the Rise of a National Language* (London: Methuen).

——— (ed.) (1974a), *Language in Kenya* (Nairobi: Oxford Univ. Press).

——— (1974b), 'The Classification and Distribution of Kenya's African Languages', in Whiteley (1974a: 13–68).

WILT, T. L. (1989), *Bukavu Swahili: A Sociolinguistics Study of Language Change*, Ph.D. (East Lansing, Mich.: Michigan State Univ., Dept. of Linguistics).

WOLFRAM, W. (1969), *A Sociolinguistic Description of Detroit Negro Speech* (Washington, DC: Center for Applied Linguistics).

Index

CPSIA information can be obtained at www.ICGtesting.com
Printed in the USA
LVOW070628180112

264405LV00002B/2/A